Snapshot

Getting to know someone a little is better than not knowing them at all.

Colin Curruthers

Contents

Dedication

To the readers of this book, I hope you laugh as much as I laughed whilst writing it.

Acknowledgments

I'd like to thank my family and friends in writing this book. Without your inspiration, guidance, technical knowhow and ongoing support, I would never have reached the end.

About the Author

Colin Curruthers was born in the late 60's. He grew up and studied in the North of England, eventually carving out a career for himself as a local government officer. His lived experiences up until this point were varied, being funny, outrageous and dark, providing plenty of content to draw upon for this novel.

Preface

Dip into the lives of......

Shy perfectionist, Wayne Spinner, finds himself in an adult world for the first time after being coerced by his mother into working in a textile mill situated around the corner from their family home in West Yorkshire. Life in this harsh industrial environment is made slightly easier after Wayne is taken under the wing of a more experienced worker who goes by the name of Kit Kat. However, Wayne can't rely on Kit Kat forever. His main nemesis, Sandra Arkwright, an experienced textile weaver, who takes a dislike to young Wayne, is waiting in the wings to make his life hell. Life in the textile mill is monotonous, and Wayne simply lives for the weekends. His hard-earned weekly pay packet of £63.00, enables him to start travelling around the country to watch his favourite football team, meet like-minded supporters and absorb himself in football culture. Constantly questioning himself whether he is employed in the right environment for him, he secretly enrols onto a course of further education to help secure himself a better future, only to find he is useless at exams, so he seeks reassurance from an imaginary friend - an orange orangutang called Terry. The question is, have the duo done enough to propel Wayne out of the mundane world of textiles and onto something better?

'The weekends were what I craved for. I'd transform from the shy factory worker with low self-esteem into somebody else. Meeting like-minded football supporters on the trains and at the

games each Saturday lifted my spirits. I loved the camaraderie and the banter. I suppose it was like being in a large family but without having the biological ties.'

....

Easy-going character, Glen Finnan, isn't winning at life. Since finishing school, he's bounced from one disastrous job to another. So far, he's tried his hand as a trainee plumber, a furniture deliverer and working in a factory that manufactures cardboard boxes. When his latest job lasts just under 30 seconds, and he ends up with an unwanted pair of steel-toe cap safety boots, it leads him to try something else other than seek work. He returns to education and starts studying for a degree. To supplement his student grant, he applies for part-time work at a local supermarket. Provisions department supervisor Nan Postlethwaite is blown away by Glen's creative ideas at the interview. Ideas that he plagiarised from a magazine five minutes before entering the interview room! To Glen's surprise, Nan holds him to one of his grand plans – a shopping delivery scheme for the elderly. To his astonishment, he materialises as her right-hand man and is given the responsibility of championing the flagship delivery scheme. The scheme lands Glen and his colleague, Robin, an eccentric provisions assistant who can't seem to stop humming, in lots of sticky scenarios. This doesn't concern Nan. Her ulterior motive is to outdo Gladys Smart, her arch-rival from the Derby branch, who has no answer to Nottingham's flagship scheme. After successfully taking the supermarket to another level, what does the future hold for Glen?

'I stated that if the service was to grow at a similar rate, a second delivery van would be required within three months. Gladys Smart was twitching and shuffling about in her seat. This was uncomfortable listening for her, and she'd had enough. Derby branch was being blown away by this flagship scheme, and she couldn't cope with this.'

....

Self-confessed airhead Daphne Dapper was coasting through life without a care in the world. Never been one for taking things seriously; her favourite motto is 'whatever happens, happens'. Obsessed with collecting wacky earrings, wearing red shoes and eating mint-flavoured sweets, sets Daphne apart from the rest. Jobless and still living at home with her parents, whom she seems to have very little in common with, her Uncle Roger comes to the rescue and offers her a role as a Mystery Shopper in the family business. Her first assignment, at a Berni Inn, ends in complete disaster after she destroys the tropical fish tanks after drinking too much Spanish wine! After her parents are unfortunately trampled to death by a crash of Rhinos whilst on safari in Kenya, Daphne is thrust into a life of independence. A situation she isn't accustomed to. One day, whilst decluttering her deceased parents' bedroom, Daphne stumbles across a mysterious wooden box at the back of a wardrobe. The contents of the box change her life forever.

'Thanks to you, Daphne, the Berni Inn on Newcastle Road no longer has any tropical fish left in its fish tank. You lost your balance during one of your dancing routines and fell into it,

dragging it off its stand and onto the floor. The surface of the restaurant was full of neon tetra, guppy and siamese fighting fish, flapping about helplessly.'

Chapter 1: Wayne Spinner

I am what I am!

My name is Wayne Spinner. It's the mid-eighties, and I'm a twenty-five-year-old textile weaver from West Yorkshire. I live with my parents in a two-up, two-down terraced house built in the early twentieth century. My parent's house is just a three-minute walk from the textile mill where I work. On a good day, I can sprint to work in just over a minute, as I've timed myself, but this experiment was carried out only out of curiosity. The proximity between home and work has its benefits, as it's handy for nipping home at lunch and break times or if I've forgotten anything, but this is a rarity. It also has its drawbacks, as despite living three minutes away, there is no escape from the unmistakable noise of the working looms from within the mill building. I've often wondered what the noise levels are like for those homeowners who live closer to the mill than me.

If you happen to spot me going to work, I would invariably be wearing my cotton green smock jacket, jeans and Adidas Samba trainers [other training shoe brands are available]. Adidas Samba is my 'go-to' trainer of choice. I don't know the exact reason for this, probably because I'd seen some of the boys at school wearing them and have liked them ever since. When I was younger, every time I requested a pair from my parents, I would be bitterly disappointed with the outcome. On one occasion, as my mother set off on a shopping trip, I gave her strict instructions that the trainers I wanted were black with three white stripes down each side, only for her to return with non-branded black trainers sporting two white stripes on either side of the laces. I broke down and ran up to my bedroom crying. She didn't care, though. Thankfully, nowadays, I have the financial resources to buy my own trainers. Just for the record, I own another pair of Samba's, but these are in much more pristine condition. These are ready and waiting for out-of-work activities, such as going to the pub or the football. For those individuals who saw me on a regular basis [and don't have an eye for detail], they would mistakenly think I didn't have any other footwear to wear and maybe feel sorry for me. This isn't the case, though.

Aside from my work clothing, I'm nothing special to look at. I'm average height at five feet, nine inches, pale complexion, slim build, green eyes and wavy ginger hair. My hair is probably the feature that makes me stand out in a crowd. Goodness knows how I have ended up with ginger hair, as the rest of my family don't seem to share this look. I must have been adopted or something! I was once described as looking like Ali Campbell [lead singer of the pop group UB40] and, within the same 24 hours, 'as having a punchable face' by a drunken guy in a nightclub. Make of that description what you want. My slim build doesn't come naturally. It's something I have to work at through diet and exercise. The motivation behind the weight management resulted from my school days. It was a throwaway comment by my PE Teacher who shouted: "Why don't you track back Wayne, you fat bastard?" as I laboured in midfield during a school football match against our local rivals, a catholic school down the road. The comment cut deep, and I've not forgotten it ever since. Oh, and I should mention that my favourite colour is green [not sure why], and that I despise the colour red. This loathing of the colour red has developed since leaving school. Maybe it's because I'm conscious red clothing doesn't suit my pale complexion and ginger hair. It never used to bother me as a youngster, and I would quite happily parade around the local football recreation ground in my red Welsh replica football shirt, the one with the Admiral logo on each collar, as I pretended to replicate the wing play of former Burnley and Welsh International, Leighton James.

If I had to describe my character, it would be a 'shy perfectionist with low self-esteem'. I'm quiet and a little bit nervous around other people. I strive for flawlessness, and other people's evaluations mean the world to me. If you throw into the mix that I'm polite with good manners, you may start to question whether my type of character was a natural fit for the workplace environment I have found myself in. But here I was, in a hot and noisy industrial factory five days a week, as part of the mill workforce, many of whom couldn't find work elsewhere.

Sitting down with a career advisor and assessing job opportunities that suited my character didn't appear to cross my radar whilst growing up. I don't recall such conversations at school with the likes of Mr Benham or whichever teacher volunteered to take on this advisory role. Conversations such as:

"Have you thought about a career working for Royal Mail, Wayne? I think it would suit your personality rather well. You need to be physically fit; it's not too taxing on your brain, and for large parts of the day, you'd be working alone. And at the end of each day, you'll have a sense of achievement as your mailbag will be empty! Ideal career choice for a shy perfectionist with low self-esteem, wouldn't you say?"

Unfortunately, the planning of my career fell to my mum whose advice was for me to trawl around local factories and ask them outright whether they had any jobs going. I recognise this wasn't the best advice to give a 16-year-old ginger teenager with low self-esteem, but the emotional pressure she placed on me was unbearable. So, to appease my mother, I found myself frequenting factories that made furniture, factories that made wallpaper, various textile mills and other unreputable establishments where you didn't require experience or qualifications. My time spent in these establishments was brief. It consisted of a quick question to the secretary in reception.

"Have you got any jobs going?" I would ask in a soft West Yorkshire accent before thrusting a bit of paper with my telephone number on it in the direction of the secretary and then bolting out of the door and heading for home as quickly as I could.

You wouldn't have got away with this approach nowadays; it's all online applications, but back in the mid-eighties, it was considered acceptable, certainly with the employers I was approaching. Once back home and having completed the mission set by my mother, I knew I could relax for a while as the emotional pressure would dissipate.

Shaving and interviews don't mix

I wasn't convinced my mother's job-hunting strategy would bear fruit until one Friday afternoon, the phone at home began to ring. It was the secretary at the textile mill across the road. I was being summoned to go and have an informal chat with them, as they had a vacancy. The secretary had noted my address and due to it being so close to the mill, asked if I could come across to the mill the same afternoon.

"Of course I can" I said, mainly because my mother was breathing down my neck during the phone call.

I had an hour to get ready. I know what I'll do, I thought. I'll have a shave. I'm not sure why this crazy thought came to my mind. I'd never shaved before. Maybe it's because I thought I was about to move from an adolescent world into an adult world by landing this job. My dad didn't possess a dry electric shaver, so I had to make do with an old-fashioned shaving brush and razor. The end outcome wasn't great. I looked like the dog's dinner and needed to patch myself up with Elastoplast to conceal my sliced-up face and to stop the blood dripping onto my freshly ironed shirt. My mother pushed me out of the door and uttered the words:

"This is your big chance; don't come back until you've got the job."

Arriving at the mill, I climbed up some stairs and headed towards reception. I remembered exactly where the reception area was from my previous visit a week earlier when I was enquiring about work. The reception area was dark due to the oak wall panelling. There were various textile-themed photos placed strategically on the wall, probably taken in the mill during its heyday. The secretary caught sight of me through a sliding screen next to the office door. She slid the screen back.

"Hi, I'm Wayne; I'm here for the job interview," I said nervously.

The secretary was a little taken aback by what was standing in front of her.

"Yes, we were expecting you. Are you ok?" she said, as she stared intently at my face.

Unknown to me, the shaving damage was much worse than I thought, and blood was oozing through the Elastoplast. The secretary turned her attention to the employment application form she had in her hand. As she passed it across, she said:

"Have a seat and fill this in, then return it to me. Let me know if you have any questions."

The application form was pretty basic. The only detail I struggled to provide was my National Insurance number, which I couldn't remember. As I passed the form back to the secretary, she quickly inspected my face, probably to make sure my wounds hadn't deteriorated any further. She then turned and walked towards the back of her office before disappearing into an adjacent room with a sign on the door which said, 'Office Manager'. Five minutes later, she returned.

"We'd like to offer you the job. It's a labourer's job. It's 9:00 – 5:00, Monday to Friday. The starting salary is £63.00 pounds a week. How does that sound?"

I couldn't believe what I was hearing. This company actually wants to employ me. My mother's job-hunting strategy has worked.

"Yes, I'm ok with that," I said.

I didn't have the confidence to say anything else, so I left it at that.

"Ok, see you on Monday at 9:00 am. On arrival, ask for Mr Golding, the Shift Manager."

As soon as I arrived home, I immediately assessed my face. No wonder the secretary gawped at me a lot; I was a mess. It didn't stop me from landing the job, though.

Kit Kat's Trainee

Over the weekend, I pondered what lay ahead. I wondered what kind of tasks a labourer had to do and what had happened to the person who'd had the job before me. I also wondered if I had beat off any competition to land the job. Probably not. Monday morning soon came around. I arrived at the mill at 8:55 am, then went through a red wooden door with a sign on it saying 'Employees Only' before climbing a fleet of stairs that led into a busy warehouse area. The first thing to hit me was an earthy smell, probably produced by the cotton being used to produce the fabric. This smell was going to take some getting used to. A man wearing a royal blue cotton workwear coat approached me from across the warehouse. He looked to be in his early sixties and was wearing glasses. His hair was shiny as a result of the healthy dollop of Byrlcreem that had obviously been applied earlier. He was also wearing some kind of cologne, but the scent of this was overpowered by the Brylcreem.

"I'm Mr Golding," he said as he stared at the half-healed shaving lacerations on my face.

"You must be Wayne?"

But before I had a chance to reply, he said,

"Follow me, we'll get you started."

I followed him to the other end of the warehouse. We were about to go through some huge rubber doors and into the main weaving shed when he turned to me and gave me a tiny box containing disposable orange earplugs.

"Don't do what the new guy did last week and push them in too far. He hasn't seen them since!"

I didn't quite get the joke, but thought I'd laugh anyway. We pushed our way through the doors and into the main weaving shed. Now I understood why I was given the earplugs. The noise levels were seriously loud. We wandered past some lockers and into a storage area that housed various containers, drums and other storage tubs. All of a sudden, this older-looking guy entered the storage area.

"Right, I'll leave you in the capable hands of George. He'll show you the ropes. Any problems, give me a shout."

And then off he went, in the direction of the warehouse. There in front of me was George. He was wearing some old grey dungaree overalls over a peach-coloured t-shirt. He was almost bald, apart from some tufts of sandy hair at the back, resembling a clown. His other distinguishing feature was that he either had huge feet or was wearing oversized shoes.

"Hello, I'm George, but most people call me Kit Kat. Are you Wayne?"

"Yes, that's me," I said anxiously. "Why do people call you Kit Kat?" I asked.

"It's because it's my favourite biscuit," he replied swiftly. "Now grab a broom from over there, and I'll show you what to do."

As I returned with a broom, I noticed the broom George was leaning on had the following words written in black marker pen on the Broom Head: KIT KAT'S BRUSH - KEEP OFF!!

The job wasn't difficult to pick up. Basically, all we had to do all day was to sweep the floor. The white-coloured dust created by the textile process was everywhere, and our job was to curtail it. This wasn't easy, as the fibres swirled around in the atmosphere and landed at will to create a snow-like blanket on the floor, ceiling and machinery. I soon noticed Kit Kat wasn't very talkative, nor did he provide any direction about how to do the job. Maybe he felt he didn't have to. When he wanted to relay a message, his preferred method was to mime it. His miming actions were effective, and I always understood them. Maybe, over the years, he learnt this was the best way to communicate in such a noisy environment. The textile looms were arranged in rows, and we soon got into a routine. He would be sweeping one aisle between the looms whilst I was sweeping another. Kit Kat's sweeping action was different from mine. He seemed to position his frame side on, whereas I was definitely more front facing. At the end of each aisle, we would scoop up our pile of fibres, using an abandoned piece of cardboard as a makeshift shovel, and throw them into one of the large bins dotted around the shed. I noticed the aisles that Kit Kat had swept always looked cleaner than mine, but I couldn't work out why.

I felt safe working alongside Kit Kat. He had soon worked out that I was shy, and he watched out for me. As he wasn't really one for communicating either, I didn't know an awful lot about him. This changed one Saturday afternoon. I had walked into town to go and buy a pair of football boots. My 'go-to' brand was Patrick, as worn by Kevin Keegan during his spell at Southampton. I was pleased with my purchase and thought I would give myself another treat by going to the Wimpy Café in the Arndale. Deciding what I was having to eat wasn't difficult, as my order was exactly the same every time I went there. Double Cheeseburger, French Fries and a Coca-Cola. As I waited for the food to arrive, I got my new football boots out of their box and began to give them the once-over.

"Have you been spending your hard-earned wages?" said a voice behind me.

On turning around, it was Kit Kat. His weekend look was very different from his weekday look. He was wearing a blue cotton sports jacket and a flat cap.

"Do you mind if I join you?" he asked pleasantly.

"Feel free" I said.

He sat down opposite me and ordered a Knickerbocker Glory and a pot of tea for one. Whereas it was difficult to get two words out of him at work, that particular afternoon, he wouldn't stop talking. He talked about the jobs he'd previously had. Interestingly, he used to work in the Parks Department at the Local Council and was responsible for keeping the parks safe and tidy. That probably explained why he was so good at sweeping after clearing all those leaves around the parks for many years. He explained he loved working outdoors, but nowadays, he would probably struggle to cope with the conditions during the winter months. He told me about the cars he'd owned, favourite places in the UK he'd visited and about his pets. He also talked a lot about his wife, whom he lost to cancer five years previously. I sensed he missed her terribly. Working in the textile mill was his way to help him combat loneliness and social isolation. As a result of the chance meeting that afternoon, I felt my bond with Kit Kat grew stronger.

Having a social life is rather nice

Earning a weekly wage allowed me to broaden my horizons. I now had a social life. I had been a keen football fan for as long as I could remember and had always dreamed of watching my beloved Aston Villa play live. This was now a possibility. However, for someone with my demeanour, the thought of travelling to unfamiliar places was quite nerve-racking. I decided to take the plunge and selected a game against Southampton as my first visit to Villa Park. I think the game ended in a draw. After that, my weekend trips to the football became regular. I even started going to matches where Villa was playing away from home. Football supporters from other clubs would be milling around Leeds Railway Station every Saturday morning. There would be supporters from teams such as Chelsea, Tottenham, QPR and Derby, all setting off for the day, not knowing whether the day would end in victory or defeat. I was soon on speaking terms with these other supporters, and we'd sit together on the train for part of the journey before we splintered off in different directions around the country, wherever our team was playing. If we bumped into each other on the way back, and we often did, there would be a few beers on the go. One of the Chelsea contingent, called Tank, had a reputation for being a bit of an ale can and, on one trip between London Euston and Leeds he attempted to break his own personal record of consuming 21 tins of lager. As we pulled out of Doncaster, his previous record wasn't in danger of being beaten, but then he somehow got his second wind, and by the time we got to Leeds, he had consumed 23 tins, beating his personal best.

As a reward, we all chipped in and bought him a Chicken Tikka Masala, Pilau rice and garlic naan bread from the Indian restaurant. He was chuffed with that.

If I wasn't spending my weekly wage going to the football, I'd be spending it on clothes. Being part of the football scene also meant I needed to look the part. Travelling around the country, I'd look to see what other fans were wearing. Some of them, known as 'Casuals', prided themselves on dressing in smarter clobber than the average football fan, wearing tracksuits, Lois jeans, cagoules and pristine trainers. I was influenced and wanted to be like them. It wasn't long before I was sporting brands such as Stone Island, Burberry, Aquascutum, Fred Perry, Lyle & Scott, Sergio Tacchini & Lacoste. The weekends were what I craved for. I'd transform from the shy factory worker with low self-esteem into somebody else. Meeting likeminded football supporters on the trains and at the games each Saturday lifted my spirits. I loved the camaraderie and the banter. I suppose it was like being in a large family but without having the biological ties.

Back in the mill weaving shed, I had settled into my role, and other employees were getting used to me being around the place. I'd get the occasional nod from some of the more friendly textile weavers or strike up conversations with one or two of the Creelers [a Creeler's duties were to ensure the correct yarn was by the loom for each production run]. The Creelers were mostly female, and I would watch them with interest as they tied the end of one yarn bobbin to another. It was important the looms had an endless supply of yarn, otherwise they would stop. One of the Creelers was a middle aged woman called Carol. She had a heart of gold and was a really lovely person. She supported Everton and would always ask me about my weekend and my trips to the football. Because she knew I followed Villa, she would always watch out for their result every Saturday teatime. Sometimes, if she needed to stop a loom to attend to a bobbin, she would allow me to press the buttons to start the loom up again, but only if nobody was looking. The satisfaction of kickstarting the loom into action was infectious, and I wanted more. Not realising that one day, that aspiration might come true.

Another worker I became friendly with was Paul. He worked in the factory, as did his younger brother and his dad. I was never entirely sure what Paul's role was. I would occasionally see him pushing a trolley around containing boxes of yarn. I'm sure he did more than that, though. His dad worked in the bowels of the factory in the cellar. He seemed to push giant trolleys around all day, transporting materials to different departments. On his left hand, he had three fingers missing, leaving only his index finger and thumb. It didn't hold him back, though. The younger brother was called Nick. I soon learned that he couldn't be trusted. He approached me one morning, whilst at work, saying he had been given a 'hot tip' in the 2:15 pm race at Goodwood and that he would put a bet on for me. He finished his shift at 2:00 pm. I gave him two pounds and didn't think much more about it. I checked Teletext later that day and noticed the horse had actually won at 10/1. When I saw him the following day and asked for my winnings, he said he'd arrived at the bookies too late to place the bet and gave me my two pounds back. I had it on good authority from another worker called Big Al that he was spotted in the bookies cheering the horse home and was seen collecting his winnings from the counter. I thought it was a real bastard's trick and was always wary of him following that experience.

It was Paul who introduced me to alcohol. We'd regularly go to a Working Men's Club called the Carlton for a game of snooker and a few pints. I didn't know the difference between one pint of beer and another, so I just downed whatever was in front of me. Judged by the speed I was getting drunk, I think it was the strongest lager on tap: a beer called Tennent's Extra. It felt good to be 'one of the boys', though. Paul did his best to look out for me. He knew there were characters within the mill workforce who would give me a torrid time if I wasn't careful. This consisted of people like Dumbbell Dan and Sandra Arkwright, a gobby middle aged woman with a wicked tongue. Up until now, they had kept their distance, but I could sense trouble ahead.

New role, new nickname and a Sci-Fi Vacuum

I was three months or so into the job and all was going ok. I had settled down into a routine, both at work and outside work. This changed one Monday morning. On arriving at work, Mr Golding was waiting for me in the warehouse area.

"Wayne, we are really pleased with your work so far," he said.

Straight away, I knew the next word was going to be 'but', and I was right.

"But I need you to help me out with something else. The Managing Director has created a new task, and you are the chosen one. I've had a word with Kit Kat, and he is happy to release you from your sweeping duties. Now follow me."

Before I'd had time to absorb this information, I was on the coat tails of Mr Golding, and we were marching through the warehouse towards the big rubber doors leading to the main weaving shed. Once past the lockers, we reached a storage area next to the Tackler's Cabin. Mr Golding ushered me in, and there in front of me was a brand-new vacuum. It was silver with blue trim and resembled R2D2, the robot character in the Star Wars franchise.

"This cost a lot of money Wayne; make sure you look after it. Make sure that roof is spotless."

Then he rushed off in the direction of the warehouse. Charming, I thought to myself. Is he not even going to show me how to use it? Obviously not. He was more interested in flirting with the female weavers. Next to R2D2 was a connectable hose and an eight-foot plastic tube, which was inserted into the hose. I'd better test the vacuum out, I thought. The Managing Director and Mr Golding were relying on me.

R2D2 wasn't difficult to operate, and I soon got to grips with it. The job entailed dragging it down each aisle of looms and pointing the plastic tube upwards, and sucking off whatever fibres I could. These were mainly off the overhead lights and pipework. The only drawback was the R2D2's lead. It wasn't long enough! There were a number of plug sockets placed strategically around the shed floor, but however hard I tried, there were certain parts of the shed I couldn't reach. Therefore, I had to improvise by attaching a small brush to the end of my plastic pole, brushing it off, then sweeping it up all the time, ensuring clumps of fibres didn't fall on the working looms. I soon realised that in my new role, I was much more prone to get covered in dust. Therefore, I started to wear a one-piece nylon boiler suit for protection. This was something I had to purchase myself, as when I approached Mr Golding and requested help with personal protective equipment, his response was:

"You must be joking, Wayne", before walking off in the direction of the warehouse.

The new role gave me a sense of independence. It was also my first opportunity to manage my own workload in a workplace setting. In my mind, I divided the shed floor into areas and then tried to cover a certain area each day. If I didn't quite finish cleaning the intended area, I would do extra the following day. That was the downside of being a perfectionist. I would still cross paths with Kit

Kat, as we often worked in the same areas of the shed at the same time. He would acknowledge me with a smile and a 'thumbs up' signal before getting his head down and continuing sweeping. Where we were once the same in our role, we were now polar opposites, as his job required him to 'look down' all day, whereas mine required me to 'look up'.

The other thing to mention was that when sweeping the floor, you didn't really get in anybody's way. Dragging along a large vacuum along the aisles was a different matter, as people couldn't get past me if they needed to. One such worker was Sandra Arkwright. She made it plainly obvious that I wasn't welcome near her set of looms with my vacuum. She was a smallish woman with a rubbery face. She had a right gob on her and was one to stay clear of. When I started overhead cleaning in her vicinity, she used to look at me in disgust. This didn't do my self-esteem any good at all. I also noticed that when I was near her set of looms, she would choose that moment to clean her looms down with the compressed air pipe, blowing dust from the looms in my direction and covering me. She never acknowledged me or attempted to strike up a conversation with me. She treated me with utter contempt. Maybe she just didn't like ginger people, I don't know.

Sandra Arkwright wasn't the only worker I had to be on my guard against. Dumbbell Dan was just as bad but for different reasons. He was called Dumbbell because of his love of the gym and, in particular, free-standing weights. This was obvious to see when you saw his physique. He wasn't shy about showing it off, either. His favourite workwear was a vest top, which not only showed off his bulging muscles but also his wide range of tattoos. Dumbbell was a complex character. Sometimes, he would be nice, but most of the time, he was nasty. Even when he was being nice, there was always the possibility he could turn and do something untoward to you. His muscly physique suited his role in the mill. He was one of the Roller Carriers. Their job was to remove fabric from the looms once the rollers were full, replacing the full roller with an empty roller. Some of the rolls of fabric would be huge, and it would require a significant amount of effort to lift them. Dumbbell embraced it though and saw it as a challenge. For him, it was additional training and an opportunity to test his strength. Similar to Sandra, for some reason, he had it in for me. If he was coming along the aisle with his roller, and I was in the way, he would smash his roller into R2D2 rather than waiting and asking me to move out of the way. That used to happen regularly, sometimes half a dozen times in one shift. He simply just enjoyed tormenting me. He also had other tricks in his armoury as part of his bullying regime that I would have to endure further down the line.

I had now been working in the mill long enough to have struck up conversations, albeit short ones, with quite a few of the workforce. I would bump into other workers in the break room or other areas of the mill, such as the tackler's cabin, warehouse, cardroom or loading bay. What I began to notice was that nobody referred to me by my first name. Weirdly, everyone referred to me as 'Snorkel'. They would say things like:

"Here comes Snorkel" or "how's it going, Snorkel?".

Even Mr Golding started calling me Snorkel! It was really weird. I just went along with it, though. One day, I was in the breakroom having a cup of coffee with Paul, and my curiosity got the better of me.

"Why does everybody call me Snorkel?" I asked. Paul smiled.

"It was Kit Kat who came up with that name. He was watching you one day as you cleaned the roof with your long plastic pole. He was at one side of the shed and you were at the other. From a distance, and through the haze caused by the loom emissions, it appeared like you had a huge snorkel attached to your head. Do you mind?"

"No, not really", I said. "In fact, I quite like it".

I think that having this nickname helped me integrate into the factory quicker. Good old Kit Kat. I think his creative thinking did me a favour.

Away days and the Cheese Sandwich challenge

As much as work was going ok, I constantly looked forward to the weekends. It was a chance to leave the noise and dust behind and live a little. Travelling up and down the country to watch football gave me a real buzz. I soon realised that watching Villa play away from home was more of an adventure and gave me a bigger adrenaline rush. I visited away grounds such as Tottenham, Chelsea, West Ham, Queens Park Rangers, Sunderland and Newcastle, amongst others.

The emotions of the day could be broken down into segments. Reaching the opposition's stadium was the first challenge, especially if it was my first visit to a particular stadium. Working out which tube or bus to catch once you had left the mainline train station was always tricky. This was where I tended to rely on railway station staff for directions. They were usually very helpful. Sometimes, it was possible to walk from the train station to the stadium. It was just a case of identifying a group of people who looked like they were going to the football, then following them. I had a nose for it. On reaching the stadium, the next test was to find the away end. I always took the approach that it was best not to look conspicuous whilst doing this to avoid making it known you were an away supporter.

Once through the turnstile and into the away end, the travel nerves evaporated. I was now surrounded by fellow Villans with the same mantra as me. Thousands of them. I didn't know these people personally [apart from little Barry from Lancaster, whom I was on speaking terms with after meeting a few months earlier on a trip to Coventry], but we were all there for the same reason.......to see Villa win. No matter what the outcome of the game, the travel nerves kicked in on the return journey home, certainly until I had reached the mainline station where I would board the train for Leeds. Even though I was literally retracing my steps from the stadium to somewhere like London Euston, the thought of getting lost or ambushed by away supporters was a thought that was constantly in my mind. It wasn't until I boarded the train I could then relax. Often, I would treat myself to a four-pack of McEwan's Export from the buffet carriage and catch up on the scores from the day's other fixtures.

The train journey back to Leeds was unpredictable. Sometimes, it was quiet in the carriage, whereas other times, it would be rowdy, with booze-addled football supporters having loads of banter and a singsong. When it was the latter, not all travellers appreciated the noise, and they would vacate to another carriage, generally being jeered by the revellers as they moved from one carriage to another.

The strangest thing I saw on one of my train journeys happened on the way back from Euston after a game against Chelsea. I was travelling back with a Leeds-based Chelsea fan called Penguin. I'm not entirely sure how he came to have this nickname. He certainly didn't look like one. Maybe he was similar to Kit Kat and had a soft spot for confectionary. We were sat in a bay of four seats, the ones with a table in the middle and two seats on either side. A guy boarded the train at Peterborough and sat down opposite us. He had a long face and a centre-parting hairstyle, which didn't flatter him. When he removed his huge overcoat, you could see it was far too big for his wiry frame. He had no intention of making eye contact and seemed oblivious to us being there. On his lap, he had a plastic shopping bag that was weathered, probably due to its age. He started to delve inside the bag and began to open what looked like a loaf of white bread. It wasn't. It was a pile of uncut sandwiches. He pulled out the first one. He peeled back the top slice of bread to reveal the filling. I'm not sure if that was for his benefit or ours. Probably his, as I don't think he knew we were watching. The sandwich filling was thick slices of orange cheese, probably Red Leicester or something. There were no condiments, like pickles or anything. As he bit into the first sandwich, Penguin leaned towards me and tried to whisper:

"He'll never eat all them, you know."

Penguin was now on his fifth can of lager, and he was the kind of guy who got louder the more he drank. Therefore, his attempted whisper was more like an announcement, really, and it alerted other passengers at the next table who clocked on to this sandwich-eating challenge. The sandwich man began to attract quite an audience but was unaware of it. Over the next forty minutes or so, one by one, he munched through each sandwich he pulled from the bag. It was difficult to comprehend how someone so thin and wiry could eat so much. As he finished off the last sandwich, he pulled out the empty loaf bag and screwed it up into a ball. Mission complete. Penguin was the first to his feet and gave the guy a round of applause. Within seconds, others followed. Soon, half of the carriage was emersed in the celebrations. Strangely, the sandwich man didn't seem to react. He just sat there staring into space. As the train pulled into Newark, he slipped back into his huge overcoat and left the train.

Stepping off the train at Leeds station after returning from the football, I was always on a high. I felt a real sense of achievement that I'd travelled hundreds of miles to an unfamiliar town or city to watch a match and then return to home territory unscathed. As I was leaving the station and heading into town towards the pub or the chippy, I'd feel a sense of superiority over other people I came across. I'd think to myself, "so, what have you achieved today?" or "I bet you haven't done much today, probably just stayed here in Leeds and done something boring. It's about time you challenged yourself and had a little bit more adventure like me." I'm not sure how much these thoughts and my arrogance were fuelled by beer, adrenalin or a mixture of both. One thing for sure: I always noticed this air of superiority had dissipated the following morning, and I was back to being a shy perfectionist with low self-esteem.

Goodbye dear friend

Monday mornings soon came around. I would once again team up with R2D2, and we would do our best to keep the upper area of the shed clean. Mondays were usually spent daydreaming about the escapades from the previous weekend. This nulled the boredom as I stared upwards for eight hours at the dusty ceiling. The rest of the week was spent daydreaming about my next adventure. I would always have something lined up for the following weekend; otherwise, the week would just drag. By this point, I had been working at the mill for about twelve months. During this time, I had progressed from floor sweeper to roof sweeper. This was probably classed as a sideways step as I hadn't seen an increase in my weekly pay packet. The regular pattern to the start of the working day would be that I generally reach my locker by 8:50 am or thereabouts, get changed into my one-piece nylon boiler suit, and then head for the storage area to pick up R2D2. I would always stop off at the other storage area, the one where Kit Kat stored his broom, just to pop my head in and say hello. He tended to arrive at the mill about 8:30 am and have a brew before starting work. He would generally be standing leaning against his brush, probably contemplating the day ahead, before starting work at 9:00 am.

One particular Monday morning, just after Christmas, something out of the ordinary happened. I was on my way to collect R2D2 before starting work for the day and on passing the storage area where Kit Kat would normally be, there was no sign of him. I wasn't too concerned at first, but it was the same again on Tuesday and Wednesday morning. I asked those workers I chatted to regularly, like Carol and Paul, if they knew where he was, but nobody seemed to know. As I rule, I kept out of Mr Golding's way and avoided interaction if I could help it. But when he didn't turn up on a Thursday morning, I plucked up the courage and went to see him. As usual, he was flirting with some of the female weavers [the pretty ones].

"I haven't seen Kit Kat this week. Is he sick or something?" I asked nervously.

"I don't know, Snorkel; I hadn't noticed as I've been busy in the warehouse all week."

Pull the other one, I thought. You've been fraternising with the female staff as usual.

"I'll make some enquiries with the girls in the office and see if they have heard from him", said Mr Golding.

"Ok, thanks", I replied before carrying on with my duties.

Later that day, just after lunch, I was cleaning the overhead pipes at the top end of the shed. Suddenly, I felt a tap on my shoulder and there was Mr Walton standing over me. Mr Walton was Mr Golding's deputy. He had big bulging eyes, huge nostrils and a massive forehead. There wasn't much room for anything else on his face apart from that. He ushered me out of the shed towards the warehouse. I could only presume it was news of Kit Kat, so I followed him.

"Mr Golding mentioned you had been enquiring about

George", said Mr Walton. "Mrs Shady from the office has tried ringing him, but nobody answered. She is going to try ringing again later. If we don't hear from him, and he doesn't turn up in the morning, we'll move to plan B," he said.

He didn't go into detail about what Plan B was, so I was none the wiser. Before the conversation ended, I happened to mention that I knew he had a spare key to his house, as he once mentioned he had locked himself out of his house but used the spare key to get back in.

I was really tired the following morning and didn't feel too well. I had been out to the Carlton Club with Paul for a game of snooker and a few drinks. I stayed away from the Tennent's Extra this time; now I knew how strong it was. I noticed a lot of the older guys in the club were drinking pints of dark-coloured ale [I found out later it was called Mild] and decided that was to be my drink for the night. It still, however, had the same impact as Tennent's, and I was plastered by closing time. Despite being hungover, I arrived at work as normal and put on my boiler suit. As I walked towards the storage area, I was praying Kit Kat would be standing there, leaning against his brush. Sadly, the storage area was empty. All I could do was go and pick up R2D2 and continue with my work. I was worried and felt something was wrong. It was a gut feeling I had.

I had just finished my mid-morning cuppa and was trying to remember where I had left R2D2 when I felt a tap on the shoulder. It was Mr Walton, and once again, he ushered me towards the warehouse. I followed just like I had done the previous day. Only this time, we stepped across the warehouse, through a door and towards the office. There, waiting outside the office were two police officers. One was short and plump, and the other was tall and thin. The tall one resembled Rodney Trotter from the television sitcom Only Fools and Horses. Mr Walton looked at me.

"We are struggling to get in touch with George, so to try and move things forward, I have asked the police to help. Do you mind assisting these officers, Wayne?"

I didn't come across Mr Walton very often, so I was surprised he even knew my name. I noticed he didn't call me Snorkel, though.

"You mentioned something about a spare key when we spoke yesterday." I nodded sheepishly. "If you could let the officers know about this, it would be appreciated."

As we turned to go down the stairs to leave the mill building, Mr Walton shouted: "I hope things go ok."

I don't think he held out much hope, though.

Being in a police car was something new for me. As we drove to Kit Kat's house, the officers chatted about random stuff, such as what they had watched on the telly the previous night, only to pause if something came through on their police radio. I got the impression they were both newbies and of the same rank. The Rodney Trotter lookalike seemed like he was the quieter of the two and less confident. Through listening to them I worked out he was called Roy, and his colleague was called Rob. We soon reached Kit Kat's place. Like me, he lived in a two-up two down terraced house. The sight of the police car sparked interest from the neighbours, with one or two looking through their windows to see what was occurring. I thought Rob and Roy might have asked me to stay in the car, but they encouraged me to get out. Straight away, Rob headed for Kit Kat's house and tried the door handle. He turned to both of us and shook his head. Then he signalled we should make our way round to the back of the house. This meant walking to the end of the street, then turning left past the gable end of the top house and turning left again down the back street. As we walked, I began to feel like I was part of their posse.

Then Roy started making conversation,

"Did George ever mention where he kept his spare key?" he asked.

"I think he kept it in one of the outbuildings in the back yard," I said hesitantly.

"What, the old coal house?"

"I think so", I said, as I desperately tried to recall the conversation we'd had weeks ago when he said he'd locked himself out of his house.

"Ok, we'll have a good rummage around the coal house and see if it turns up."

Luckily, the backyard gate wasn't bolted. Roy started to explore the old coal house whilst Rob tried peering through the windows. He'd only been searching the coal house for about 30 seconds when he shouted:

"Gotcha!" and turned to us, holding a key in the air.

Unexpectedly, Rob responded by giving him a high five. This behaviour confirmed my suspicion that these guys were definitely a couple of rookies. I doubted the likes of Sherlock Holmes and Dr Watson would behave in such a way! I followed them as we worked our way back round to the front of the property. The neighbour's interest in the situation had continued. One neighbour was now standing on her doorstep; she was that keen to know what we were up to. Just as Rob put the key in the keyhole, he turned to me and said, "We'll take it from here. You'd better wait outside."

Maybe I'd underestimated these rookies; perhaps they 'had' listened at police training school.

"Ok, you both go for it," I said.

They both entered the property, closing the door behind them. As I stood waiting outside, I started to think about my chance meeting with Kit Kat in the Wimpy Café in the Arndale and how talkative and happy he was that day. These thoughts were short-lived as Roy soon appeared back at the front door. His face was as white as a sheet, and he struggled to get his words out.

"Wayne, it's bad news, I'm afraid. George has passed away. Come and sit in the car with me whilst Rob makes a few calls."

I already felt sick from all the Mild I'd drunk the night before, but this news made the feeling significantly worse. Roy wasn't expecting what I said next.

"Can I see him?"

Roy was flummoxed and didn't see this question coming. He was unsure how to respond. His mind was racing, and he was trying to recollect what he had been taught at police training school. He really should have said no, but he didn't.

"Just for a couple of minutes, but don't touch anything," he said firmly.

I followed Roy into the house and down the hallway. As we entered the living room, we were hit by a distinct odour. Roy gestured towards the armchair. He was really struggling with the situation, as I don't think he had seen a dead body before. Sure enough, there was Kit Kat slumped in the chair. He was wearing his work clothes. He had half a cup of tea on the table beside him. He'd obviously been getting ready for work when he died. There was some discoloration on his face. He'd been deceased five days now, and nature was beginning to take its course, hence the smell in the room. His eyes were open, but they seemed to be looking downwards. A weird thought crossed my mind. Kit Kat spent all his time looking down at work as he swept the floor, and he was still looking down, even though he had passed to the other side. I couldn't stop staring at him; I was fascinated. I was so engrossed I hadn't noticed how much this was having an impact on Roy. He was sweating like crazy and retching. The retching had a rhythmic beat to it. Next, he made a weird noise and the contents of his stomach hurled towards the floor and covered Kit Kat's shoes and the bottom of his overalls. It looked like Roy had been on cornflakes for breakfast. Poor Kit Kat, as if he hadn't been through enough, he was now covered by Roy's insides. All the commotion, brought in Rob from the kitchen. He was on his radio organising for an ambulance to come to the house. He couldn't work out why I was in the living room and why Kit Kat was now splattered in sick.

"I suggest you two both go outside and wait in the car," he said in a stern voice.

He wasn't very happy. We both left the room immediately and headed for the car. It took about an hour before all the necessaries were taken care of and we were able to drive away from Kit Kat's house. Rob and Roy thought it was for the best if they dropped me off at home and suggested I take the day off. They then went to the mill to break the news to Mr Golding.

Kit Kat's death hit me hard and was on my mind for weeks. I had presumed it was a heart attack. The police confirmed this a few days after we had found him. I had to go to the police station and provide a statement; it was all pretty informal. On a day-to-day basis, there were too many triggers that reminded me of him. These were just little things, which I knew were part of his routine. Somehow, I had to try to put this behind me and move on.

Fortune Telling in the Garden

A couple of months after Kit Kat's death, my days of sucking fluff and dust from the shed roof came to an end. Mr Golding asked me if I fancied a change and if I would like to be a Creeler. Old Edna, on the red shift, had recently retired, so there was a vacancy. It would mean shift work [6:00 am to 2:00 pm one week, followed by 2:00 pm to 10:00 pm] the next. These shifts were known as 'earlies' and 'lates'. It would also mean a pay increase. My £63.00 a week would rise to £84.00 a week. This was the bit I was really interested in. I had my eye on a new Sergio Tacchini Tracksuit top, amongst other things, so this extra cash would really come in handy. I would also be able to distance myself from Sandra. Although we would be on the same shift, I would be working away from the rubber-faced cow on the other side of the shed. I would just need to ensure I avoided her at break times.

It was my friend, Carol, who mentored me in my first couple of weeks of being a Creeler. I was really nervous at first. I was responsible for 36 rapier looms and had to ensure they didn't run out of yarn and that the bobbins of yarn were replaced at the appropriate time. This meant constantly patrolling the looms. I was conscious the weavers who managed these looms were so used to having old Edna around that they wouldn't take to me. Luckily, I needn't have worried about that as they all confided in me that she was well past her best, and they were glad to see the back of her.

Working shifts changed my routine. I much preferred the early shift, where I started at 6:00 am. I despised the back shift. I loathed the wait before going to work at 2:00 pm. On the early shift, I would be home just after 2:00 pm. This was ideal if I had something planned, but this was rare. The usual schedule was to get showered, rid myself of the dust and aroma of the shed, make a quick sandwich [this was always cheese and cucumber], and then go to bed until teatime. On the early shift, my half an hour breakfast break started at 9:00 am. As I lived so close, I generally jogged home for some marmalade on toast and a mug of tea. One particular morning, as I approached the house, I noticed a lady walking up the garden path. I could only see the back of her at first. I caught her up before she had a chance to ring the doorbell. We looked at each other for a split second. She looked to be a good age, and her skin was dark olive in colour. She wore a long-fringed skirt and high-heeled boots. Her fringed shawl covered her white ruffled blouse. Her outfit was complete with a red headscarf and hooped earrings. She was carrying a basket of homemade flowers with white petals. The penny soon dropped. She was of Romani Gypsy Heritage.

She looked me up and down and gave me a warm smile.

"I hope you will give an old lady a little bit of your precious time", she said in an unusual but friendly accent. "You look like a kind child, and something tells me the stars are in your favour."

I didn't know what to make of this woman. My initial instinct was to push past her, say, "No thanks", and then bolt into the house.

I didn't, though. Being an Aston Villa fan, I was well aware of our local rival [Birmingham City] and that in 1906 a Gypsy's curse was placed on St Andrews by Romany people who were angry at being moved from the site for a new football ground. Since then, the club has had generations of struggle and a lack of success.

"I've just popped home from work for half an hour. I'm on my breakfast break," I explained, hoping she would bid me farewell and come back another time.

Unfortunately, this tactic didn't work. She smiled again and, this time, handed me a flower from her basket. She looked at me closely.

"Allow me to read your fortune, my child."

I knew there would be a cost for her service, so I tried to bluff my way out of it. "I'm afraid I don't have any money", I said.

Her eyes narrowed, and her psychic powers kicked in.

"You are a child who is never without money", she said.

Blimey, I thought. She must have known I was saving up for a Sergio Tacchini Tracksuit top, and I had some money stashed in my bedroom cupboard. I had been rumbled, so rather than lie again, I decided to go for it, as I didn't fancy suffering the same fate as Birmingham City. She waited patiently outside as I went to get the cash.

When I returned, I was clutching £25.00, two slices of marmalade on toast and a cup of tea. She wasn't interested in the toast and made it clear she was about to start the reading with a bow of the head. There was no sign of any Tarot cards or anything. Nor did she ask to see the palms of my hands. I don't know whether she had these in her repertoire, but on this occasion, she opted for face reading. Her dark brown eyes surveyed every aspect of my face. The information that was being transmitted from my face into her mind was 'on the button'. She described my characteristics perfectly. It was as if I had known her all my life. She then progressed to future happenings and talked about relationships, marriage, children, career prospects and living a long-life. She finished off the reading by stating:

"One day, you will own a red car of your own".

I was very pleased with what I had been told, apart from the stuff about having a red car. I despised the colour red, so there was no way I would choose that colour of car. What was she thinking? A second bow of the head was her way of telling me the reading was over. She then held out her right hand as she waited for payment. Gold rings covered her fingers. I handed over £25.00, and she gave me one of the homemade flowers from her basket.

"Bless you, child", she said as she headed out of the garden gate and up the street.

The really amazing thing was that a few years later, I bought a Vauxhall Nova car. I was so fixated on purchasing the model I wanted that I didn't register that the car was red!

Ups and downs

One of the advantages of working shifts was that I was able to go to the football more often. I wasn't able to watch any midweek games when I worked 9:00 am – 5:00 pm, but shift work changed all that. Finishing at 2:00 pm meant I could travel around the country to watch Villa play. There was always the option of swapping shifts, too, if the game was taking place when I was on the late shift. Of course, this meant working a late shift, going home to sleep for eight hours, and starting another shift at 6:00 am before setting off to the match. Night matches under the floodlights took me to away grounds such as West Brom, Birmingham City and Wolves. I also experienced the fantastic atmosphere of European nights against the likes of Inter Milan and Juventus. You couldn't beat it.

Football ski hats were the fashion, as were football lapel badges. I became obsessed with the badges and would buy one every time I went to a match. I built up quite a collection, including badges of teams from lower leagues, such as Bury and Darlington and teams in Europe, such as Bayern Munich and Ajax.

Due to travelling back so late from games, there were occasions when I didn't get back to Leeds that evening and found myself sleeping at train stations. Then, I'd catch the first train home the following morning. I'd sometimes be woken up by the transport police in the middle of the night along with the waifs and strays, who were using the station as a place to put down their heads for the night before being moved on.

I'd only been a Creeler for a few months when I put my name forward to learn how to weave. Through spending so much time working alongside the weavers, I'd begun to pick up the basics. I knew how to stop and start the looms; I knew the difference between warp and weft breakages and I could tie a weaver's knot. The advantage I had in my favour was that Mr Golding knew how reliable I was. He didn't speak to me very often, but he fully understood my character and that, given the chance, I wouldn't let him down. A couple of months after expressing an interest in weaving, he beckoned me to the shift manager's office. This was a raised structure with big Perspex windows where the shift manager spent most of his time. It had an excellent view of what was going on across the whole weaving shed. I had never actually been in the office before. It was the office where, every Friday, we formed an orderly queue outside to pick up our wage packets. I followed Mr Golding up some steps that led into the structure.

"Have a seat, Snorkel", he said.

As I listened, I noticed he had a badly damaged nose and was wearing his replacement glasses. This was because he had been headbutted by Joyce Wilson's husband at the works Christmas party a few nights earlier. Mr Golding had a reputation for flirting with the female weavers and Mr Wilson had decided to take matters into his own hands when he found out his wife was involved. Mr Golding continued,

"We are looking to train a weaver and I noticed you had put your name forward for this. Is this something you are still interested in because we need someone to start training on Monday."

"Yes, I'd really like that", I said as I stared at his fractured nose.

"Ok, that's great. Do you know Tommy, the small guy with the beard? He'll be training you. Report to him first thing Monday morning" [it was now Thursday afternoon].

"Ok, thanks for the opportunity, Mr Golding. I won't let you down."

"Make sure you don't", he said as I left his office.

I was normally buzzing on Fridays because I generally had something lined up for the weekend. But that particular Friday, I had a 'double buzz'. Not only did I have a juicy trip to Sheffield Wednesday to look forward to the following day, but I knew my career in the textile industry had just moved to another level. I also knew that my pay packet would increase to a minimum of £120.00 per week. I was on the up.

Word soon got round that I had been promoted. I knew this wouldn't sit well with the likes of Dumbbell Dan and Sandra Arkwright. Sandra was the first to show her feelings. She had to walk past my work area to reach the break room. As she did so, coffee cup in hand, she stopped and gave me the death stare. She wasn't happy that we were soon to be on par as she had always looked down on me as if she was far superior. Dumbbell Dan took his frustrations to another level. He approached me from one of the storage areas. He had a smirk on his face. I didn't notice he had one hand behind his back.

"Hey Snorkel, what's this I've heard about you going weaving?"

Just as I was about to answer, suddenly, he thrust forward the arm that was behind his back and towards my face. He was holding a handful of green coloured grease, the type used to lubricate the textile machinery. The attack was over in a split second. The grease went into my mouth, up my nose. My face was covered in it. Dumbbell thought it was a great prank and walked off laughing. No other workers witnessed what had just happened. I stood there in shock. Although I felt like crying, I remained composed and wandered off to the toilets to get cleaned up. As I looked in the mirror, I saw a shy young guy with low self-esteem staring back at me. I thought to myself, I wasn't like this at the weekends. I was more outgoing. I was more confident in my own skin. Maybe I didn't belong in this environment. Maybe this environment was curtailing me and I could do better. Maybe this place was only for the likes of Dumbbell Dan and Sandra Arkwright. According to the reading from the Romani gypsy lady, I had a better career ahead of me. Well, here I was in a backstreet mill with a bunch of bullies and no clear escape plan. This was the first time these thoughts had come into my mind, and they weren't the last.

Broken Bones and Barnsley Away

My first day as a trainee weaver soon arrived. My mentor was Tommy Wands. Tommy was short, bearded and always had his hairy chest on display. He smoked roll-ups and always seemed to have a Tupperware of sandwiches on the go. He was the only person in the shed who used an army-style white enamel mug for his tea. Tommy was a bit of a show off and was always bragging about how good a weaver he was. His ability didn't always match up with his confidence, though.

"Hey, Snorkel, watch how fast I can get those three looms going", he would say to me.

And ten minutes later, he would still be trying to get the first loom started. It was hilarious. He had a great sense of humour, and he took the mickey out of me at times; I didn't mind, though. I gave as good as I got. I was pretty relaxed around Tommy.

A couple of weeks into the training, we were stood at the top of the shed chatting. We were right next to one of the fire exits. I was leaning against the wall but wasn't concentrating on what I was leaning on. All of a sudden, we were given the fright of our lives as the fire alarm started to go off. It was deafening. I presume the volume had been set so high so that it had to overpower the noise of about 250 textile looms. It was then I realised that I was leaning on one of those red Fire Alarm Call Points, the ones which state 'in case of fire break glass'. I hadn't actually broken the glass, but the pressure I must have placed on it was enough to set it off. Tommy looked at me in panic as he knew what had just happened.

"Follow me", he said.

Along with all the other workers, we made our way out of the mill. We all congregated in the freezing cold outside. I was trying extra hard not to look guilty. Eventually, the Fire Brigade turned up and turned off the alarm. They then carried out an inspection of the fire alarm system but couldn't come up with a reasonable explanation as to why it went off in the first place. Only me and Tommy knew that, and that's the way it stayed.

I spent approximately four weeks being mentored by Tommy until I was confident enough to weave on my own. Tommy then returned to his Helper Weaver role. This was kind of a floating role that supported other weavers and covered for breaks and such like. I was allocated set 12 and was to be responsible for twelve state-of-the-art weaving looms powered by rapier technology. My set was located in the top right-hand corner of the weaving shed near to the Tacklers cabin. This was handy if there was an issue with one of the looms as I hadn't far to go to seek assistance to fix it. The tackler who was responsible for set 12 was called Kenny. He was a cheerful fella and had the look of the actor Michael Caine.

Weaving could be challenging at times. The aim was to make sure the looms were running as much as possible over an eight-hour shift, and you were paid on performance. The two main reasons a loom would stop would be for a weft breakage [this was indicated by an orange light on the loom] or a warp breakage [this was indicated by a red light on the loom]. On some shifts, the looms would run like clockwork, but these were few and far between. More often than not, you would spend eight hours just chasing orange and red lights. It could be demoralising at times, as you would start a loom, thinking all your looms were running, only to turn around and see five more stopped. It was endless. The climate in the shed had to be humid. The natural cotton fibres require moisture from the atmosphere to help with the weaving process. The humidity was created by sprinklers attached to overhead pipes, and these created a fine spray of water. Working near the sprinklers when you were full of dust and fibres wasn't very pleasant.

My promotion to weaving had meant an increase in my weekly pay packet and this was most welcome. At around that time. I also started generating additional income from an unexpected source. One day, I was approached by a guy from the warehouse called Eddy. He was a friendly guy and loved the banter, especially if it was football related. He wasn't a good-looking guy by any stretch of the imagination. He was also going bald with a comb-over hairstyle. Somehow, though, he had managed to bag himself a Spanish wife who was really attractive. They had a corner shop and she used to run this whilst he was at the mill.

"Hey Snorkel, your dad collects the Football Pools Coupons, doesn't he?" asked Eddy.

"Yes, that's right", I said.

"Is there any chance he can start collecting mine? That old fella who currently comes to the mill collecting the pools is very hit and miss, and I want somebody more reliable."

"Yes, I'm sure that would be ok. I'll bring you some coupons tomorrow."

As I wandered back to my looms, I recalled seeing the old fella that Eddy mentioned. I'd only seen him briefly, but from memory, he must have been in his seventies and had a look of the British journalist Alan Whicker. He generally wore a Trilby hat, a trench coat and carried a wicker shopping bag. He shuffled around the mill at a snail's pace.

Sure enough, the following day, I arrived at the mill with some pool coupons for Eddy. He filled them in and I took them home along with the money and gave them to my dad. Word soon spread. Other workers in the mill began to approach me. This included some of Sandra's associates which she was none too happy about. They too were fed up with the old guy with the shopping bag. It wasn't too long before I had built up a bank of enthusiastic customers. Because I was taking home so many coupons, my dad put me on commission. Thursdays were extremely busy, as I had a steady flow of customers to deal with whilst trying to keep all my looms running. My percentage efficiency on Thursdays never climbed above 70%, but I didn't mind. The commission I was making through the pool coupons was enough to cover my train fare to Birmingham and back, which at the time was £12.00. The Alan Whicker lookalike eventually packed in coming as all his customers had moved allegiance to me because I provided a reliable and efficient service. He was last seen standing in the middle of the mill scratching his head and wondering where all his customers had gone.

I'd only been weaving a few months when I had an accident away from work. I was at the sports centre playing badminton with my friend Tim when it happened. I rolled my ankle and heard a crack. It was pretty painful, so we stopped playing and he dropped me off back home. I didn't think it was too serious, so I didn't bother going to A&E. Big mistake. I was on the early shift and the alarm went off at ten past five as normal. I had completely forgotten about the accident the previous night. I threw the covers back, spun around to get out of bed and put my injured foot on the floor to stand up. The pain that shot up my leg was excruciating. It was so bad I yelped. Maybe this wasn't a sprain, after all, I thought. By lunchtime that morning, the bottom part of my leg was in Plaster of Paris, and I was signed off work for ten weeks. I had broken my ankle in two places.

Although I was incapacitated, it didn't stop me from getting out and about, especially to the football. I set my sights on an away match at Barnsley. The trek was only from West Yorkshire to South Yorkshire, and for someone on crutches, I thought this would be doable. The trip didn't get off to a good start. As I was crossing the road approaching Leeds train station, both my crutches slipped off the kerb. It took me completely by surprise, and I lost my balance and fell into the road. Thankfully, the cars managed to quickly swerve around me rather than running me over. Undeterred, I picked myself up and made my way to the station to catch my train. The walk from Barnsley train station to the football ground was quite tiring, even though most of it was downhill. For part of the walk, I recall the terrain underfoot being this slagheap-type material. It was also freezing cold, and I hadn't put enough layers of clothing on. Being fashionable was more of a priority to me in those days rather than being warm. I reached the football stadium nice and early, probably about 45 minutes before kick-off. There weren't too many fans milling about. Standing up for ninety minutes in my condition in the freezing cold temperatures was going to be an issue.

Outside the main stand, I spotted a steward and approached him. He was an old, doddery fella wearing a flat cap and an orange fluorescent vest on top of his overcoat. My guess was that he had been a steward at the club for a long time, but I could have been wrong.

"I've got a broken ankle and don't think I will be able to stand up for 90 minutes. Where in the stadium would you recommend I sit?" I asked.

In a strong Yorkshire accent, he said,

"Folla uz".

We went through a door next to one of the turnstiles and walked down the side of the pitch to the bottom corner of the ground. Initially, I couldn't work out where he was taking me to. We turned left and up a ramp with a gentle incline that led us up to an elevated structure with Perspex windows. It was a designated area for disabled supporters. Inside, there were enough seats for about fifteen people.

"Sit thi sen darn," he said.

Then he handed me a pair of headphones. I popped them on to find they were tuned in to the local radio station.

"Ahl be back i' eur minute."

As I waited for him to come back, I could see that the other people in the space were severely handicapped. They were excited and decked out in red and white football gear, but I'm not convinced they fully knew what was going on. Within a few minutes, the old Steward was back.

"Gerr these daahn theur", he said, as he handed me a meat and potato pie and a cup of Bovril.

"How much do you want for these"? I asked.

He just winked at me and then shuffled off to attend to someone else. I couldn't believe my luck. Instead of leaning on my crutches in the freezing cold, here I was, in a toasty warm space with a brilliant view and filling my face with the best cuisine Barnsley could offer. I felt slightly guilty though, as I felt like a fraud. I only had a couple of broken bones and would be back to normal in a matter of weeks. The other supporters had lifelong disabilities and were far more worthy of these fantastic facilities than I was. Still, I didn't ask the old steward for this generous hospitality; he offered it. The match finished 2 – 0 to Villa. I decided to leave ten minutes before the end to get ahead of the crowd. I knew I had an uphill walk on crutches to get to the station. I timed my getaway just right as I just about managed to avoid being stampeded by hordes of other supporters. As I headed back towards Leeds on the train, I contemplated how the day had unfolded and how everything had worked out in my favour. I was really grateful to the steward for his kindness and a couple of days later wrote a 'thank you' letter to the club for their generosity. I have had a soft spot for Barnsley football club ever since.

Fisticuffs in the Weaving Shed

I had now been employed at the mill for a couple of years. Apart from Dumbbell Dan and Sandra Arkwright, I got on well with the other workers. Nobody referred to me by my Christian name; everybody just called me Snorkel, even though my roof cleaning days were behind me. I didn't mind, though, as it reminded me of Kit Kat. I was doing ok, apart from the nagging thoughts I had from time to time about the future. I pondered all sorts of things, such as whether I would be a textile weaver for the rest of my working life, what other types of jobs were out there that would suit me, and how could you access these jobs. Then, the nagging thoughts would fade away, and I would start daydreaming about something else.

The company was constantly recruiting new staff, especially for menial type jobs such as cleaning and working in the warehouse. I noticed one of the new recruits was hired as a loom sweeper. A loom sweeper's job was to clean the loom after an empty weaving beam had been removed. The cleaning regime was to dowse the loom down by spraying it with purple coloured cleaning liquid, then blow the loom down with compressed air before rubbing it down with old rags. The new recruit was overweight with a heavy mop of jet-black hair. At first impressions, he came across as being arrogant. He didn't look the type to be rushed, either. Due to his physique, he was given the nickname of Roly Poly, but by whom, I never found out. He was aware of this label but didn't seem to mind.

He'd only been working in the mill a couple of weeks when I began to notice a strange pattern. I'd often look up to find him staring at me. When I caught him staring at me, he would try and stare me out. Sometimes, I would catch him staring at me even if he was on the other side of the shed. It was all a bit odd. I also noticed that when one of my looms needed cleaning, he was always at the front of the queue to clean it. The other loom sweepers never got a look in. When he was cleaning one of my looms, he would purposely try to cover me in debris by pointing the compressed air pipe in my direction. I could see him smirking behind his disposable facemask. I soon came to the conclusion that he didn't like me for some reason. The feeling was mutual.

Early one Thursday morning, this dislike for one another came to a head. I had been home for my breakfast. It wasn't quite half past nine yet, and I decided to spend a few minutes in the breakroom before going back to set 12 to start weaving again. I entered the break room to find Roly Poly sat there on one of the benches. He was alone. I sat down across from him. I expected him to start staring at me, and he did. I felt quite tired that morning and wasn't as laid back as normal. In fact, I was quite grumpy.

"What are you staring at?" I asked.

There was no reply, but he continued to stare. His big brown eyes were full of hatred. I raised my tone,

"I said, what are you staring at?" Still, there was no reply.

As I wasn't getting a reaction, I reached for a discarded newspaper on the table between us. The headline on the front page was 'DNA Match-up is a billion to one'. It crossed my mind that this might be an interesting article. I was just about to start reading it when Roly Poly decided to speak.

"Have you had your hair cut?"

"What if I have?" I said in a resentful tone.

"I'd ask for your money back if I were you, it's shite."

I saw red, threw down the newspaper and sprung to my feet. He also got to his feet, but not as quickly as me. I moved away from the table and bench. So did he. In my mind, this confrontation was only going in one direction. I was so angry I didn't even consider where I was [at work]. I clenched my right fist and then punched him in the face as hard as I could. He made a groaning noise and stumbled to the floor. His fall was cushioned by his flabby body. I didn't think he would get up, but slowly, he got to his feet. His nose was bloodied. Instead of throwing a punch in my direction, he opted to wrestle me, which I thought was an odd tactic. He flung his arms around me. We were like two wrestlers moving backwards and forwards around the break room. Because our bodies were slamming into each other I was picking up an unpleasant aroma of garlic and a cleaning fluid from my opponent.

We were extremely lucky that no other worker entered the breakroom during the melee. Then, our luck ran out. Together, we fell against the breakroom door. It was a sliding door and wasn't designed to open upwards, but on that occasion, it did, due to the fact that 25 stone of body mass had just smashed into it. Directly outside the breakroom was the staff locker area. There were eight rows of connected lockers, and unfortunately, during our sumo-style wrestling match, we stumbled into the row of lockers directly outside the breakroom. The effect was similar to that of pushing over a row of dominos. Only these dominos were twelve feet long and seven feet high. Each locker toppled against the next, with the last row smashing through the window of one of the storage areas. This chain reaction of the lockers falling over signalled the end of the fight. We both picked ourselves up. In the space of a few seconds, we had caused carnage. What we hadn't considered was whether anybody was using their locker when they toppled over. Our only priority at that moment was to make ourselves scarce and hope we hadn't been spotted. This was rather unlikely, given the racket the lockers made as they fell into each other. As quickly as I could, I returned back to set 12. Roly Poly and his bloody nose hurried away in a completely different direction.

It wasn't too long before the management were made aware of the incident and were stood by the lockers inspecting the damage. Some of the workers were taking an interest and had wandered over to take a look. There was a lot of scratching of heads followed by finger-pointing......with some of the fingers being pointed in my direction. At first, I thought I might have got away with it especially as I saw Roly Poly being dragged into Mr Golding's office. Twenty minutes later, I could see Dumbbell Dan approaching me. He wasn't quite as smug as normal and was covered in bandages and dressings after he'd had some form of treatment to remove his tattoos. By looking at the state of him, I thought he hadn't had the tattoos removed via laser surgery. It looked like he had saved himself a few quid and tried to do it himself. He was a mess and looked to be in a lot of pain.

"You need to go to Mr Golding's office. You are in big trouble, Snorkel," he grunted.

Then he walked off. I trundled across the shed in the direction of the office, not knowing what my fate would be. I questioned why I had behaved that way. How had I got so angry? Why couldn't I control this anger? I shouldn't have punched someone whilst in the workplace.

As I arrived at Mr Golding's office, Roly Poly was just leaving. His nose was swollen and red. He'd also been crying. As our paths crossed, he muttered,

"You're fucked, Snorkel."

During his interview with Mr Golding, he'd obviously 'stuck the boot in', which I fully expected. Now, it was my turn to sit in the hot seat. Mr Golding was fuming. His complexion had changed colour with anger. In no uncertain terms, he told me how disappointed he was with me. He was also extremely surprised by my behaviour. Based on the evidence [Roly Poly's damaged nose] it was clear that it was me who had been throwing the punches. I accepted that and explained how sorry I was. I tried to defend myself and made it clear that I had been provoked and that I had perhaps gone over the top. I didn't mention that I may have been influenced by a documentary about West Ham's Inter City Firm [ICF], I'd watched a few nights earlier. I would have totally lost him. I just sat there on tenterhooks, awaiting my fate. When my fate was revealed, it was a complete surprise. Amazingly, I had kept my job. But only just. He explained that my behaviour 'was totally out of character' and that was the only reason he had decided to give me a second chance. He made it clear that a repeat performance would not be acceptable, and if it happened again, I would be down the road. The same message was given to Roly Poly.

Max to the rescue

The day after the fight was a Friday, so it was nearly the weekend. The feeling of getting away from the dust and the clattering of looms was great. It hadn't been a great week for me, and to make matters worse, there was a rumour circulating around the mill that redundancies were on the horizon. All the workers were talking about it. If you were in the breakroom or at the coffee machine, the conversation would be,

"Have you heard that they are going to be laying people off?" or something to that effect.

Workers were beginning to get worried.

The following day, I'd pencilled in a trip to Birmingham. Villa were at home to Millwall. My train fare had been covered by my football pools commission, so it always felt like the travel was free. This left surplus money for other essentials, such as more lapel badges or a steak pie supper at the end of the day. The usual footie fans were mingling around Leeds station. We had a catch-up before setting off in different directions around the country. I loved the buzz at Leeds station on a Saturday morning. The feeling of excitement and anticipation. I wish I could have bottled it. That particular Saturday, I was wearing my blue Lyle & Scott sweatshirt, jeans and my beloved Samba trainers. I had noticed a correlation between wearing the Lyle & Scott sweatshirt and Villa winning, hence the decision to wear it. On the journey down, I stared through the train window at the passing scenery. I couldn't help but mull over what had happened at work over the last couple of days. How was it that this shy perfectionist with low self-esteem was getting so worked up that he started throwing punches at other workers? Had I changed so much? Why had I behaved like this? What should I do about it? By the time I arrived at Birmingham New Street station, I'd worked out what to do. It was something I suspected for quite a while. I had to leave the textile industry and try something else, which was in a completely different environment. I was going to need some advice on how to do this, though.

My usual routine on home matchdays was to arrive early in Birmingham and have a look around the Bullring indoor market before catching the train out to Witton. Listening to the locals who ran the market stalls was fascinating. Their stalls were ladened down with things like fruit & vegetables, household goods, tapes & records and other bric-a-brac. I was in awe of their confidence as they shouted above the crowds as they peddled their wares. Some of the stallholders had the customers eating out of the palm of their hand. It was really impressive how persuasive they could be. For example, customers would be looking to buy one punnet of strawberries and leave the stall with three!

That particular day, I'd had my ear pierced at a booth in the market. It was something I had been considering for a while. I knew I would be teased at work, but I could cope with that. I wandered through the market, and a stall I hadn't seen before caught my eye. It sold jewellery. The stallholder looked to be in his mid-thirties, wearing a denim jacket, with bleached blond hair shaped in a mullet style. I was the only person browsing. He glanced up, then carried on sorting his stock, which seemed to be more of a priority. Next to me appeared a rather attractive female who also started browsing. She looked to be in her mid-forties. She stood out. She was classy and sophisticated and was wearing high-end clothing. Her arrival at the stall sparked the attention of the stallholder. Although he clearly didn't stand any chance whatsoever of dating the woman, this didn't stop him from trying.

"Hey blondie, yaw place or moy-un", he said, in a strong Brummie accent.

She was flattered, blushed and slowly glided away to browse at another stall. Then he looked at me, smiled and said:

"Yaouw win sum yaouw lose sum" before carrying on organising his stock.

Although it hadn't worked on this occasion, this was the best chat-up line I'd ever heard.

Unfortunately, that afternoon, my lucky sweatshirt didn't work, and my winning streak came to an end as Villa was beaten by Millwall 2 – 1. On the way back, a guy called Max boarded the train at Wolverhampton. He was one of the regulars at Leeds train station most Saturday mornings. We all knew him as Max but weren't sure of his proper name. That seemed to be the normal thing to do. You just used to latch onto the names everybody else used rather than find out the person's proper name. Anyway, Max supported Tottenham. He looked to be in his early thirties, wore glasses and was short with dark hair, which was starting to go grey. Max didn't swear. He didn't drink. And he didn't follow fashion. He was very sensible. He always had a Gola sports bag with him, one of those shoulder-length ones. Inside, he would have a selection of food to see him through the day, a flask of coffee and a transistor radio. Max never visited the train station buffet or food vans outside the football grounds like the rest of us. He would also keep his matchday programme in the sports bag. He was the only person I came across who would buy two copies. One programme would carefully be placed in a plastic wallet, and the other was for reading. I am presuming the ones that ended up in a plastic wallet would form part of a collection he was building up.

Max sat down on the seat opposite to me and placed his bag on the table. I noticed he was out of breath and perspiring when he first boarded the train. A few minutes had passed and his breathing rate had now returned to normal.

"Did you nearly miss catching this train, Max?" I asked.

"Yes, I had to leg it across Wolverhampton town centre", he said. "A car slammed on its brakes as I dashed across the road. It hit me, but my sports bag cushioned the impact, and I was able to get to my feet. I'm really lucky to have caught this train. I could have ended up in A & E, or even worse, been killed."

If it had been anybody else telling this tale, I may not have believed them, but this was Max, and he was as honest as the day is long. He even managed to verify his story, as when he delved into his sports bag for something to eat, to his amazement and mine, he pulled out an apple that had split in half following the collision with the car. It wasn't a surprise that his flask was broken, too.

Max was good company on the journey back. We mostly chatted about his adventures watching Tottenham. He mentioned he worked at the local college in the Support Services team and that he had been there since leaving school. I talked to him about my job and admitted how the previous week had unfolded. I explained I would like to change my career path but wasn't sure how to go about it. He said that there were people at the college who could help me and that I should call in the following week. He pulled out a notepad and pen from his trusty sports bag and jotted down his work phone number before passing it across. I promised him I would call him on the following Monday after I had finished work and organise to make an appointment.

A couple more cans of McEwan's Export later, and we pulled into Leeds train station. We were greeted by the unmistakable railway station smell - there are slight variations to this smell, but overall, it smells the same, like creosote. The stuff that they soak the railroad ties in to preserve them. Fuelled by four cans of McEwan Export and buoyed by some potential support to increase my chances of leaving the mill, I was on a high.

The following week at work was pretty eventful. The rumours about redundancies that had been circulating were confirmed by management. Every worker received a letter explaining that orders of fabric from the factory had been in decline for many months and the outlook was looking bleak. As a result, they were informing every employee that they were at risk of being made redundant. With this in mind, it looked like my conversation with Max might be quite timely. I wasn't downbeat like many of the workers. At least I had started to plan my escape route.

As agreed with Max, I gave him a call on the Monday afternoon after I had finished work and we arranged a day and time for me to go to the college to discuss my options going forward. I was to attend the college at 3:00 pm on the Friday of that week, and when I arrived at the reception, I had to ask for someone called Lesley. He encouraged me to make some brief notes beforehand that covered what I wanted to say and take along any copies of certificates or qualifications that may be useful.

The day soon arrived when I was due to visit the college. I was quite anxious about it. That particular day, set 12 was running like clockwork, and the shift dragged. It got to just before 1:00 pm, and I was standing leaning against one of my looms watching old Judith. Judith was an elderly Scottish lady whose job was quality controller. She checked the quality of the fabric and cloth being woven and, if necessary, reported any faults. She had been doing the job for years. Judith stopped loom number 222. She knew how to separate out the ends from each shaft and move the rapier along in slow motion to check for faults. If a fault was spotted, she would stop the rapier and place her middle finger under a number of ends where she suspected the fault was, lift them up and inspect them closely. It was something she had done hundreds of thousands of times before. On this

65

particular occasion, something went badly wrong. I am not sure how it happened but whilst she had her hand inside the loom checking the ends, the rapier flew across at high speed, taking her hand with it. Judith made a noise like I had never heard before. It was a helpless yelping sound. I only looked for a split second but could see she had gone from five digits to four digits in a flash. There was no doubt more damage to her hand, but now wasn't the time for a closer inspection. Judith needed my help and fast. I sprinted away from the loom to look for assistance. I knew that the First Aider was called Cindy, as she had treated me a few weeks earlier when I cut my hand with some scissors. I quickly scanned the shed but couldn't see her. My next thought was to sprint towards Mr Golding's office to tell him about the incident. Luckily, he was there. I blurted out what had happened. He instructed me to go into the warehouse and inform Mr Walton who was to ring for an ambulance. Then, I had to track down the First Aider. I did as I was told, although Cindy didn't look too impressed as she was just about to sit down and have a hot chocolate she'd bought from the machine.

By the time I got back to loom 222, there was quite a crowd of workers gathered round Judith to see if she was ok. Through the crowd I could she was slumped over the loom. It looked like she had been sick too, probably due to the shock. It was difficult to carry on weaving with all this commotion happening on set 12. It just didn't feel right. Not with Judith being in such a predicament. All in all, she was probably there for another twenty minutes before she was cut free. She was escorted out of the shed in a wheelchair by one of the paramedics. Part of the rapier that had caused the damage was still wrapped around her hand. This would need to be removed at the hospital under anaesthetic.

Judith's accident had distracted me from thinking about my appointment at the college later that afternoon. I didn't have time to go home for my usual cheese and cucumber sandwich, so I headed to the college straight from work. I arrived in good time, reported to reception and asked for Lesley, as instructed by Max.

"Lesley will be with you shortly," said the receptionist.

A couple of minutes later, a slim-looking lady with frizzy auburn hair and small round glasses came wandering down the corridor towards me. She was very smiley.

"You must be Wayne", she said. "Duncan mentioned you would be dropping in to see me this afternoon."

I looked at her blankly. Who the heck is Duncan, I thought. Then I realised that Max's first name must be Duncan, and he was probably called Duncan Maxwell or something.

"Oh right", I said, as if I knew exactly who she was talking about.

"Follow me Wayne; let's go and grab a coffee and have a chat and see if we can help you in any way."

We made our way along a corridor and through a library area before reaching a space outside some offices and classrooms where there were some comfy chairs and a coffee machine. Lesley chatted to me all the time we walked. She was really friendly. I don't know whether it was Lesley's manner or the after-effects of witnessing the accident at work, but I felt a lot calmer than I thought I would. I also couldn't help but notice how clean the college was in comparison to the environment I worked in on a day-to-day basis. I spent nearly an hour with Lesley.

She was keen to know my current situation, any previous qualifications and my thoughts on career plans moving forward. She explained that what the college could offer would work alongside my full-time job. But there would need to be a degree of commitment from my end if this was to work.

By the end of the hour, we had a plan in place that I could work towards. I was to undertake an Open College course called 'Study Skills'. This was designed to help me feel more confident about learning. In addition, I was to study for my GCSE Maths as I hadn't achieved this at school and this would be a prerequisite for any higher-level courses I wanted to attend in the future or jobs I applied for. The plan was for me to do the majority of the studying at home and attend College once a week, tying it in with whatever shift I was on. That afternoon, I left the college building full of hope and pleased the visit had gone well.

Redundancies looming!

The following morning, I was up early as I was travelling to Crystal Palace to watch Villa. I spotted Max at the train station and thanked him for setting up the meeting with Lesley. He said he was more than happy to help and wished me good luck with my studies. He also mentioned that if I had a problem with any of the coursework, I should give him a call.

The train journey down to London gave me time to think. I thought about: old Judith's hand and how she was, the proposed redundancies at the mill; and my forthcoming educational and learning challenge. I probably would have pondered these thoughts all the way to the capital, but I was distracted by a girl who boarded the train at Grantham. She sat on the seat opposite me. She had a gothic look. She was wearing distressed denim jeans with a black T-shirt, combat boots, and studded bracelets. Her accessorises included moon and star-shaped jewellery and black lipstick. Her makeup was very elaborate, dramatic, and, in some cases, extreme. Her mission between Grantham and London King's Cross was to plait some strands of the jet-black hair that swept across her face.

For the next ninety minutes or so, I was mesmerized as she painstakingly divided the hair and crossed strands over each other, time and time again. She knew I was watching but didn't seem to mind having an audience. Similar to me, I got the impression she was a perfectionist. The plait had to be immaculate and look like whatever image she had drawn up in her mind. If it wasn't, she had no qualms in dismantling it and starting again. I enjoyed watching this girl. She had a presence.

But there was one thing I didn't understand. It was her fingernails. They were all about an inch long. It wasn't the length of them that concerned me. It was how dirty they were. They were packed with black grime and looked disgusting. It looked like this build-up of grime had been there for some time, too. My mind started racing as to why this might be the case. Maybe it was a rebellious statement to complement her style. Maybe it was a sponsorship challenge to ignore nail hygiene for 12 months. I didn't have the answer. Give it a couple of minutes, with a small scrubbing brush and some hot, soapy water and, this could be sorted. Maybe she was going to tackle the nails when she got home? I would never know. All I knew was when it came to prioritization; she seemed more interested in plaiting a few strands of hair than sorting out her manky digits.

The trip to Crystal Palace was a pretty dismal affair, with the game ending in a draw. During the match, I stood next to a couple of Villa fans who were nonchalantly smoking marijuana. This was the first time I'd come across the use of drugs in public before. I listened to them as they recalled a story from two weeks earlier. They were driving to an away game at Ipswich when another car pranged into them. The driver of the car had no intention of stopping and drove off, so they set chase after it. After chasing the car for six miles or so, they realised it wasn't going to stop. In frustration, one of the guys wound down the window and threw the first thing he could lay his hands on at the other car. This turned out to be a spider wrench and it caused some serious damage to the other car's door. Under the influence of the weed, the guys thought the story was hilarious and recounted it over and over again. By the end of the game, most of us who were stood in earshot knew the story off by heart.

On the tube, on the way back to Kings Cross after the game, I found myself in a carriage with a young homeless guy. He was probably in his mid-twenties and he was hunched over one of the train seats, asleep. The front of his trainers was badly falling apart, revealing his green socks. I reckon the socks hadn't come into contact with a washing machine for at least six months. The stench coming off this guy was remarkable, and I wasn't even sitting next to him. His situation made me put things in perspective. I thanked my lucky stars that I had a job and that I had a roof over my head. I wanted to wake him up and give him a few quid, but the disgusting odour got the better of me, so I kept my distance.

Over the next couple of weeks, the atmosphere in the mill felt different. The banter levels dropped due to the impending redundancies. The rumour was that the workforce was to be reduced by 20 percent. It was noticeable that some workers' behaviours changed. Some of those who had a reputation for being lazy suddenly stepped up a gear. To save her own skin, Sandra Arkwright cut back on her tea breaks. She made sure the mill management team was aware of this at every opportunity. If I happened to come across her in the break room [which wasn't very often], she made her feelings known to those who were listening that junior weavers should be the first names on the redundancy hit list. She looked at me as she said it. She was poison. The threat of redundancies didn't play on my mind too much. I was still living at home with my parents and would likely still have a roof over my head should I become a redundancy casualty. However, I'm not sure what their reaction would be if my £17.50 weekly board and lodgings contribution per week suddenly stopped.

I had now started my part time courses at the college. Any downtime I previously had was now being taken up by studying. Instead of frittering away my spare time, I was absorbing information about things like research techniques, academic writing styles, equations, ratios, and fractions. Lesley had stressed that it would be really hard work combining part-time study and full-time work, and she was right. The hard work wasn't going to stop me, though. I was committed, determined to do well and, most importantly, enjoying this new challenge. The one thing I had to ensure, though, was that my part-time study should remain private and that nobody at the mill was to find out about it. The last thing I wanted to do was to 'let the cat out of the bag' and to give more ammunition to the mill bullies, such as Dumbbell Dan, so they could taunt me more than they already did.

Redundancy survival and the big Snooker challenge

One evening, on the late shift, I was on my customary 9:00 pm tea break. In the break room were Tommy Wands and little Jim Briggs. Little Jim was about five feet tall with rosy red cheeks. He was similar to Mr Golding in that he conditioned his hair with Brylcreem. He was also about four feet wide, which was not surprising, as his favourite food was steak pudding and chips. He used to tuck into this particular dish at least four days a week and would generally follow it up afterwards with apple pie and custard.

Little Jim's role at the mill was to ensure all the factory machinery was well lubricated. He carried an oil can and cloth everywhere he went. When I first started working at the mill, he was a bit standoffish for the first few weeks. I just thought he was shy or maybe wanted to keep himself to himself. Then he discovered we had something in common and all that changed. He became aware that his wife and my mother attended the same church every Sunday. He broke the ice one day when I clocked on for work. I arrived at my locker and was carrying a plastic bag that contained my overalls and some snacks. I heard a voice behind me say,

"I hope you haven't got your prayer mat in that bag."

I turned around to see Little Jim grinning at me. Before I had a chance to say anything, he piped up,

"I understand you come from a family of churchgoers," he said mischievously.

I started laughing. And from that moment on, we got on like a house on fire.

The other thing we had in common was that we used the same barbers. The barber's name was Godfrey. He had a shop in the open-air market. He was very popular. One Saturday morning I was sat in Godfrey's barber shop waiting for a haircut. This was the type of establishment where you didn't make an appointment. You just had to work out who was in front of you in the queue and who was behind you. There was no background music or casual conversation either. Just the sound of Godfrey's scissors snipping men's hair.

The shop was really busy that morning, with up to ten other blokes waiting for a trim. In front of me in the queue was a balding guy wearing a Hawaiian shirt. Once he'd vacated the barber's chair, I jumped into it. As I was a regular at Godfrey's, he knew I always went for the short back and sides look, so just clarified whether I wanted my usual. I quickly nodded to avoid having to speak in front of the ten or so punters behind me. Godfrey had only been clipping away at my wavy ginger locks for a couple of minutes when the silence was broken by a big booming voice from the back of the shop.

"Hey Godfrey, make sure you give young Snorkel a belter of a haircut. He's going on the beer tonight, and he'll want to be impressing the ladies!"

Little Jim's funny remark went down well with the rest of the guys in the shop. I was laughing too, but at the same time, going

74

bright red and warm with embarrassment. Unfortunately, Little Jim's remark distracted Godfrey too, and his Saki's nicked my right ear, causing it to bleed. Godfrey was very apologetic about the blunder and patched me up before I left the shop.

Initially, the conversation with Tommy and Little Jim during the tea break was about Scottish Judith. News had come through from her son that she had lost two fingers through the accident, and more surgery was required to save another finger, which had severe tendon damage. One thing was for sure. As this was an industrial accident, a compensation claim was on the horizon. As I was the only witness, I would need to be interviewed as part of the process. This was something I wasn't looking forward to.

As with most conversations that Tommy was involved in, he was generally bragging about something or other. On this occasion, the subject was snooker. By the end of the tea break Tommy had claimed he was so good he could go toe to toe with someone of the calibre of Steve Davis. As we left the break room, a snooker match between Tommy and Little Jim was being mooted. Within 45 minutes this singles match had now developed into a doubles match. Little Jim had roped in Henry Daley, one of the managers in the warehouse, and yours truly had been roped in to partner Tommy.

Tommy had recruited me without doing any research whatsoever. Little did he realise, I was below average when it came to snooker. The date for the match was the following Thursday at 7:00 pm. The venue was the Pigeon Club, a working men's club, where Little Jim and Henry Daley were members. Little did we know at the time what the consequences of the snooker match would be.

The day arrived when workers found out if they were to be made redundant. It was the same day as the snooker match. The banter and build-up surrounding the snooker match was a temporary distraction for some of us, away from the gloomy mood that had developed around the place. Tommy didn't seem to be phased by the imminent redundancies. He was too focused on the snooker match. He talked about nothing else. He seemed obsessed. The plan was for us to leave work at 2:00 pm, go home and rest before meeting up at a snooker club in town at 5:00 pm for a couple of practice frames to get ourselves warmed up. We were all set. We just needed to avoid being made redundant first.

The actual process of how people found out they were to be made redundant hadn't been made clear to us. We soon worked it out, though. In a nutshell, if Mr Golding was walking in your direction, your 'number was up'. It was that simple. At 1:00 pm, the process started. From set 12, I had a decent view across the whole shed. I watched as Mr Golding walked in different directions to inform workers that they were to be let go. Sometimes he would disappear in the warehouse to deliver the bad news, then reappear a few minutes later. Those unlucky to have lost their job were each handed a white envelope. No doubt, this confirmed their fate in black and white.

As I dealt with a weft break on loom 224, I watched Mr Golding stride towards a weaver called Wilco, whose set of looms ran adjacent to mine. Wilco was trying to get one of his looms started. He could sense Mr Golding getting closer and closer to him. With each stride, Wilco's face turned redder and redder. It wasn't very pleasant to watch. He was handed his letter by Mr Golding; then he set off in the direction of the lockers to collect his belongings. As he walked past set 12, tears rolled down his rosy cheeks, and then, in a fit of frustration, he flung his scissors and reed hook to the floor.

By 1:30 pm, Mr Golding's work was done, and he went back to his office. Maybe he had been through this process before, as he didn't seem to show any remorse. I guess carrying out tasks such as this was part of his role. It seemed like me, Tommy and Little Jim had somehow managed to keep our jobs. I couldn't believe it. I had only been a weaver for a short time, and with the incident with Roly Poly on my disciplinary record, I was convinced my name would be on the redundancy list. I had lived to fight another day. I also had a snooker match to look forward to that evening.

I followed Tommy's instructions and arrived at the snooker club by 5:00 pm. The club was located in a huge underground basement beneath some shops. The only way to access it was through an open-ended shopping arcade. Inside the club, it was dimly lit, with about ten full-sized snooker tables and a couple of pool tables. There was also a bar. Tommy was already there when I arrived. He was wearing a checked shirt, jeans and cowboy boots. He was pacing around the table, weighing up which ball to pot. I noticed there were the remains of a pint of lager on the nearby table next to the coat hanger. His first comment when he saw me was,

"It's your round, Snorkel."

I trundled off to the bar and ordered two pints of lager. I also asked the guy behind the bar how long the table was booked for. He confirmed it was until 6:30 pm.

"Your mate has been here since 4:00 pm. He'll be lucky if he lasts until 6:30 pm, though, at the rate he is knocking those lagers back. This will be his fifth pint."

"Blimey, I didn't realise that. Thanks for letting me know," I replied.

I carried the drinks back to the table. Tommy had racked up the balls for a new frame. We began the practice match. We didn't play for points. The intention was to get a feel for the snooker cue and pot as many balls as we could in the time we had available.

I'd only been at the snooker club for about 20 minutes, and a couple of things were quite noticeable. Tommy was nowhere near as good as Steve Davis by a long chalk. To put it bluntly, he was average at best. The second thing I noticed was more worrying, though. The Tommy I was with at the Snooker club, was a far different Tommy I was used to at work. In the mill, he was a nice guy to be around. He loved the banter and enjoyed a good laugh. He also poked fun at himself. He wasn't at all like this in the snooker club. He was serious and agitated. He was also very quiet. The only noise he made was a tutting noise every time he missed a shot, which was virtually every time he went to the table. By the time it was 6.30 pm and time to head to the Pigeon Club to meet Little Jim and Henry

Daley, Tommy had consumed in excess of ten pints of lager. The build-up to this eagerly anticipated snooker match was not going well.

We arrived at the Pigeon Club via a taxi. Little Jim was waiting at the entrance to meet us. He was dressed in a dark blue blazer and white shirt. He must have nicked himself shaving as there was a smidgeon of blood on his shirt collar. He was also wearing a pair of red trouser braces, which hugged his protruding stomach and held up his black slacks. He smelled fresh and was Brylcreemed up. It was unusual not to see him wearing overalls and carrying an oily cloth.

"Here they are. Steve Davis and Jimmy White," he shouted before following this up with his unmistakable laugh.

As this was a 'members club', he needed to sign us in. He introduced us to a guy called Ron, who was sitting at a table just inside the club entrance. He completed the necessaries and then Jim led us through to the main room in the club. Henry Daley was stood at the bar waiting to be served.

"What's your tipple Gents?"

"Two lagers", shouts Tommy, whilst inspecting the snooker table in great detail, trying to give the impression he was looking for something specific and he knew what he was doing.

I soon worked out that the Pigeon Club was on another level to the Carlton Club that I sometimes visited with Paul. This place had more of an exclusive feel to it, and the clientele seemed more upmarket and less welcoming. You could tell by how Little Jim and Henry Daley interacted with other members of the club, that they were well respected and fitted right in. Those members present [about 30 of them] somehow seemed to know about this snooker showdown and had turned out in force to cheer on their own. I couldn't see any posters around the place advertising the 7.00 pm showdown, but there might well have been. I began to develop pre-match nerves. Now I knew how Aston Villa players felt when they stepped out at the likes of Old Trafford and Anfield. This definitely felt like an away match.

We'd agreed from the offset that the snooker match was best out of five. It only took a few moments before I knew what we were up against. The opposition was good and certainly knew their way around a snooker table, particularly Henry Daley. The way he held his cue and paused at the front and back of his stroke was very classy. Little Jim, on the other hand, was luckier than anything else, but when it came to using the Spider rest, he was red hot. Due to his height, he didn't have the reach, like the rest of us, so he was reliant on this accessory and used it several times every frame.

Every time one of them went to the table they would either pot a ball or put us in a snooker. We were getting slaughtered. The fact that Tommy was sinking more pints than he was snooker balls wasn't helping our cause. He was now slurring his words and finding it difficult to walk in a straight line. Little Jim and Henry had noticed this, and so had the opposition fanbase. I was beginning to feel quite tipsy myself but trying not to bring attention to it.

Unsurprisingly, the first frame went to them by a margin of 70-plus points.

"Come on, Snorkel, we can still win this," blurted Tommy, but his words were too incoherent and slurred because of the alcohol consumption.

His attempted rousing words of encouragement had little effect. Henry Daley had got the bit between his teeth and was sinking balls for fun. He was unplayable. Together, him and Little Jim were like a well-oiled machine, whereas we resembled a car engine that wouldn't start. We were getting annihilated and lost the second frame to go two frames to nil down.

Just before the start of the third and crucial frame, a man behind the bar brought out a huge tray of chips and buttered bread rolls. This was most welcome. Not only was I starving, but it paused proceedings and gave us a break from the humiliation of the snooker. I tucked into the food but noticed Tommy didn't bother; he continued to swill back the lager. The break in proceedings didn't make any difference. Little Jim and Henry continued where they had left off. As each ball disappeared into the pocket, our chances of victory faded away. A break of 32 by Little Jim helped them clinch the third and crucial frame and victory was theirs. We all shook hands. Little Jim had a big grin on his face.

"Same again next week," he bellowed before giving us another helping of his instantly recognizable laugh.

Tommy, in his drunken state, then proceeded to make a half-hearted attempt to rack up the snooker balls for the start of another game. Fortunately, we talked him out of it. He was absolutely hammered. As he slumped into a chair next to the snooker table, he muttered to himself,

"We can still win this Snorkel; they are there for the taking."

It was heading towards midnight before we left the club. Little Jim and Henry Daley lived a few streets away from the club, whereas I lived about half a mile away. I wasn't really sure where Tommy lived. The night was cold, and the sky peppered with stars as I staggered home. I knew I'd had too much to drink as I couldn't walk in a straight line. I was also conscious I had to be up for work in just over five hours' time. I needed my bed.

Hangover from hell

It only felt like I had been asleep for about an hour before my alarm clock started buzzing. I hated the sound of the alarm clock at the best of times, but that particular morning, the levels of hatred were off the scale. I considered rolling over and going back to sleep, but as Henry Daley was part of the management team, I had no choice. I had to turn up for work. Besides, I was conscious I needed to show some loyalty to the company after the recent round of redundancies. The effects of the alcohol hadn't worn off from the night before. I felt dreadful. My head was banging, and I wanted to vomit. Everything was a struggle, even getting myself dressed. Minor things, such as the textile odour smell coming off my jeans, amplified my tender state. I had eight hours of work in front of me, and a deafening textile mill was not the place you wanted to be when you were still smashed and had a terrible hangover. This was something I was going have to face and somehow get through it.

It wasn't a surprise to see Little Jim waiting for me by the lockers. He was grinning like a Cheshire Cat and started mimicking someone playing snooker as I approached.

"Lambs to the slaughter," he bellowed, as a reference to the night before, then burst out laughing. "I see your partner in crime is too ashamed to show his face," he went on.

By that, I presumed he meant Tommy wasn't in yet. I was so ill I couldn't be bothered to engage in a conversation, so just smiled, or made a vain attempt to, before heading in the direction of set 12. It was obvious Little Jim wasn't feeling the effects from the night before. His was his normal cheery self, and his complexion was as rosy as ever. In comparison, I was so pasty I looked like I had been locked in a room for 12 months with no sunlight. I approached set 12 and said a little prayer. I needed the looms to run well. Unfortunately, my prayers weren't answered. Set 12 ran me ragged. It was weft and warp breaks all the way. By eight o' clock, I had thrown up twice in the gent's toilets. This was to the amusement of some of the workers who were in there at the time. The toilets doubled up as a hiding place or place to have a quick smoke, so some of the workers used to congregate there. At times, getting through the shift felt like torture, but somehow, I managed it. It would have been much easier if my helper weaver had been around to assist. Unfortunately, this hadn't been the case. Tommy hadn't turned up for work.

The following day, Villa were away at Portsmouth. Although I had recovered from the hangover, I hadn't planned on making the trip to the south coast. It was a long way to go, and I wanted to focus on my college work. I had earmarked the Saturday to work on my Study Skills modules and the Sunday to focus on the GCSE Maths. With dreaded maths exams on the horizon in a few weeks' time, Lesley had given me some previous maths exam question papers to practice on. She had explained that I would need to sit two exam papers. Each paper would last ninety minutes. The first paper was a non-calculator exam. I was growing in confidence in topics such as geometry and measures, ratio and proportion, and probability and statistics. The topic I struggled with was algebra. I simply didn't get it, despite how hard I tried. If I had been struggling with a topic a few years earlier, I would have simply thrown in the towel. But not anymore. I was now a little bit more mature and had developed a resilience to succeed. I also had people at the college, like Lesley and Max, willing me to do well. The support was there. I just needed to ask for help if I needed it.

We were working the late shift the following week. With the immediate threat of redundancy now dispersed, I was hoping the week would be more positive than the previous one. I was also expecting to see Tommy. As we started the shift at 2:00 pm, there was no sign of him though. It was a complete mystery. His attendance record was generally excellent. Little Jim, who generally knew everybody's business, was also in the dark about his whereabouts. He just shrugged his shoulders when I asked him if he knew where he was.

The looms on set 12 purred during that shift. This was rare. I couldn't let this opportunity pass me by, so I took out the maths revision notes I had in my pocket on the off chance I would get a chance to look at them. It wasn't an ideal environment for revising but I tried to absorb the information the best I could. I wasn't normally one for getting sidetracked, but I couldn't help think about Tommy's behaviour on the night of the snooker match. It was abnormal. Why did he drink so much alcohol too? I was now beginning to wonder whether he managed to get home safely. I hoped he was ok. Then my eyes diverted back to my revision notes, and to questions like a class has 12 boys and 17 girls, write the number of boys and the number of girls as a ratio.

Tuesday was college day. When I was on the late shift, I generally turned up about 10:00 am. Lesley was her usual smiley self. A couple of weeks earlier we had been chatting about what my career options were, going forward. One of the things we had discussed was quitting working in textiles and undertaking a full-time further education course, as from September. Together we had identified some potential courses including a BTEC Diploma course in Leisure Studies at a college in a nearby town. She had agreed to explore this on my behalf. Lesley relayed that following a phone call with the course leader, they were interested in meeting me to discuss the course in more detail and give me a tour of the college at the same time. They were aware I was studying for my GCSE in Maths, and had explained that passing this, was a prerequisite for the BTEC course.

This news from Lesley was really exciting, yet also daunting and filled me with dread. Exams were not my thing. The thought of the GCSE Maths exams made me sick. It was now only eight days away from my first exam too. And I still hadn't cracked algebra. We agreed that I would get the exams out of the way, and then deal with making an application to undertake the full time BTEC course. For the next couple of hours, I practiced algebra questions with Lesley before heading off to work.

The days leading up to the first exam were filled up with either work or revision. I had managed to hide the fact that I was undertaking part time study away from the other workers. I hadn't even mentioned it to those workers who I was really friendly with, like Carol, Paul and Little Jim. I felt it was best to see this though on my own and give it my full focus and attention without the added pressure of other people knowing about it, or in some cases, making fun of me.

The day before the exam, Carol pulled me to one side during the shift. She knew about the snooker match and how worried I was about Tommy. "I bumped into Tommy's mother-in-law yesterday morning whilst I was shopping in town," she said. "It's not good news, Wayne."

Carol was the only person in the mill who referred to me by my Christian name instead of my nickname.

"Tommy was an alcoholic in recovery. He'd been sober for a couple of years. He'd made a promise to Jackie [his wife] never to drink again. Something triggered him to start drinking again on the day of the snooker match. Jackie has asked him to leave the family home because she has had enough of him. She simply couldn't cope when he was back on the booze. Nobody has seen him for over two weeks now."

I couldn't believe what I was hearing. I had no idea he was a recovering alcoholic. I suppose it's one of those things you might not want to broadcast, for obvious reasons. For the rest of the shift, I tried to get my head around the news. My emotions were all over the place, I was angry one minute and sympathetic the next. I also felt guilty, as I was part of the event which may have triggered the relapse. I asked myself, what could I have done if I had known he wasn't supposed to drink? Probably nothing. I guess it's down to him to remain sober. Why did he choose that bloody night to go on a bender, though? And where has he been for the last two weeks? I hoped he was ok.

Examination day woes

The day of the first GCSE Maths exam arrived. My 5:10 am alarm went off as normal. I turned on my bedside light and lay there staring at the ceiling. I felt sick. I knew the day ahead was going to be a real test. I know you shouldn't 'wish your life away', but I wanted it to be the following day, as then, the current day, including the exam, would all be over. That was my 'go-to' thought in situations I didn't want to face, as for a split second, it gave me some comfort. As I lay there, I played out in my mind how I wanted the day to unfold. It was as follows. Go to work; set 12 purrs all day; squeeze in last bits of revision; go home for a quick wash and change; arrive at the college by 3:00 pm; and blast through the exam. The way I wanted the day to unfold, in comparison to the way the day actually unfolded, was poles apart.

When I arrived at set 12, all the looms but two were stopped. Afram, the weaver who ran the set on the night shift, shook his head as I approached him. He looked hot and flustered. You could tell by the dust on his work clothes he had been in a battle for the last eight hours.

"They are running like pigs" he said, as he walked past me on the way to the lockers.

 Oh shit, that's all I need, I thought.

If an experienced weaver like Afram couldn't keep the looms going, what chance did I have? Twenty minutes into the shift, I was so absorbed in trying to get the looms running that I hadn't noticed something significant. It was Carol who tapped me on the shoulder and pointed it out.

"Tommy's back," she said, pointing in the direction of set 10.

I stopped what I was doing immediately. Through the haze of the mill fog, I could see a figure in the distance. It didn't look like Tommy, though.

"Are you sure that's Tommy?" I asked. "It is," replied Carol.

"He's in a mess, and he has no money. He came to the mill yesterday afternoon and begged them to let him come back to work. Reluctantly, the management said yes, and have agreed to sub his wages so he can try and get back on his feet."

I didn't know how to react. Of course, I was pleased he was back at work, but what did this mean going forward? Not just for me, but for everybody, now we understood he had a drink problem.

Over the next few hours, I worked my socks off, trying to keep the looms running. The intensity of the work meant I didn't have time to think about Tommy's reappearance or even cram in any last-minute exam revision. I was unsure about whether I should try to strike up a conversation with Tommy or leave him be. Carol suggested I should give him space and not pester him. I thought that was sound advice, but at the same time, I didn't want him to think I wasn't there for him. I, therefore, decided to pitch it somewhere in the middle. I knew he didn't have any money, so I thought I would sort out some food for him.

On my 9:00 am break, I dashed home and made numerous slices of toast, wrapped them up in tinfoil, before sprinting back to the mill. I walked towards him. He was at the back of a loom tying a weaver's knot. Tommy was unrecognisable. He had lost the beard and looked really gaunt. The clothes he was wearing weren't his usual attire. He was probably relying on handouts or something. But for his gold filling and the tattoo of a swallow on his left hand, I would have thought that the Tommy stood in front of me was an imposter. But it wasn't. It was definitely him. As I handed him the tinfoil package, his sad eyes looked past me, rather than at me.

"I thought you might be hungry, mate," I said before wandering off towards set 12. I was devastated.

The rest of the shift was challenging. The looms didn't behave themselves. Maybe it was because it was a really warm day. It was pushing 27C outside. I had noticed a pattern that the looms seemed to run better when the weather was cooler outside. For eight hours, I don't think I managed to have all 12 of them running at any one time. I certainly didn't have time to look at the revision notes in my pocket, either. I occasionally looked in the direction of Tommy. I was hoping he might come over and have a word with me, but it never happened. He kept himself to himself.

At 2:00 pm, I sprinted home, got myself cleaned up and headed for the college. I managed to get there at 2:45 pm. The exam was due to take place in the college sports hall. I was familiar with the venue as I had played five-a-side side football there many times. Inside the sports hall, it was sweltering. I took my seat at one of the tables. There was approximately 200 to choose from. I chose one facing the sports hall wall, as I felt I would be less distracted. On the table to my left sat a guy with blond hair. He was wearing a Dutch national football shirt, jeans and Reebok trainers. Then I looked to the table on my right and there was a guy who looked exactly the same and wearing the same outfit. I couldn't believe it. I had seated myself between identical twins. It was uncanny. I was aware that some parents preferred to dress their twins alike when they were toddlers. Potentially, it could be a faster way to shop since they only have to pick an outfit and look for the corresponding size, but these guys looked to be about 18. Maybe they had started out wearing identical outfits and just wanted to continue enjoying the symbolism of their unique status as twins for a bit longer.

I was sweating profusely. I could feel droplets of sweat rolling down my forehead. My yellow Lacoste polo shirt was soaking. Suddenly, the exam invigilator started to speak. After some brief instructions, he then asked us to turn over our exam paper and commence. I took a deep breath, picked up my pen and made a start. The first question was:

Janice has three coins in her pocket and they are all different from each other. Jeremy has three coins in his pocket and they are all the same as each other. Jeremy has twice as much money as Janice. What are the coins they each have?

I spent a couple of minutes trying to work it out but couldn't. Lesley had drilled it into me to 'pass' on questions I was struggling with and then return to them later. With this in mind, I started passing on question after question until I could find something I could answer. All the time, I was getting hotter and hotter. It was a combination of the heat in the sports hall and feeling hot as a result of the panic and stress caused by the exam. Finally, I came across a question I could answer comfortably. It was:

Petra and Stephan share £240.00 so that Petra gets one third of what Stephan gets. How much do they get each?

This gave me a little bit of confidence. I now needed some momentum, but sadly, that never came. For the next hour, I found myself going backwards and forwards through the paper and picking off questions sporadically. With twenty minutes to go, Double Dutch [the identical twins] stood up at the same time and left the sports hall. Either they had breezed through the paper, or they had bombed. By the look on their faces, it wasn't the latter. I had at least ten questions which I hadn't even attempted.

"You have ten minutes left," the invigilator announced.

With the unanswered questions, I randomly guessed at the answers rather than leaving them blank. The last unanswered question in my paper was about probability. The invigilator brought proceedings to a close.

"Please, can you put your pens down and stay seated until your papers have been collected!" he shouted.

I was absolutely exhausted, not to mention relieved. I had given it my all and couldn't have done any more. Then I realised something. I pushed back my chair to stand up. I had been sweating so much I had created a small puddle on the floor. Oh, crikey, people are going to think I have got so stressed that I have pissed myself. Quickly, I manoeuvred the chair over the damp patch to try and conceal it before making a sharp exit out of the building. The day hadn't unfolded like how I hoped it would, but I had got through it. Just.

Hanging around with an Orangutan called Terry

That evening, I mulled over how I thought the exam had gone, and this continued into the following day whilst at work. As I trudged from loom to loom, I could think of nothing else. The effort I put in wasn't in question. What I needed help with was how to manage myself better when under exam conditions. I recalled Max telling me that one of his cousins struggled with exams and decided to seek help. She found a book in the library about how to cope with exams. She adopted some simple strategies to reduce exam stress and, by all accounts, cruised through her next exam. My mind was made up. I was going to visit the library the following day and see if I could find a book that would help. My second exam was just over a week away.

Over the next few days, the mill management monitored Tommy's attendance. He was either turning up for work late or not turning in at all. When he did turn in, I continued to supply him with rounds of toast. My mother was having to buy extra loaves from the supermarket to keep up with demand. She even threatened to increase my board and lodgings to cover the cost. It wouldn't have bothered me if she had. I wanted to help Tommy and this was the only way I knew how.

Eventually, those in charge at the mill decided to terminate his employment. He'd once again turned up for a shift late. He was boozed up and unsteady on his feet. Mr Golding and Mr Walton gave him the news when he arrived. Tommy went ballistic. He started hurling abuse at the management and shouting he was the best weaver the mill had ever seen [typical Tommy] and that he would burn the place to the ground if they sacked him. Mr Golding and Mr Walton couldn't handle him in this mood and so called the police. The police officers who arrived were Rob and Roy, the same ones who handled the incident with Kit Kat. Tommy had to be escorted off the premises. I'm pleased I didn't witness any of this, as it would have been heartbreaking to watch. I began to wonder if I would ever see Tommy again.

In the library, books about Coping in Exams were scarce. In fact, there was only one available to borrow. According to the librarian, the library stocked about seven books that covered this subject, but the other six were out on loan. It did cross my mind whether two of those books had been borrowed by Double Dutch, and the consequence of this, was that they were able to leave the first exam with 20 minutes still in the tank. On closer inspection of the only remaining book available, I noticed it had last been loaned out over six years ago. On the inside cover, somebody had written in pencil 'this book is shite'. I didn't let that put me off. I took it out on loan. I was desperate.

When I arrived home, I looked at the book in more detail. The book had spiritual connotations and emphasised how it was possible to integrate mythical creatures into our psyche and lead a more fulfilled life. You were encouraged to create a fictional animal in your mind and build up a relationship with it through subconscious communication. The overall idea was that you were supposed to feel mentally stronger by having this creature within your soul. The book gave examples of situations in our lives, when we might need to be at our strongest, mentally, and this included scenarios like sitting examinations, job interviews or the build-up before having a serious medical operation. My immediate thought was that it all sounded a load of codswallop. Surely, this mumbo jumbo wouldn't work. But what other options did I have? I needed to pass the GCSE Maths to be able to access the BTEC course or a better job. Otherwise, I might end up being stuck in the textile mill forever, and that's not what I wanted. Decision made. I was going to go for it.

Within a few minutes, my imaginary animal was created. I felt it would make more sense if I created something that was a similar size to me. It would feel more real, than say communicating with a tiny mouse or something. The creature I created was an orangutang. I called him Terry and gave him a cockney accident. The cockneys I'd come across always sounded confident and thought that's the kind of character you need on your side in an exam. I began to introduce my new imaginary companion at different points throughout the day.

At first, it felt a little bit weird. I started off by having conversations with Terry at home, where it was private. For example, in my mind, I'd read out a maths question, provide a rationale for the answer and then ask Terry what he thought and he would respond. After a couple of days, I progressed to using my new technique in other places. Terry and I discussed what horses to back when I went to the bookies and we chatted about which drink to order when I went to the pub. Not only was Terry a great sounding board, he was also my guardian. One particular day, I was alone in the breakroom and in walked Sandra Arkwright. It was very rare we bumped into each other on a break so one of us must have been out of sync. I normally would have sat there and absorbed her verbal abuse, without saying anything back. But not on this occasion. The conversation was as follows.

"You were lucky to keep your job the other week when they were making redundancies. If I was in charge, it would have been last in, first out." [Sandra]

"Ask the rubber-faced cow if she has ever been bullied whilst at work." [Terry]

"Have you ever been bullied whilst at work, Sandra?" [me]

"What's it got to do with you?" [Sandra]

"Tell her, you have been reading an article in the newspaper about bullying in the workplace." [Terry]

"I was reading an article in the newspaper about someone who was bullied at work. The bully was reported to management and lost their job." [me]

"What are you telling me for?" [Sandra]

"Don't answer her question. Ask her what she would do if she lost her job because she'd been accused of bullying someone." [Terry]

"What would you do if you lost your job because you'd been accused of bullying in the workplace?" [me]

Sandra made a dismissive noise, accompanied by a shrug of the shoulders.

"Now stand up, and as you walk out of the breakroom, tell her you are being bullied at work and are thinking of reporting the person to management." [Terry]

"I'm being bullied and have been ever since I arrived at this place. I'm fuckin sick of it and I'm going to report it to management." [me]

As I walked in the direction of set 12, I couldn't believe what I had just said. I didn't have any intention of reporting her for bullying, but she didn't know that. It felt so good to stand up for myself for a change. It was going to be interesting to see how she handles me next time our paths cross too. I also recognised that a leopard cannot change its spots, so the conversation may have been a waste of time. I would have to wait and see.

The day of the second maths exam paper soon arrived. This time, the exam was 9:30 am and it coincided with me being on the late shift, which was ideal for me. Unlike last time, I didn't have the issue of taming set 12 beforehand and then having to rush to the college. I could take my time. Lesley had phoned me the day before to offer me words of encouragement. I thanked her for her support. However, I declined to tell her I would have an imaginary companion by the name of Terry, in the exam room next to me. I hadn't said a word about this to anyone. People would think I was going doolally. Maybe I was.

I arrived at the college at 9:15 am. After the experience of the previous exam, I didn't want to tempt fate, so I opted for a table at the back of the sports hall, a good 30 yards from where I had sat before. I also decided to wear the thinnest T-shirt I had in my wardrobe to avoid any chance of overheating. The t-shirt was merchandise I bought at a Fleetwood Mac concert 'Greatest Hits Tour', a few months previously in Manchester. From the back of the sports hall, I had a view of everyone. Double Dutch were once again on the front row. Although I could only see the back of them, they looked to be wearing Ajax football club shirts instead of the bright orange shirt worn by the national team.

In comparison to last time, my anxiety levels were totally different. Although I was sat there on my own, physically, I knew that spiritually, this was going to be a team effort. The exam invigilator went through exactly the same process as he had done just over a week ago and then asked us to turn over our exam paper and commence. I flipped over my paper and picked up my pen. The conversation inside my head started as follows.

"Here we go, Terry. Are you ready?" [me]

"Ready as I'll ever be. Now, question one looks tricky, so try looking at question two first. And don't forget to show your workings." [Terry]

"Got it covered." [me]

"Question seven is about probability. You tend to do well with probability questions, don't you?" [Terry]

"I sure do." [me]

"Does the sequence of numbers look right on question 16?" [me]

"Check your answer again, just to make sure." [Terry]

"Will do Terry." [me]

We managed to sustain this pattern of communication for the next eighty minutes or so. It was a fantastic team effort. With ten minutes to go, all the questions had been completed so there was time to quickly revisit all my answers. On the ninety-minute mark, the invigilator brought proceedings to a close. As he started to go around each table to collect the completed papers, I sat there with a smile on my face. I couldn't believe how much easier it was this time around. I didn't panic, I didn't perspire, and I wasn't mentally exhausted. In fact, I felt quite fresh. The only similarity to the last time around was that Double Dutch again left twenty minutes before the end. I left the sports hall, then managed to have a quick word with Lesley before making my way home. She was delighted I had got through both exams and we agreed to meet the following week to discuss my progression route.

That afternoon at work, I was chipper. I was also relieved to have got the exams out of the way. Even though I didn't know the result of the exams and study skills course, I was proud of what I had achieved. Studying part-time and holding down a full-time job had really challenged me. However, I felt I had risen to that challenge. The result of all my hard work would materialise in due course. In the short term, I now needed to give some serious thought to what I was to do next in terms of career progression. For the next couple of days, though, I just wanted to chill out and do nothing. I think I'd earned it.

The following morning, I went to the library to return the book I had borrowed, the one about Coping in Exams. I perched myself on a comfy chair away from the other people in the library and said my goodbyes to Terry. It was a brief chat, with Terry doing most of the talking.

"Terry, thanks for everything you have done over the past week or so. I don't think I could have got through this without you." [me]

"No problem, Wayne, it's been a pleasure. If you ever need to call on me again, don't hesitate to ask. Good luck with your exam result. I'm sure you'll smash it. Until next time." [Terry]

"Thanks again. See you around." [me]

As Terry disappeared from my psyche, I wondered whether we would ever cross paths again. I chuckled to myself as I was convinced his cockney accent had softened a little through hanging around with me over the last few days. I opened the front cover of the book to once again reveal the graffiti on the inside page. I knew I shouldn't, but when the librarian wasn't watching, I decided to alter it. After my input, instead of reading: 'this book is shite,' it now read 'this book is highly recommended,' followed by 'Orangutans rock!' Pleased with myself, I left the library and headed for home.

The Last Shift

The following week, with the help of Lesley, I confirmed my interest to join the full-time BTEC course at a neighbouring college. This involved completing a rather lengthy application form as part of the process. I also needed to provide a reference, and Lesley duly obliged. The college made contact with me about attending a site tour, but unfortunately, I had to decline, as it clashed with work. As we headed into the summer months, life was less hectic. The football season was now over so my weekends were pretty quiet. This suited me as I knew I needed to save some money, especially if I continued with my plan and left my job to go to college full-time. As each week went by, I started squirreling money away. With the money I earned from the pools round, and not going to the football, I was saving nearly £70.00 a week. I was happy with that.

The last week of August was a scorcher. This was the week I would finally find out the results of the courses I had undertaken. I headed to the college in anticipation. I didn't arrive until 10:00 am. I assessed the students who were loitering around. Some were ecstatic, whilst others looked forlorn. I wondered which camp I would end up in over the next few minutes. I approached a table in the college reception area and was handed two white envelopes by a junior member of the Support Services team. I didn't open them immediately. I wandered down a corridor in the direction of the college canteen. Just outside the canteen, there was a meeting space with some comfy seats next to some imitation plants. I sat down. Firstly, I opened the Open College Study Skills envelope. I had obtained 3 credits at level 3. I didn't show any emotion, but deep down, I was chuffed. Now for the big one. I took a deep breath and ripped into the envelope containing the GCSE Maths result. It read: Wayne Spinner has obtained a Grade C in Mathematics GCSE. I was speechless. I was delighted. I had passed the exam. It wasn't the greatest grade in the world, but I didn't care. It was what I needed to leave the mill. All my hard work and revision had paid off. I had also been rewarded for not giving up. I could have easily thrown in the towel after that first exam paper, but I didn't. I persevered and got there in the end. I went into the canteen and bought myself a custard tart and a coffee to celebrate. Lesley was in there, and so was Double Dutch. They were wearing matching red polo shirts and looking chuffed with themselves, so I could only presume they had also passed the exam.

Lesley came over, congratulated me and gave me a big hug. "When I get back to the office, I'll tell Duncan", she said.

"Please do," I said, happily. When I finally left the college, I was absolutely buzzing. Nothing was going to spoil this day, I thought. Sadly, I was wrong.

Later on, I arrived at work ready for another late shift. I had only been at set 12 for a few minutes when Carol approached me. She looked at me with her big, droopy eyes. I could see she had been crying. I sensed now wasn't the time to inform her of the news of my academic achievements.

"Wayne, something dreadful has happened. Tommy has died. He was found dead this morning. He had been living in a bedsit in town for the last few weeks. One of the tenants in the flat found him."

I was stunned and just stood there. I had never received news like this before and didn't know what to do. I was trying to absorb it, but I couldn't. I just kept having flashbacks to the night of the snooker match. Carol put her hand on my shoulder whilst at the same time wiping her eyes with her handkerchief. She was also fond of Tommy. For the remainder of the shift, we looked out for each other. We also exchanged anecdotes about Tommy. The things about him that had made us laugh. It helped make what was an awful situation feel just a little bit better. That particular shift flew by.

I had the weekend to soak up the highs and lows of the previous day. The death of Tommy had overshadowed my academic achievements. There was no doubt about it. I smiled as I daydreamed about him. His constant bragging and how he covered for me when the fire alarm went off in the weaving shed. Then I stopped smiling and thought about the snooker match. It was that fucking snooker match that changed everything. If I had known how things were going to turn out, I'd have tried to do something about it. It was impossible to know, though. Going forward, I knew I had to focus on the good times I had with Tommy and the relationship we built up. Dwelling on the negative stuff and his addiction to alcohol was not the way to go.

The college that had offered me a conditional place on the BTEC course was informed of my GCSE grade and followed this up in writing by confirming my place on the course. I wrote back to accept their offer. The course was due to start in just over three weeks. For the next couple of weeks, I had the occasional wobble as to whether leaving the mill was the right thing to do. Then I'd look across the shed and see the likes of Roly Poly, Dumbbell Dan and Sandra Arkwright and soon come to my senses. Staying at the mill was not the right thing to do.

On the Monday of my final week, we were on the early shift. I knew I had to give a week's notice about leaving my job and handed Mr Golding my resignation letter at the start of the shift. I don't think he realised what the content of the letter was and just shoved it in the top pocket of his work overall. At some point during the shift, he must have read the letter as I was summoned to his office. As I sat down opposite him, he said,

"Now, what's all this about Snorkel? This letter suggests you are looking to leave. Is this right?"

"I'm afraid it is, yes. I've decided to go to college full-time to do a course", I said.

"Oh, I see. We don't want to lose good weavers like you. Is there any way I can change your mind?" he added.

"Not really. I've had to work really hard to get on this course, and now I'm really looking forward to it."

"Ok, well, we'll be really sorry to see you go. I'll ask the girls to write you a reference, as by the sounds of things, you might need this further down the track. One last thing. Does anyone else know it is your last week here as an employee?" he went on.

"Not that I'm aware of," I said.

He then winked at me as if to say 'Mum's the word'; I won't say anything then.

It was a great feeling to be on the verge of leaving. I decided to tell those closest to me that Friday would be my last day. These were people like Carol, Paul and some of those who I collected the football coupons from. They were surprised I had handed in my notice, and they were even more surprised that I was going off to college rather than leaving for another job.

Friday soon arrived. I walked into the shed, knowing this would be the last time I would experience the noise and smell of a textile mill again. Over the week, set 12 had been running on average at 66% efficiency. This showed that I wasn't working at full throttle like I would normally do. I didn't care, though. Nobody seemed to notice either. I reminisced about Kit Kat, Judith's accident and Tommy. Carol brought in a chocolate cake she had baked. She had decorated it with the words, "Sorry you're leaving Wayne." This confused most people as nobody knew who Wayne was. If the name on the cake was Snorkel, people would have recognised it instantly.

My last shift had been quite pleasant, with nothing untoward happening. With fifteen minutes to go, I was dealing with a weft break on loom 222 when I felt someone approaching me. It was Sandra Arkwright. The rubber-faced cow looked to be in a determined mood. She'd kept out of my way since I had warned her off [with the help of Terry] a few weeks earlier, so I was slightly surprised she'd come up to me. Her persona was aggressive, and her face was inches from mine. She must have just downed a cup of coffee as she stunk off the stuff.

"Hey Snorkel, what's this I've heard? You and your fancy ideas about going to college. All you know is how to weave. Mark my words; you'll be back here within six months." Then she sped off in the direction of the lockers.

Within a few minutes, it was 2:00 pm, and my time working at the mill came to an end. As I said my goodbyes to the other workers and walked up the backstreet home, those cruel words from Sandra rattled around my head. Deep down, though, I secretly knew that my future was brighter than hers.

Chapter 2: Glen Finnan

What you see is what you get!

I'm Glen Finnan. I'm twenty-eight years old, from Nottingham, and I've just started my final year at university studying Sport, Health & Leisure with Media. Some people may describe this as a 'drinking man's degree,' but I don't. I'm taking it very seriously. I guess that I am in the category of being a mature student, as I was over 21 years of age when I started the course.

I'm five feet, ten inches tall, with spiky sandy hair and my nose is thin and sharp. My standout feature is my front teeth, which are super big and long. In some quarters, I have picked up the nickname of 'Wallace' as I am thought to resemble the good-natured, eccentric inventor from the Wallace and Gromit franchise. However, whereas he loves cheese, I absolutely despise the stuff as it brings me out in a rash. Last time I ate some feta it gave me a prickly sensation all over my body, which lasted for days. Regarding my teeth, I've recently been doing some online research about cosmetic dentistry, but I don't see anything that will work without making my teeth look even bigger.

People who know me may describe me as being laid back or having a pretty relaxed character. I feel I kind of suit the name Glen, as most of the other Glens I have come across in my lifetime have been pretty chilled-out guys, too, without a care in the world. The truth is that although I come across as if I couldn't give a monkey's, I have an inbuilt, steely determination to do well that others cannot see or feel. Despite having the determination to do well, I wouldn't describe myself as 'winning at life.' This is a phrase I keep hearing, and I'm going to use it in this context, but I don't really know what it means.

I'm the type of person who is a stickler for routine. For example, I have cereal for supper every night. I have always done as long as I can remember, and maybe I always will; who knows? Currently, my 'go-to' cereal is Rice Crispies. I'm no stranger to a cereal combo either, with Corn Flakes and Weetabix being my preferred choice. I tend to stick to brand names when it comes to cereals, as I find supermarket's own brands just don't cut it for me. Each to your own though.

Whilst on the subject of food, I am very pernickety about 'sell by' and 'use by' dates on food. I'm also not over-keen in other people making food for me either, as it makes me queasy. At times, this is pretty difficult to avoid, especially if I buy a meal in a pub or I'm at somebody's house, and they offer to make me a sandwich or something.

If this is a phobia [and I'm not sure if it is], I know exactly when it started. It was a friend's birthday party when I was about ten, and I consumed a rogue egg and cress sandwich. It's amazing how such a minor event can stay with you for the rest of your life. Maybe one day, I should seek out some form of therapy to be able to deal with it. Then I could comfortably eat somebody else's food anytime, anyplace, anywhere.

For some unknown reason I've always been pretty health-conscious. I've had various gym memberships over the years. I'm also no stranger to 'working out' at home. I went through a stage where I was obsessed with doing lots of sit-ups before I went to bed. It got so bad that I wouldn't be able to get to sleep until I'd done 600 sit-ups before hitting the sack. In those days, I had a stomach like an ironing board.

The one thing I have been naturally blessed with is speed. I'm not sure if I have inherited this gene or what, but I have always had this natural ability to run really fast. The first time I noticed it, was in the 100 metres sprint in the first-year sports day at senior school. It was a hot afternoon in June and I recall I was drawn in lane three. The other guys in the race hadn't seen me run before, so they had no idea what was in store. As the race got underway, I flew out of the blocks and accelerated away. At about the seventy-metre mark, I looked to my left, then to my right and with the remainder of the field trailing behind me by some distance, I dropped down a gear and cruised home sporting a big goofy grin on my face.

"You'll run for England at the Olympics one day!" shouted Mr Caine, the PE teacher.

Unfortunately, that prediction never came true. Mr Caine had a reputation of being a drinker and a gambler, and it wouldn't have surprised me if he'd placed a wager on me at the bookies to win Olympic Gold after that Sports Days performance. More fool him.

As well as bringing me success at school sports days, my speed has got me out of trouble on the odd occasion. One day, I was merrily going about my own business, probably walking home from the pub or something, when I decided to spit the gum I was chewing up into the air and then volley it before it touched the ground. I'm not sure why this challenge came to my mind, but it did. I counted to three, then blew the gum in an upwards trajectory. As it began its descent, I swung back my right leg and then thrust it forward as hard as I could, making a perfect connection with the gum when it was about a foot off the floor. However, there was one thing I hadn't accounted for. I had forgotten I was wearing slip-on-shoes. As the gum flew in one direction, my slip-on shoe flew at speed in another direction.

Unfortunately for me, it flew across someone's front garden and straight through their living room window! Like a coward, I didn't hang around to see what happened next. Even though I was now only wearing one slip-on, I bolted like my life depended on it until I finally reached home, where I kept a low profile for a couple of days.

Rumour has it that the man who owned the house carried out a door-to-door search in neighbouring streets, asking the males in the house if they owned a pair of Clark's Slip-On shoes and if they were willing to try on the stray shoe. It was very much like the Cinderella fairy tale but without the happy ending.

Outmanoeuvred by an orchid-pink Sofa

It was never an ambition of mine to return to education as a twenty-something-year-old adult. I seemed to have drifted in this direction because I couldn't seem to hold down a job or establish myself in a career that I was interested in. I've had more jobs than I care to remember. Some of them, more memorable than others.

When I first left school, I landed a job working in a furniture store. A guy I knew from school called Gordon was already working there, put in a good word for me. The furniture store was based in a redundant church building. The furniture on sale was priced reasonably, but that's because it was of a 'certain quality'. The job entailed furniture deliveries in the local area and rearranging the warehouse as new furniture arrived. When we weren't doing those tasks, the gaffer [Alfie] gave us odd jobs to do, which all seemed to revolve around tarting up the old church. This included painting the internal woodwork and disposing of unwanted items left by the previous owner.

The most unpleasant task we were given was one which included treating the church roof rafters. We had to climb up some long ladders with pressurised industrial-sized spraying containers strapped to our torsos. The container was full of this claret-coloured liquid, and our job was to give the rafters a jolly good soak. I didn't ask what we were doing, I just followed Alfie's instructions in order to keep my job. No health & safety assessments were undertaken or anything.

For some reason, I always got the feeling that Alfie much preferred Gordon to me. I was left in no doubt that this was absolutely true when an incident occurred whilst out one day on a delivery. We had to drop off a three-seater velvet sofa with an oak base exterior to one of the posher dwellings in the neighbourhood. The sofa was orchid pink and it was one of the most expensive pieces we had in the warehouse. As we pulled up outside the property, I began to wonder why the occupants were shopping in our establishment. If you were to go off the size and appearance of their property alone, it looked like they were minted and could have afforded to shop at one of our competitors whose stock was far grander than ours. They had obviously not taken that approach, though.

As was the norm, Alfie drove the van and Gordon and I were responsible for carrying the furniture into the house. It was late October on a Tuesday afternoon, and the light was fading. It had been raining heavily for days, and it was tipping down that afternoon too. As Alfie sat in the van and watched us, we tried to manoeuvre the sofa into the front porch of the house. For some reason, the sofa didn't have a protective plastic cover over it, and therefore, we needed to get it inside the house pretty sharpish before it got wet. Gordon was at the front and started to work his way backwards into the porch. I was holding the other end of the sofa, but due to its length, I was stood in the muddy garden.

"Get a move on, you idiots!" shouted Alfie from the comfort of the van.

I knew his comment was probably aimed at me, but I tried not to let it affect my concentration. Suddenly, without letting me know, Gordon unexpectedly twisted the position of the sofa to create a better angle for himself. This completely took me by surprise, and I lost my grip. My end of the sofa dropped into the squelchy mud. The arm of the sofa, which was previously orchid pink, was now mud brown! The noise from the wind and rain was soon dwarfed by a high-pitched shrieking noise from inside the van. As I wrestled with the weight of the sofa in the sludge and rain, I swiftly felt a whack around my head.

"Get in the van, you bloody moron!" bellowed Alfie, as he took my place.

I trudged across the garden and jumped back in the van. I looked back towards the house. Beyond the raindrops, which trickled down the van window, I could see Alfie apologising to the man who had bought the sofa. I am not sure how the discussion went, but within a couple of minutes, Alfie and Gordon were carrying the muddy, wet sofa away from the house and in my direction. The back shutters of the van were opened, and the sofa was carefully placed and secured. Alfie jumped into the driver's seat, but he didn't say anything; he just scowled at me before we sped off back towards the furniture store.

That evening, I replayed the incident over and over in my head. I was just caught by surprise, and it was a complete accident. Alfie didn't see it that way. He was thinking about the sale he had just lost.

I thought it best not to return the following day and left the job with immediate effect, even though I was owed at least a week's wages.

I think you've all done very well…….

Another job casualty I can remember was my experience on a Youth Training Scheme [YTS]. This scheme was brought into operation in 1983 and intended to provide school leavers aged 16 and 17 with the opportunity to seek a recognised vocational qualification through on-the-job training. I don't actually recall how I became involved in the scheme. Maybe I had said in passing that it might be useful to learn a trade or something, and my careers advisor latched on to this and signed me up.

I was being taken on by a local building firm. The gaffer was called Derek, and he was supported by a band of sullen-looking guys. Most of them looked like they weren't too far off retirement age, apart from one guy who was called Laurie who looked to be a couple of years older than me. It was Laurie who Derek decided to team me up with, probably because the other more experienced guys didn't want to be lumbered with the new recruit.

Derek's firm had won a contract to renovate some of Birmingham's run-down terraced properties. The house we were working on was in a terraced row overlooked by a canal. Derek didn't like getting his hands dirty. He tended to drop in unexpectedly, have a word with this second in command, Baz, and then disappear for the rest of the day. He was probably trying to secure further building contracts in the city or something. Me and Laurie gelled straight away. I think he welcomed having someone around who was nearer his own age. I'd only been there a couple of weeks when Derek rocked up in the works van and told all his workforce to collect their tools because they were going off to another job. Laurie and I were instructed to stay put and continue to work at the terrace house by the canal.

I was grateful that Laurie was with me, as I wouldn't have had a clue what to do. He directed proceedings and I was happy to follow. Our days consisted of knocking down walls, removing bathroom and kitchen fixtures and fittings, bagging up rubbish and other general labouring tasks. It was filthy work. In essence, we were the lackeys who were gutting the house for when Derek's band of merry men decided to return and undertake the skilled work like plastering, joinery and plumbing.

The worst task we carried out took place on a hot summer's afternoon. We had to lay rolls and rolls of this yellow-coloured fibreglass insulation stuff in the space under the roof eaves. As the name suggests, the material consists of extremely fine glass fibres. With the sun beating down on the house roof, the space we were working in was roasting. I was wearing polycotton work overalls, which slipped over my jeans and T-shirt.

The introduction of the overalls was an effort by my mum to cut down on her washing regime. Normally, it was ok wearing overalls, but on this particular day, the extra layer did me no favours at all. Because it was so warm, I was perspiring pretty badly. The fibres in the atmosphere in the eaves space were overwhelming, covering me and getting inside my clothing. It was really uncomfortable like somebody had poured itching powder all over me. I couldn't wait for the working day to come to an end so I could get out of the itchy workwear and get showered. Following this experience, I now have a real problem with fibreglass insulation. If I see a discarded piece lying around, I have a shivering sensation. It's just another phobia to add to the list.

Every Wednesday, Laurie worked on his own, as that was the day I would attend the local college on day release. At college, I would meet up with the other 'no-hopers' who hadn't done particularly well at school. Here, we could access the fully equipped workshop and get some practical experience, albeit in a safe environment. We learnt how to cut, weld and assemble pipes. It was all entry-level stuff to begin with. This was followed by tasks such as fitting and repairing various household appliances. The more complex stuff, such as reading and interpreting blueprints or plumbing installation plans , was too much of a stretch for us novices and something we would tackle further down the line. College days were a good laugh and a nice break from the labour-intensive days at the house by the canal.

Due to us spending so much time at the house, we began to get to know some of the neighbours. They took an interest in our project and would often enquire how we were getting along. One of the neighbours was called Raymond. He lived next door to the house that was being renovated. Raymond was in his late seventies. He was slim with a thin pointy nose, and when he spoke his face used to scrunch up. He was always smartly dressed in a shirt, tie, jacket and slacks, which didn't seem to fit with the modest lifestyle he led and the run-down area he was living in. He also had a campness about him. He would pop in most days and see us, often bringing us treats that suited Laurie's palette but not mine.

"I think you've all done very well, very well indeed," he would say.

These words of encouragement would make us smile and would motivate us for the rest of the working day. Raymond was a really nice fella and ever so kind. He even once let Laurie use his outside lavatory for a number two.

"I can't believe it," he said when he came back from next door. "I've just wiped my arse on newspaper, as that is all he has; square pieces of the stuff hanging on a piece of string on the door."

The thought of that made me laugh all afternoon.

Our morning walk to work was along the canal. We'd both pick up the canal towpath at the same point and wander on together. The walk generally consisted of Laurie talking about a girl he fancied called Debbie. If he was looking for advice on the matter, I wasn't in a position to help as I had no experience with the opposite sex. It didn't stop him from bringing the subject up every morning, though.

As each week went by, we seemed to have less urgency to get work, probably because the rest of the gang was deployed elsewhere, and we had been left to our own devices. One particular morning, after Laurie had droned on about Debbie for a good twenty minutes and his inability to entice her to the local pub for a drink, he started trying to scare the ducks on the canal. He would pick up stones or whatever he could lay his hands on and throw them so they would narrowly miss the ducks but send them into a panicked frenzy. Laurie thought it was hilarious, and with each throw, his stones were getting bigger and bigger. The next thing, he launched a stone missile the size of a cabbage towards one of the ducks. I don't think he realised how big the stone was. Maybe he wasn't concentrating and he was still thinking about his latest knockback from his beloved Debbie. Anyway, the stone landed right on top of the duck. The duck didn't even have time to quack! It disappeared under the water.

"Oh shit! I think I have just killed a duck," said Laurie.

I didn't say anything; I just started running as fast as I could, taking into consideration I was wearing oversized work boots and in my work overalls at the time. Laurie soon followed.

As we approached the point where we left the towpath, we could see the street below and that there was a gathering of people outside the house we were renovating. On closer inspection, it was Derek and his band of merry men. Laurie turned to me,

"Holy shit, I didn't realise the gaffer would be turning up this morning."

I looked at my watch, and it was 9:30 am. We are supposed to have clocked in an hour ago. As we sheepishly walked towards them, Derek's second in command [Baz] was the first to have a go.

"Are you two allergic to mornings?" he shouted.

This resulted in the others sniggering. Then it was Derek's turn to read us the riot act. If we were hoping for sympathy, it never came. He was fuming. His face went a purple colour, and he continually pointed his finger at us, well, mainly at Laurie anyway, probably because he was more senior. He bellowed that they had all been locked outside the property for the last hour when they could have been working and that we had betrayed his trust. He also asked how many times this had previously happened over the last few weeks.

Old Raymond tried to intervene and save our bacon, but even his favourite phrase: "I think you've all done very well, very well indeed," had no effect whatsoever, and Derek continued with his rant.

It did cross my mind once or twice to mention we were late because we had been too busy murdering the local wildlife but thought better of it. Eventually, Derek seemed to run out of things to say to us and turned his attention to the others. He gave some instructions to Baz before driving away in the works van. It was only 9:45 am in the morning and so far, we had massacred a duck on the canal and managed to get ourselves sent to Coventry by our work colleagues.

If I thought the day couldn't get any worse, I was wrong. That evening, I was out cycling and managed to fly over my handlebars and fracture my shoulder. Under doctors' orders, I was signed off work for ten weeks. I wasn't much use to Derek and the gang with a gammy shoulder. Sadly, during this time I was off, Derek's firm went out of business, and I had no job to go back too. Consequently, I lost my place on the Youth Training Scheme.

Making cardboard boxes with Elvis

I remember one job I had, albeit for only a short time, was working in a factory that made cardboard and other sorts of packaging. The company was based out by East Midlands Airport. I was recruited along with a batch of other guys on a temporary contract at the start of Summer. In addition to myself, the new recruits consisted of Geoff, another guy called Geoff, and Shaun. One of the Geoffs [the older one], resembled singer-songwriter Elvis Costello, so we referred to him as Elvis. He was in his mid-forties, and his favourite word was 'gotcha.' He said it at every opportunity, although I sense he didn't actually know he was repeating the word so often.

The other Geoff was much younger and in his early twenties. He was daft as a brush, lacked concentration and was easily distracted. Geoff and Elvis seemed inseparable. They would arrive together for their shift in a taxi, work next to each other, have their breaks together, and then leave together in a taxi after the shift. Initially, I thought they were father and son, but after listening to the banter between them, it seemed to be the job that had brought them together.

Shaun, on the other hand, was quite different. He was a mature student who was trying to earn a few quid over the Summer. He was a nervy type with thinning hair and unsure of himself. Despite trying his best to fit in, he never seemed to quite gel with the rest of us.

We were all recruited as Packers, on a temporary contract. There wasn't much to the job. We were each shown to a workstation and given a handheld glue gun and packs of cardboard. The packs of cardboard had been manufactured in another part of the building and dragged across on a pallet. Essentially, each piece of cardboard, when laid out flat, was an unassembled cardboard box. At one end of each piece of cardboard, there was a thick red line running down its edge. At the other end of the piece of cardboard was a flap where the glue had to be applied. Our job was to glue the opposite ends of each piece of cardboard together and then stack them in batches of twenty. The trick was to avoid burning your hands with the hot glue.

The work was as boring as hell and I suspect a large number of employees had trodden the same path before us. Some of whom may have then gone on to work in other departments in the factory. These departments included paper making, board production, box conversion, printing, design and commercials. Although Elvis had only been there a couple of days, he already had his sights set on working in other departments as these were much better paid.

Watching our every move was the shift supervisor. He was about six foot, slim, with bleached blond hair and an earring. The noticeable thing about him was that he had a very distinct walk. Elvis's description was bang on, when he said: "He walks like his arse is chewing a toffee."

We were fascinated by the way he walked and couldn't understand why he didn't try to adapt it so it would bring less attention to himself.

Geoff and Elvis seemed to settle in very quickly. They instantly got to know the layout of the factory and were soon on speaking terms with other employees. It was as if they had worked there before! They soon worked out a system for fag breaks too, and knew where people congregated. This seemed to be at the far end of the factory and on the other side of some shutter doors next to some pallets. Fag breaks seemed to be on the hour, every hour. Toffee Bum didn't seem that concerned with Geoff and Elvis and their regular fag breaks. He was more interested in me and Shaun. He watched us like a hawk. We couldn't understand why, and it was quite unnerving.

As the weeks rolled by, we got to know Geoff and Elvis better. The banter between them was pretty funny. It was definitely a love-hate relationship they seemed to have, with the 'hate feelings' only lasting a matter of minutes before they were back on track again. Despite Elvis's regular fag breaks, I noticed he was a hard grafter. His ratio of gluing and packing boxes outstripped the rest of us by some distance. One day, we were chatting, and he explained that after deducting his taxi fares [to and from work], rent, and household bills from his weekly wage, he was left with £12.00 to live on. This did make me wonder whether it was worth his while to actually work at all and whether being unemployed would be an easier option. He didn't seem to take this option though and kept turning up regardless. Fair play to him.

Our contracts were due to finish at the end of September that year, after working all Summer. During our final week, on a Thursday afternoon, Toffee Bum came marching over.

"Anyone for overtime on Saturday morning, 6:00 am – 12 noon?" he barked.

"Gotcha," said Elvis, who seemed to answer on behalf of the other Geoff as well.

"What about you, Glen?" he asked as he looked me up and down.

"Count me in", I said.

I thought the extra cash would come in handy. When we had done overtime previously, it had been pretty relaxed. Shaun also agreed to the overtime when Toffee Bum asked him.

We didn't leave the factory until 10:00 pm that Friday night, as we were on the late shift. This meant we would only be away for eight hours before we were due to start our overtime at 6;00 am. Shaun and I were always pretty punctual and arrived bang on time. There was no sign of Geoff and Elvis, though. It got to just past 6.30 am when Elvis arrived. He was on his own. He was unshaven and looking pretty dishevelled, to say the least.

"Where have you been?" I asked.

"I've been on the nest all night." said Elvis. Me and the missus invited our next-door neighbour round and we made a blue movie!"

"Oh, right," I said, not really expecting a response like that.

On closer inspection, his eyes were bloodshot, and his creased white T-shirt was inside out. There was also a pungent smell of garlic coming off him too, which, if you got too close, nearly knocked you out. Based on his smell and appearance, it was difficult not to believe what he was telling us. However, I couldn't quite work out how he had managed to fit in a garlic-flavoured dish into his packed schedule. Anyway, after a quick cup of tea, he was soon gluing cardboard boxes as if his life depended on it.

As we approached 12 noon, Toffee Bum came waltzing around the corner and was heading in our direction. He was marching straight towards my workstation. What does he want? I thought. He got within ten feet of me and beckoned me over with his finger so I was out of earshot of Elvis and Shaun. I'd never had the pleasure of being so close up to him before. There was an aroma of Old Spice coming off him, and his last meal was definitely fish-based.

"I've been watching you," he said in a husky voice.

Don't I know it, I thought to myself.

"I think you have got potential and could have a bright future here," he continued.

Then he slipped me a piece of paper with a telephone number on it and departed towards the part of the factory where the printing took place. Elvis was over like a shot.

"What did Toffee Bum want?" he asked.

I was still floundering as to what had just happened.

"I think he has just offered me a permanent job," I said.

I could immediately see that Elvis was disappointed. Deep down he was hoping for further work in the factory, whereas I wasn't really bothered.

"What are you going to do?" he asked.

"I'm not sure; I'll have to think about it."

I don't know why he chose me above the others. Maybe he'd sensed my inbuilt steely determination to do well rather than the laid-back attitude he witnessed daily.

As we worked our way towards the exit, Toffee Bum stood at the door. He acknowledged me as I went past by winking at me. It didn't take me too long to consider Toffee Bum's job offer or whatever offer he had put on the table, and I never returned to the factory that made cardboard. I've often wondered what happened to the Geoff, Elvis and Shaun, though.

Serving Queen and Country

The job I did for the shortest amount of time is one I am unlikely to forget. I was contacted by a guy from the job agency I was linked to at the time. He was called Paul Peas. I'd never met Paul before. I had just spoken to him a few times previously on the phone. Based on these brief conversations I had formulated a mental picture of what he might look like. My guess would be he was medium build, pasty complexion, with jet black hair, but whose hair was greasy again the day after washing it. He struck me as the kind of guy who would always opt for a novelty tie to go with his suit. He was an excellent salesman and, at the same time, an excellent bullshitter!

"Hi, Glen; a vacancy has just come up, and I think it would be ideal for you. It's within travelling distance from your house, it's 9:00 am-5:00 pm, Monday – Friday, and it's indoor work."

What's not to like? It all sounded pretty reasonable so far, I thought.

"It's a cleaning job, and it's linked to the armed forces. They need someone to start first thing Monday morning [it was currently late Friday afternoon]. Are you up for it? I have explained to the employer [I noticed he didn't refer to them as the Armed Forces] that you would be an ideal candidate. By giving it a go, you'll not only be helping me out, you'll be serving Queen and Country."

It's at this point that I should have requested a copy of the job profile and description, but I didn't. I had been out of work for a few weeks since I was let go from a job in a shoe factory [I only lasted one day], and my savings were running out. Reluctantly, I said yes and accepted the job offer. Paul was ecstatic, as I think his role was commissioned based and every time he coerced someone into work, he got a few extra quid in his pay packet. He quickly gave me instructions for my first day before ending the call.

"The address you need to go to is Unit 13, Castle Lane Industrial Estate. On arrival, ask for Craig. Oh, and make sure you wear steel-toe-capped boots and clothes you don't mind getting dirty."

I sat down on the stairs and absorbed Paul's instructions. If this was a job linked to the armed forces, shouldn't I be heading out to an army barracks? The nearest one to me was based out at Chilwell. And why did he say I should ask for Craig when I arrived? Should I not be asking for a Private, Corporal, or Sergeant or something? I was beginning to smell a rat.

That weekend, I thought I had better go to the Famous Army & Navy Store in town, as I didn't own any steel toe cap safety boots. Luckily, they had a size that fitted and I just had enough money to buy a pair. The assistant in the store said that if I was wearing them every day, as I thought I would be, they would be guaranteed for between 6 – 12 months. She also warned me that sometimes it can take a while to 'break them in.'

Monday morning soon arrived. Following a ten-minute bus journey, I arrived at the address given to me a few days earlier by Paul. Unit 13 was an innocuous-looking building. It didn't have a company sign or logo on the outside or anything like that. Through the main door was a small reception area, which wasn't particularly inviting. It wasn't carpeted and had been kitted out with a solitary piece of furniture: a battered black leather sofa that was ripped in several places. The only other thing I noticed was a door at the other end of the reception area, which looked to have been kicked a few times.

I started to feel uneasy. This didn't strike me as an operation run by the armed forces. I wondered what I had signed up to, as according to Paul, this gig would 'suit me down to the ground'. Suddenly, the main door behind me opened. A sheepish looking guy walked in. He didn't say anything to me, nor did he make eye contact. He didn't sit on the crappy sofa either. I suspected he was a new starter like myself. If he was, he hadn't followed the instructions about what to wear. He had turned up in a brand new pair of Nike Air Max 90 and was wearing white jeans. The next few minutes were awkward as we stood there in silence to await our fate.

Suddenly, the 'kicked-in' door at the far end of reception sprung open. In came a stocky-looking guy with closely shaved hair and a facial scar. This must be Craig, I thought. Craig didn't have time for pleasantries. He looked at me,

"You must be Glen?"

"Yes, that's right", I answered.

"And you must be Brian," as he looked at the guy in the white jeans.

He tried his best to say yes, but nerves seemed to get the better of him, and he just made a funny croaking noise.

"Put these on and follow me" ordered Craig, as he handed over our workwear.

It was a silver-coloured chemical coverall suit. The type you might see someone wearing who was visiting the area where the Chernobyl nuclear disaster took place. Only this was made out of foil material, similar to what you get when you complete the London Marathon.

We quickly jumped into our fancy workwear and followed Craig through the 'kicked-in' door. What I saw next was astonishing. The space was sizeable and dimly lit. There were dozens of people in makeshift booths made from plastic sheeting, each holding pressure washers that were pointed in the direction of ex-army ammunition boxes connected to the pipework above by long chains. Now I understood Paul's comment about the role being linked to the armed forces. This company must have won a contract to clean and maintain the ammunition boxes or something. Or perhaps he was just trying to make the job sound sexy by dropping the 'armed forces' comment in.

The toxic cleaning liquid was hitting the boxes with some vigour, forcing the boxes to spin round. The drainage system in place obviously couldn't cope with the volume of toxic liquid being used, as we were up to our ankles in the stuff. I immediately thought about Brian's brand-new Nike Air trainers. They didn't stand a chance in these conditions. Craig led us towards one of the vacant booths. As we strode through the pools of cleaning liquid, I was having serious doubts and wasn't sure I could go through with it. How have I arrived at this? I thought. I am in what can only be described as a hellhole and about to start one of the shittiest jobs on the planet. Surely, I could do better. Fuck this, I'm leaving, and I did a U-turn and headed back towards the reception area. In the reception area I got out of the coverall suit as fast I could, discarding it on the battered sofa, then headed for the exit. As soon as I got outside, I legged it.

On the bus home, I pondered whether I might be included in a future edition of the Guinness Book of Records for the person who held down a job for the least amount of time. I reckon I was in that appalling space for about thirty seconds, tops. It wasn't too long before Paul Peas rung. He was furious, and he called me a time waster. He never contacted me again. That afternoon I went back to the Famous Army & Navy Store and tried to get a refund on my steel toe cap safety boots. I pretended they didn't fit me properly. The assistant knew too well that I was trying to pull a fast one and refused. So, I was now stuck with a pair of unwanted safety boots, no money and no job.

It was this experience of being recruited to one of the worst jobs on the planet that got me thinking. Maybe I should try something else, other than seek work. There was nothing to stop me. The only other options I could think of was either starting my own business or going to college. As I didn't have a viable business idea to hand,

I decided to go with the latter and I ended up undertaking some A-levels at college. Due to my interest in health and fitness, I opted for A-Levels in PE [Physical Education], Biology and Sport Psychology. I excelled and managed to get the grades required to start a university course in Sport, Health & Leisure with Media.

Impressing Nan Postlethwaite

By now, I had moved out of my parent's place and was living in a flat with my mate, Steve. I knew I would be entitled to a student grant at university, but also knew this would only stretch so far and that I would need a part-time job to supplement it. I was well aware that when it came to landing jobs, and then holding them down, my track record was awful. Maybe I would have better luck this time around, especially as I only needed to pick up something part-time.

After scanning my local newspaper, I noticed there was plenty of scope for part-time work. Shops, cafes, pubs were all offering part time hours, but the one which caught my eye was a position being advertised by a large supermarket on the outskirts of the city. Luckily, my flatmate, Steve, was going to the same supermarket the following day and he duly picked up an application form from the supermarket's customer services desk whilst he was there. I quickly completed the form, then submitted it. Within a few days I was invited for interview. The letter inviting me for interview read as follows:

Dear Mr Finnan, thank you for your application for the position of Provisions Assistant [part-time]. Your application was successful, and you are invited to attend an interview on Wednesday, 16th September, at 4:00 pm. Please confirm if you are able to attend. We would be grateful if you could prepare a five minute presentation on the following: Please explain how you would contribute to building the supermarket's brand in the future.

Securing the job interview was great news. I had a feeling there would be plenty of students and school leavers looking for part-time roles, so I would need to be at the top of my game to land the role. I couldn't wing it this time; I would need to prepare properly.

On the morning of the day of the interview, I scanned my wardrobe for something to wear. In terms of something smart, the options weren't great. I had a dark green suit, which I'd only worn on a few occasions. It had been purchased for me by my parents over a decade ago, as I needed to look smart for a family wedding we were attending. It had one of those disposable see-through cellophane dust bags covering it. I removed it from the wardrobe and quickly tried it on. To say I'd not worn it for so long, it wasn't a bad fit. I just needed a tie to go with it. I was torn between something jazzy or something plain looking. I thought the interviewers might take me more seriously if I went with a plain look and opted for a bottle green coloured tie.

Later that afternoon, I arrived at the supermarket all prepared for my interview. The instruction on the interview letter was to use the staff entrance to access the building, instead of using the customer entrance. To reach the interview room, I had to climb a fleet of stairs. At the top, there were a couple of chairs and a black coloured coffee table. On the table were a number of magazines. I was a few minutes early, so I picked up one and flicked through it. It was called Retail Weekly, and unsurprisingly, it was full of articles akin to the world of retail. I was hoping I might pick up some last-minute ideas that I could include in my presentation. I was half way through an article about the food shopping behaviours of senior citizens, when the door of the interview room opened and a short stocky women stepped out. She was wearing an embroidered supermarket apron with a huge badge pinned to it with the words 'Happy to Help' in green writing. She looked me up and down.

"Hello, young man. My name is Nan Postlethwaite," she said.

"You must be Glen Finnan?" she asked.

"Yes, that's me", I said confidently as I tried to get off on the right foot.

"Do your parents like the Scottish Highlands?" she asked nonchalantly as we sat down on either side of a table.

"Err, I'm not sure," I said.

"Don't worry, it's just me having a little joke" she said and swiftly started providing details of the role on offer.

She explained the role was working in the Provisions department. Duties would involve stocking the fridges with chilled produce such as yoghurts, cheese, cooked meats and so forth. Other tasks would include stock-taking and working on the deli. She explained that customer service was a top priority, and as she expressed this, she pointed to the huge badge pinned to her chest. It didn't take too long to work Nan Postlethwaite out. It was clear she was passionate about her job. It was also clear she was equally passionate about retail. I didn't ask, but I suspected she had worked in the retail sector for a long time, possibly even with the same company. She was the type of character who was no nonsense and would call a spade a spade. She had no qualms during the interview in pulling me up on a couple of things. She must have noticed my bottle green tie had shifted.

"If you are going to wear a tie, Glen Finnan, make sure it's straight," she said.

Then, partway through the interview she reached into her overalls and pulled out a tissue and handed it over.

"Blow your nose, Glen Finnan. Our customers wouldn't want a Provisions Assistant who constantly sniffs, and neither do I."

I did have a slight cold, and although I was oblivious to the sniffing, she obviously wasn't. She was inquisitive about my career to date [or lack of it] and was impressed that I had drawn a line in the sand and had decided to start afresh. She thought that was courageous. The interview was more like an informal chat really. I tried to base all my responses towards a retail setting and emphasised my qualities in things like customer service, working in teams, dealing with difficult situations, problem solving and communication. She listened intently to my answers but didn't give much away. The final question she asked was how I could contribute to building the supermarket's brand in the future. As I didn't have much to draw upon, I decided to take a massive gamble. I just hoped she hadn't been reading any of the magazines on the table outside the interview room.

"You've mentioned the supermarket's customers several times during this interview Mrs Postlethwaite [I presumed she was married as she was wearing a wedding ring], but has the supermarket ever fully considered the food shopping behaviours of senior citizens? I have some thoughts about this, that could take the supermarket's brand to another level."

I then paused to see her reaction and, more importantly, see if I had been rumbled. I hadn't. She stopped scribbling on her notepad and looked at me curiously.

"Tell me more, Glen Finnan," she said.

I then went on to reel off a number of schemes that would encourage the elderly to shop at the store, with the jewel in the crown being a shopping delivery scheme for the over 60's. Supermarket deliveries by the major supermarkets hadn't yet been introduced, so this concept was alien to her. Her little blue eyes lit up. You could see her mind racing. If she relayed some of these ideas back to the supermarket's Chief Executive, she was bound to score a few brownie points. She then went on to clarify the finer details of the role such as the contracted hours and the hourly salary rate, before she brought the interview to an end. She explained that she had further candidates to interview but would be making a final decision over the next couple of days. As I stood up to leave the room, she said,

"It's been nice to meet you, Glen Finnan. I'm sure we'll be seeing each other again."

As I descended down the stairs to leave the building, the door at the bottom burst open, and a guy stumbled in. He'd obviously been running as he was sweating like a trooper and blowing hard. He was bent over, with his hands on his knees, trying to get his breath back, but still managed to strike up a conversation with me. I could tell by his accent that he probably originated from Northern Ireland.

"Am I at the right place for the job interview?" he blurted out as he gasped for breath. "I've had to run here because the bloody bus didn't show up. I've come straight from work."

As the conversation continued, I soon found out that he worked for a rival supermarket.

"Are you busy at work?" I asked.

Still with his hands on his knees and bent over, he raised his head and looked up at me.

"Busy……I'm that busy, I don't have time to shit!!" he said.

I wished him good luck as he clambered up the stairs towards the interview room. I smiled as I left the building. I thought the guy from Northern Ireland was quite a character.

It was just after 9:00 am the following morning when the phone began to ring. I picked it up, and the caller said:

"Hello, I'd like to speak to Glen Finnan, please, my name is Nan Postlethwaite."

"Hello, Nan, it's Glen speaking."

"Morning, Glen Finnan [for some reason, she added my surname whenever she referred to me], I'm ringing you up to tell you that following your interview yesterday, I have decided to offer you the job. You were the standout candidate by some distance. I was very impressed by your interview, particularly the schemes you have identified to improve our branding. I have mentioned them to the Chief Executive already, and he is keen to implement them. Do you want to accept the job offer?"

I paused for a few seconds as I absorbed the information.

"Yes, Mrs Postlethwaite, I'd love to accept the job."

"Ok, that's great. Can you start this Saturday?"

"Yes, I'm free this Saturday."

"Splendid. See you at 9:00 am sharp. Use the entrance to the building you used yesterday when you attended the interview. Make sure you are wearing a white shirt, dark trousers and dark shoes. We'll provide you with the rest of the uniform. See you on Saturday."

Then she put the phone down. I knew it was only a part time gig to give me some extra money to get by on, but this was the first time I had been through an official recruitment process and had been successful. I had achieved something, and it felt good.

No more Yoghurts………please

It was the first day of my new part-time job. Nan was waiting for me as I walked in through the staff entrance.

"Good morning, Glen Finnan," she said enthusiastically as she handed over a green and white striped apron, a clip-on green tie and a white trilby hat.

The hat was very similar to one a fishmonger might wear.

"I had a good look at you at your interview the other day and presume you are a medium [in size]. Slip into these, and then we'll get you started."

She then proceeded to give me a guided tour of the supermarket, starting with the 'staff only' areas. This consisted of the staff canteen, locker room, offices, management areas, meeting rooms and first aid area. We walked and talked as we moved around the different spaces. It was Nan who did most of the talking. It was a relentless stream of questions as if she was building up a profile of me. I found myself answering questions about whether I was in a relationship; whether I had passed my driving test; what my interests were outside work; did I have any holidays booked, and so on.

Maybe it was something she needed to do, to understand the staff she had in her team, so she could get the best out of them. I wasn't sure, so I just played along with it. During the tour, we walked past the interview room I'd been in a few days earlier. I noticed the Retail Weekly magazine was still on the table. I made a mental note to remove it as soon as I could, otherwise my plagiarism would be uncovered.

Once we had seen everything there was to see in the 'staff only' area, we made our way onto the shop floor. She escorted me around all the chilled fridges in the Provisions Department, pointing out where everything was. Over the next few minutes, I was shown fridges packed with cooked meats, dairy products and ready meals. I was also told about what products were on special offer. That particular week it was Cheese & Onion Quiche. Based on the amount of quiche still in the fridge, sales didn't appear to be going particularly well.

Nan also emphasised the need to keep an eye on product 'sell by' dates and what to do with a product if the 'sell by' date has surpassed. I also learnt phrases like 'facing' and was given a demonstration of it. In retail, facing is the act of bringing products to the front of the shelf and making sure their labels are facing forward.

As we moved up and down the aisles, we encountered other members of Nan's team. I was introduced to Ray and Lindsay, who were all beavering away stocking the cooked meat fridges. Finally, Nan showed me around the warehouse area and where the stock for the provisions department was stored. She showed me a huge refrigeration area containing cages full of stock. The cages were on wheels and the objective was to drag them out one by one onto the shop floor and transfer stock from the cage and into the chilled fridges. Once a cage had been 'worked,' it had to be taken back to a huge refrigeration area. Then another cage would be dragged out, and the process would start all over again.

"Right then, Glen Finnan, I think I have shown you as much as I can for now. Have you got any questions?" Nan asked.

"I don't think so." I replied.

"Jolly good. I want you to work alongside Robin today. He will help you settle in. He's over there, restocking the milk and cream fridge. He's expecting you. I'll catch up with you later."

And she waddled off in the direction of the Customer Service desk. When I found Robin, he was cleaning up some milk with a blue paper towel that had spilled onto the floor. He was so engrossed in his work, that I think I startled him a little when I introduced myself.

"Hiya Robin, my name is Glen. Nan has said that you will be showing me the ropes today."

He rearranged the angle of his spectacles to get a better look at me.

"Ah yes," he said.

He appeared to mutter this to himself rather than direct his response towards me. Robin looked to be in his early 60's. He had a handlebar moustache and goatee beard. He'd lost most of his hair and the bits of hair that remained needed a good trim. His white shirt was discoloured and was veering towards a grey colour. All of a sudden, he spoke again.

"Yogurts!" he blurted out as if the word had just been catapulted into his mind.

This vocal outburst wasn't directed towards me. I think it was more of a reminder for him. Then, he set off in the direction of the large refrigeration storage area. I just followed him, as I guessed that's what he wanted me to do. I noticed he had a bouncy gait when he walked. It was difficult keeping up with him. Over the course of the next few hours between us, we worked our way through five cages of yoghurts. I'd never seen so much yoghurt in such a short space of time.

One thing that I soon noticed about Robin was that he would constantly hum to himself. His humming would be in the form of recognisable tunes. His repertoire included theme tunes from Match of the Day and the television series Z-Cars. He was quirky, and I had never met anyone like him.

It was inevitable as part of the role that there would be the occasional interruption from customers. This tended to happen at least half a dozen times a shift if you were lucky. If you were unlucky, it could be far more than that. Questions such as: "Where are the tins of rice pudding?" and "do you sell shoe polish?" were random enquiries that were thrown our way. Rather than explain whereabouts in the store the product was, Robin would bounce off in the direction of the aisle where the product was actually located, and the poor customer was desperately trying to keep pace behind him. Robin wasn't unfriendly towards customers. He just had an unconventional and slightly strange manner about him. Customers didn't seem to mind.

Nan approached me towards the end of the shift. She was clutching a piece of paper.

"How have you found your first shift, Glen Finnan?"

Before I had a chance to reply, she had answered on my behalf.

"Robin tells me you have done very well and that you are a fast learner. He was very impressed with how you worked those yoghurts. You must have done well because it takes a lot to impress our Robin. Now, let's walk and talk, as I need to ask you something."

We left the shop floor and went through a door that led into the 'staff only' area.

"Now, what are your plans for next week, Glen Finnan?" she asked.

I started to think. My brain was multitasking. On one hand, it was thinking, why does she want to know what I am doing next week? And at the same time, I was thinking, what am I actually doing next week? Eventually, my brain surrendered. I think it was fried after absorbing the vast amount of information about yoghurt brands.

"I don't have any plans next week," I said.

Then she threw me a curveball question. "Do you like the great outdoors?" she asked.

She intervened before I could respond.

"There is a staff teambuilding residential next week in the Lake District, and I have just been informed that Janice Bolton, who works on the checkouts, can't go because she has to take her mother for a chiropody appointment next Wednesday, so there is a spare place. Goodness knows why her husband can't take her mother to the appointment, but there you are. I know you have only just started, and you don't really know anyone, but would you like to go? I think it will help you integrate into the company faster."

"Yes, count me in," I said reluctantly.

"Here is your kit list", she said, handing over a piece of paper with the details on it. Be outside the staff entrance by 8:00 am on Monday morning. The minibus leaves at 8:15 am sharp," she clarified.

I left the supermarket and wandered towards home. Dark clouds were looming, so I quickened my pace as I walked. I reflected on the past few hours. It had gone well. I compared it to other jobs I'd had, such as at the factory that produced cardboard and the furniture store. This felt different. It felt like I was progressing in the right direction.

Sharing a tent with Robin......and a trowel!

The following couple of days were spent packing everything required for the trip. The kit list included things like a waterproof jacket, a large rucksack, suitable footwear, a sleeping bag, toiletries, bug repellent, sunscreen and a torch. Luckily, I had most things on the list, and I borrowed the items I didn't have from my flatmate, Steve. Linked to the residential, one or two things concerned me. Physically, I was in good shape, so I had no worries there. I would, however, be out of my routine and that did concern me. Things like, would I be able to cope without having cereal for supper? And how was I going to react if I had to eat food made by other members of the group? These things were on my mind as I wandered off to sleep.

There were a dozen of us on the minibus that set off for the lake district the following morning. Staff from different departments such as bakery, produce [fruits and vegetables], butchery, general grocery, checkouts and warehouse had all signed up to the week away. There was also me and Robin from the provisions department. I was slightly surprised to see Robin, as he didn't strike me as the outdoor type. Maybe he had been coerced by Nan. I wasn't sure. Anyway, I was pleased he was part of the group otherwise I wouldn't have known anybody. It would also give me a chance to get to know him better.

As we headed up the M1 towards the lakes, the banter on the bus was pretty positive. The conversations were varied and I listened with intent to see if I could learn anything. One of the things I overheard was why the residential had been organised in the first place. It was because Norman Archibald, the Chief Executive of the supermarket, was keen to try different ways in which to boost morale amongst the workforce. He'd personally benefitted from these types of activities in the past.

I was conscious that, apart from Robin, nobody on the bus knew who I was. This became evident when I overheard Jackie, one of the ladies from Produce, ask her colleague, Cheryl [also from the Produce Department],

"Who's the guy with the big teeth who's sat next to Robin?"

Normally, in situations like that, I would just want the ground to open up and swallow me. But on this occasion, I didn't. Luckily, for me, there was another individual on the minibus who eclipsed me when it came to distinctive facial features. That was Norman who worked in the warehouse. He had an extremely long nose. It was like a giant hot dog sausage glued to his face. Work colleagues referred to him as Pinocchio for obvious reasons. When you saw him for the first time you couldn't help but stare at it. It was truly an amazing sight.

The most senior member of our group was Nigel. He was the manager of the Butchery Department. He was thickset with a heavy mop of brown hair. Because he ranked higher than everyone else, he took it upon himself to play the role of group leader. I'm not sure whether he enjoyed this responsibility though. I noticed when he made announcements to the group on the bus, he blushed significantly. He looked to be out of his comfort zone.

Our base for the residential was at an Outward Bound Centre in the heart of the lakes. The accommodation was basic but clean. I shared a room with Robin. Through spending more time with him, I noticed there was another tune within his humming repertoire. It was the theme tune to the television sitcom Dad's Army. The early part of the residential was spent undertaking exercises to develop our communication, teamwork and problem-solving skills. We undertook activities such 'Cat and Mouse,' 'Skin the Snake,' 'Shrinking Island' and 'Human Knot.' Some of the activities required us to be blindfolded and were quite challenging.

The objective of the activities was to prepare us as a group before we set off on a gruelling four-day expedition the following day. The planned route was to include two wild camps and two pre-planned nights at different campsites. Although we would be supported by an instructor from the Outward Bound Centre, we would need to carry all our own clothes, sleeping bags, tents, cooking utensils and food. The food was freeze-dried, dehydrated and ready to eat expedition and camping meals. This was a relief as I knew I would be able to cook the food myself and my eating phobia wouldn't kick in.

The following morning, just before we were all ready to leave to start the expedition, Nigel decided to give a rousing speech to motivate the troops. During breakfast, he must have sensed the trepidation amongst the group at the prospect of the 50-mile slog ahead of us, so he took it upon himself to do something about it. His message seemed to be based on previous speeches by Winston Churchill as it included phrases like, 'blood, toil, tears and sweat' and 'we shall fight on the beaches'. He even threw in a quote from Rocky Balboa: "Let me tell you something you already know. The world ain't all sunshine and rainbows." I recognised it straight away as I'd watched all the Rocky films, some several times. Unfortunately, the speech went down like a lead balloon. There was only Pinocchio who showed his appreciation. The rest of us just stared at him. His default face colour was normally red after making an announcement, but after this failed speech, it was now burgundy.

Sadly, we were no longer a round dozen. Big Sharon from checkouts, pretended she'd turned her ankle on the 'Human Knot' activity the day before and insisted on pulling out of the residential. She reckoned she was gutted, but everyone knew she was a lazy slacker and probably had the whole thing pre-planned for weeks. Her husband Barry had to drive up the motorway to collect her. As they drove away in their Ford Fiesta, she was shovelling a Mars bar into her mouth and clutching a bar of Kendal Mint cake, which was no doubt next on the menu.

The testing terrain of the Lake District was challenging for some members of the group. One of those struggling was Nigel. He was a portly figure and found the steep inclines tough going. He probably wished he'd spent more time increasing his stamina before the trip, instead of propping up the bar at his local pub, the Wagon & Horses. Another one who was struggling was Robin. This wasn't surprising, based on what he was wearing. He was dressed head to foot in all this heavy duty canvas gear. Even his sleeping bag was primitive and seemed to be made of canvas and wool. He must have been really uncomfortable. His gear probably wasn't waterproof either. His backpack weighed far more than mine. He struggled on though. Others, such Pinocchio, and his co-worker from the warehouse, Walter, seemed to be handling themselves ok. As did Jackie and Cheryl. They seemed to spend their entire time gossiping as they walked. It was entertaining to listen too.

At the end of the third day, we settled down in a picturesque spot for our second wild camp. We were about 200 yards from a tarn with a gorgeous mountain backdrop. The mountain was called Helvellyn. I'd partnered up with Robin on the first wild camp, and he didn't seem to have a problem with us teaming up again. Even though he didn't say much, he was a nice guy to be around. For the wild camps, when it came to toileting, we had been issued with trowels. One trowel per tent. If we needed to do a 'number two', we were required to dig a small hole, do what we needed to do, and then bury the mess. At about 10:30 pm Robin and I settled down for the night. The combination of walking in excess of 10 miles a day, and all the fresh air, meant we were soon fast asleep.

Partway through the night, I was disturbed by something and woke up. I shone my torch onto my wristwatch. It was 3:10 am. I shone the torch in the direction of Robin's sleeping bag to see if he had also woken up. His heavy-duty sleeping bag was empty. I sat up and shone the light around the tent. The bottom end of the tent was unzipped and fluttering in the breeze. Where the hell had Robin gone, I thought. I switched off my torch and lay there in the dark, listening intently. As we were in the great outdoors, I could hear all sorts of weird noises, which I mostly put down to wildlife. Suddenly, I could hear footsteps followed by a shadowy figure approaching the tent. I pulled the sleeping bag over my head and prayed nothing untoward was going to happen. Then I heard someone humming the theme tune to Match of the Day. Thank goodness for that. It was Robin. He was back from wherever he had been. As he got himself back in the tent and settled, I pretended to be asleep. It wasn't long before he was snoring. I, on the other hand, was wide awake. Mainly because my stomach was rumbling, and I was in discomfort. I put this down to either nerves caused by the recent fright Robin had just given me or the corned beef hash freeze-dried camping meal I'd eaten a few hours earlier. It was most likely to be the latter.

Although I didn't want to, I was going to have to leave the warmth of my sleeping bag and venture outside to empty my bowels. As quiet as I could be, I unzipped the flaps, put on my cold, damp hiking boots, grabbed the torch, trowel and toilet roll and left the tent. I knew the tarn was directly in front of our tent, so I decided to turn left and head in that direction. I clumsily moved forward across the uneven terrain. Occasionally, the beam of light from the torch hit a grazing sheep, but they didn't seem to bother.

I was conscious about walking too far, losing my bearings, and not being able to find my way back. I'd calculated I'd probably gone about 150 yards and thought that was adequate for this type of mission. I crouched down and started tapping at the ground with my trowel. Every time I tapped, my trowel hit stoney terrain. I needed to find somewhere fast, as the corned beef hash needed an escape route. I walked a few paces forward. I tapped again with the trowel, but this time, I added a little bit more pressure. Suddenly, the trowel sunk into the earth. It was like a knife going through butter. Perfect, I thought. I started to dig a small hole. It was far easier to penetrate the ground than I anticipated. As I lifted the clod, I was hit by a horrendous pong. Then I realised what was going on. I had the whole of the Lake District to choose from and I had chosen the exact spot where Robin had unleashed the remnants of his corned beef hash a few minutes earlier. What were the chances of that? I closed up the hole and moved on a few more yards. Fortunately, I was in an area that seemed to be stone free and was able to dig a hole quite easily. In less than five minutes, I had emptied my bowels, got myself cleaned up and was back in the tent. Robin was still snoring and unaware of my adventure.

As dawn broke, I was woken up by a sheep nibbling on the guy ropes of the tent. Reluctantly, I got up and leaned out of the tent porch to check for damage. Everything was fine. Bleary-eyed, I took a moment to soak up the natural environment I found myself in. The view of the choppy blue water of the tarn, dwarfed by the dramatic ridged edges of Helvellyn was absolutely stunning. The peace and quiet was only briefly interrupted by Robin's snoring and the local bird population such as grouse and mallard. I was in a happy place.

Within a couple of hours, we had polished off breakfast, taken down the tents and left our wild campsite behind. It was the final day of the expedition and Pinocchio and Walter were in charge of map reading. It was their responsibility to lead us back to base. The mood in the group was positive. The thought of a hot shower and a cooked meal back at the Outward Bound Centre seemed to put a spring in our step. The pace seemed to be quicker than in previous days. There was probably a good reason for that. Some members of the group, such as Jackie, Cheryl and Tonia from the Bakery Department, weren't prepared to use the trowel and dig a makeshift toilet and, therefore, were keen to return as soon as possible. We covered the final 12 miles in just under three and a half hours.

After showering and jumping into fresh clothes, we made our way to the canteen area. The choice of meal was either chicken stew and rice or steak and ale pie, potatoes and vegetables. I went for the steak and ale pie option. My phobia about who had made the food and where it had come from went out of the window. I was that hungry; the food didn't even touch the sides. It did cross my mind that I had managed to last for five days without having cereal for my supper every night. For me, this was quite an achievement.

With the group fed and watered, Nigel decided to give another speech. He looked surprisingly confident in view of his recent track record. The gist of this latest speech was to congratulate us all on our efforts over the last few days. However, rather than keeping it simple, he decided to approach it from a different angle. In summary, he simply changed the words of an incredible speech given by

Norwegian commentator Bjørge Lillelien at the end of a match between Norway and England in Oslo a few years earlier. He took a deep breath, then let rip,

"It is unbelievable! We have conquered the Lake District. The Lake District - the home of giants." Then he rhymed off every mountain he could think of. Scafell Pike, Great Gable, Coniston, Helvellyn, Skiddaw, Catbells, Blencathra…………. "We've beaten them all. Alfred Wainwright, can you hear me? Your mountains took a hell of a beating!"

Then, he waited for a reaction. We all sat there staring at one another. Pinocchio, who was supping a mug of tea during the speech, burst out laughing and ended up spraying a mouthful of tea over Robin's woolly jumper. Robin didn't seem to mind, though. Once again, Nigel turned a burgundy colour. Then there was silence. It was only for a few seconds, but it felt longer. The silence was broken when Tonia from the Bakery Department asked,

"Can we go home now?"

We were soon on the minibus heading south.

The wrong joint

Starting the degree course and settling in at the University was a pretty smooth process. With me being slightly older than the average undergraduate and living off-campus, I wasn't really interested in things like Fresher's Week or joining groups like the Debating Society or Sports Society. I didn't need distractions like this. My sole focus was to try to obtain a BA Hons Degree in Sport, Health & Leisure with Media, then use this as a foundation for a new and exciting career path.

I didn't specifically go out looking to make friends; it kind of happened naturally. The student friends group consisted of Andy from Huddersfield, Dom from Bolton and Tom from Birmingham. Tom and I were a similar age, but Andy and Dom were a few years younger. Like me, the guys were all determined to do well on the course, but there was always scope for plenty of banter and micky-taking.

The first year of the degree included core modules such as Psychology of Motor Performance, Anatomy and Physiology of Exercise and Media & Democracy. The results from the first-year modules didn't contribute to the overall degree mark. Nonetheless, I was keen to do well and still gave it my all. In the first couple of weeks, as part of the Anatomy and Physiology of Exercise module, we were introduced to the 'Bleep Test.' This was a 20-metre shuttle run test to measure cardiovascular fitness and maximum oxygen uptake [VO2 max]. VO2 max is the maximum rate of oxygen your body is able to use whilst you're exercising. The greater your VO2 max, the more oxygen your body can put to use. It is a maximal test involving continuous running between two lines, 20m apart, in time to recorded beeps. It allowed us to put into practice some of the theoretical learning from the lectures about aerobic capacity.

With anything linked to running, I always fancied my chances. However, this was more of a test about endurance capacity rather than speed. Although I kept running as long as I could, I couldn't maintain the running speed set by the pre-set audio tone, and the lecturer, a guy called Neil, pulled me up, as he had recognised I had nothing else left in the tank. A young guy from Romford wiped the floor with us, recording a bleep test score of 12.7. Neil was really impressed with this score and waxed lyrical about it for months.

The core modules only accounted for a percentage of our total credits for year one. We were required to build up the remaining credits by selecting modules from a list of options. The main factor behind how I chose my option, was linked to how the module was assessed. In summary, if the module was assessed by an examination, I wouldn't touch it with a bargepole. I just didn't fancy examinations at all. As part of the degree, I knew there would be an examination waiting for me somewhere down the line, in year two or three, but for now, I was trying to avoid them at all costs. The thought of sitting an exam made me shudder. A friend of a friend had told me a story about a guy up North who reacted so badly in an exam, that he left a puddle on the floor under his chair. In an effort to improve his performance in an exam a few days later, he befriended an imaginary orangutang to assist him, and apparently, it worked.

Whether this story is true, I don't know. I had a strategy, and I was going to stick to it. Using this strategy, however, limited my options. It meant me choosing an option around Contemporary Dance. This wasn't ideal, as I had never danced in my life, but one I was prepared to confront if it meant keeping me out of the examination hall.

In the Contemporary Dance module, I made a complete fool of myself. One particular week, the lecturer split us into groups and then challenged each group to create a short dance. In order to do this, each group had to create a number of dance steps and then link the steps together to formulate a dance routine before presenting it to the other groups in the class. My group consisted of a chubby guy from Chesterfield, a shy-looking girl from Watford and a guy called Pete from Newcastle. Looking around the group, there didn't appear to be a natural leader amongst us. The girl from Watford wasn't even able to make eye contact, and, therefore, was lacking one of the basic traits required to be a highly effective leader. The chubby guy from Chesterfield looked too highly strung based on the short time I'd known him. Pete, on the other hand, was a bit of a joker and didn't seem to take anything seriously. I think he was also amused by the size of my teeth. Therefore, that left me at the helm, and the others seemed ok with this.

We were given pieces of flipchart paper and a marker pen to use to help us plan the dance. We started off by drawing forward-pointing arrows to signify steps forward, followed by arrows pointing left and right to signify steps to the left and to the right. We then introduced other symbols to signify movements, such as spinning around, turning, jumping, clapping our hands and so on. Before long, the flipchart was full of all sorts of symbols to depict the steps and movements of our newly designed dance routine.

We agreed we wanted to finish off the dance with some form of gesture which was to be delivered in unison. We wanted to demonstrate the power of non-verbal communication. The gesture we agreed on was a quizzical stance and expression that symbolised the phrase, "So, what did you think of that then?" Essentially, we wanted to create a reaction from the audience. However, we couldn't agree on what symbol to draw on our flipchart to represent the gesture we'd decided to use. Then jokey Pete pipes up,

"Why don't we draw a joint?"

The fat guy from Chesterfield nodded nervously, and the shy girl from Watford was unsurprisingly non-committal.

"Should we?" I asked.

Jokey Pete was nodding furiously whilst laughing at the same time. However, I wasn't sure what he found so funny.

As I picked up the marker pen, I was racking my brains as to how to draw a joint. My drawing skills weren't the greatest, and therefore, this would be a test for me. The group huddled around me as I got to work. Even the shy girl from Watford took a genuine interest. To add to the pressure, jokey Pete announced to members of the other groups,

"Glen is drawing a joint."

They all gathered around. I had more than 20 people watching me. They were egging me on. I sketched away for a couple of minutes. It all went very quiet. Even jokey Pete stopped laughing. I just presumed they were in awe of the quality of the drawing. Then, the shy girl from Watford spoke. This was the first time we had heard her voice.

"It doesn't look like a joint to me," she said.

Then, more comments followed.

"Me neither."

"Same here."

"What the hell is that?" were some of the remarks from those watching.

It wasn't until jokey Pete said,

"I'd like to see you getting high of that!" that I realised what I had done.

Over the years, I was so used to having a roast dinner on Sundays whilst still living with my parents that I had drawn a 'joint of lamb.' Having never smoked weed before, it had not dawned on me to draw a marijuana joint. What an idiot I looked in front of everybody. My face didn't quite go the same burgundy colour as Nigel after his failed speeches, but it wasn't far off. My fellow students thought this was hilarious. I knew I was never going to live this down!

Nottingham branch 1…..Derby branch 0…….

Back in the supermarket, Nan continued to put me through my paces. As the weeks went by, she ensured I experienced all aspects of the role. I worked all the different chilled sections within the department. This consisted of milk, dairy & eggs, chilled meats, cheese; yoghurts; pizza, pasta & pasta sauces; party food, pies, deli & dips; desserts; and ready meals. She even had me working in the back offices, where I learned to order stock on the computer system. Being the newest member of the team and only working part-time, I found this quite unusual and somewhat baffling. I thought she may have allocated tasks like this to someone like Robin, who had more experience and was likely to remain with the company much longer than me. But no, I seemed to be the chosen one. Now and again, she came out with comments like,

"What are you going to do with this fancy qualification when you finish at University?"

And,

"Is it worth your while doing all these studies when you could have a great career here at the supermarket?"

I just laughed these comments off, but actually, I was really flattered that she was giving me so much responsibility and that she valued me so much. I had never been treated this way before.

On one occasion, Nan asked me to step in for her at a Retail Manager's meeting. It was the type of meeting where managers from different regions got together every quarter. She couldn't attend because she had just had an ingrown toenail removed and was struggling to drive. I knew I didn't have any lectures on the day of the meeting and thought it would be a chance to gain some work experience whilst, at the same time, earning a few extra quid. The location of the meeting was in Cambridge. I was given the option of travelling by train or by hire car. Either way, the supermarket would cover the costs. I didn't own my own car, but I had passed my driving test when I was 18. I thought it might be a good idea to get behind the wheel again, and therefore decided to drive.

The day of the meeting should have been straightforward. Unfortunately, it wasn't. I set my alarm for 6:00 am. The plan was to set off by 6:30 am and arrive in Cambridge by 9:00 am. The alarm went off as planned. When I drew back the curtains, my heart sank; it had been snowing during the night, and there was a thick blanket of snow on the ground. The hire car, which had been delivered during the night, was covered, too. Nan had expressed I should look smart for the meeting. I had no other option, but wear my dark green suit, the one I had worn when I was interviewed by Nan a few months earlier. This time though, rather than wearing my plain looking bottle green tie, I opted for a riskier alternative. It was a novelty tie and I hoped it would give my outfit a lift. It was black with colourful pictures of Liquorish Allsorts on it. My logic was wearing a food themed tie at a Retail Manager's meeting, would be quite appropriate. To finish off my look, I applied some hair gel to liven up my flat sandy hair. I also thought I would apply some moisturiser to my face to help revive my skin as it had been feeling dry over the last couple of days. I had been given the moisturiser as part of a men's luxury face and body product care set for my birthday but had never used it.

I was about halfway through applying the moisturiser, when I heard a shrieking noise outside. I looked out of the window and realised it was the hire car's alarm that had been triggered. It was probably the weight of the snow on the car roof or something. I dashed downstairs. There on the floor, behind the front door, were the car keys. They had been posted through the letter box when the car had been dropped off in the middle of the night. I grabbed the keys and opened the front door. A cold blast of air hit me. I was conscious the deafening noise made by the alarm would wake up the neighbours. I strode as quickly as I could through the fresh snow on the footpath and inserted the key into the car lock. As soon as the car door opened, the alarm stopped.

Phew, thank goodness for that, I thought. Then I went back inside and made myself some cereal and a coffee. All we had in was Shredded Wheat, but that was fine with me. As I sat eating my breakfast, I pondered how I was going to clear the snow off the car. As I didn't own a car or have any car accessories like a car ice scraper, I had to improvise. Although it took a little bit longer, I managed to clear the snow off the car by using the brush from the dustpan and brush set which usually sat next to the kitchen bin. It wasn't until the car was snow-free that I realised the hire car was a Vauxhall Astra. We were still in darkness but due to the rays coming off a nearby streetlight, I could make out it was navy blue in colour.

Although I had the inconvenience of the snow, I managed to get away by 6:30 am, as planned. Driving on the roads leading to the motorway was a little bit treacherous. On some roads, there weren't any tyre tracks created by traffic. The driving conditions on the motorway, however, were slightly easier. The volume of traffic on the motorway had carved out tyre tracks on the inside and middle lanes. Motorists had enough sense to avoid the outside lane. Then I had a problem. I noticed my windscreen washer wasn't working. I guessed it was either empty or was frozen up. The spray from the grit, salt and dirt on the car window was making visibility really difficult. Turning the windscreen wipers on but without any water, was only making matters worse. I could hardly see anything at all. To add to this, the morning sun was beginning to rise, and the sun's glare was blinding me.

After about half an hour of driving on the inside lane at about 50mph I'd had enough and pulled off the motorway into the services. I needed to clean my windows and somehow fix the windscreen washer. I parked to the side of the main car park, next to some snowy covered land dotted with some small bushes and other greenery.

When I got out of the car, first of all, I checked the windscreen washer nozzles. They were frozen. That should be easy to sort, I thought. I knew I would be able to get a cup of warm water from somewhere inside the motorway services and defrost them. Before doing that, I thought I'd use the resources at my disposal to clean the car windows. I stepped onto the snowy-covered land next to the car. The snow was untouched. I have always enjoyed walking on snow that nobody else has stood on. I bent down and, grabbed a big handful, and went back to the car. I started smearing it on the windows to remove the combination of salt, grit and dirt. After a few seconds, I noticed the windows didn't seem to be getting any cleaner. In fact, they were getting dirtier. They were turning a brown colour. Then I realised the reality of the situation. I was trying to clean my windows with a combo of snow and frozen excrement! I hadn't seen the sign that clearly stated I had gathered the snow from a 'designated dog walking area.' Yuck. What a bloody idiot! I threw the remaining snow and faeces to the floor and headed towards the gent's toilets to get cleaned up. I wasn't aware that anybody had been watching me trying to clean my windows with dog muck, but maybe they had, as I was receiving some strange looks from people inside the services. I got cleaned up, then defrosted my windscreen washer nozzles with warm water I got from the toilets. Now the washer nozzles were working; I cleaned my windows properly and then set off again on the motorway. This trip wasn't going to plan. And it was only just after 7:00 am.

By the time I reached my destination, it was 9:15 am. I was late for the meeting. The snowy weather conditions and build-up of morning traffic approaching Cambridge hadn't done me any favours. I parked up and entered the supermarket. Nan had given me instructions on which entrance to use. She knew where to go as she had been to a meeting at the supermarket before, albeit a couple of years earlier. Once inside, I came across various meeting rooms located on the left hand side of a corridor. They all had glass walls, so it was possible to see if they were being used or not. There were various meetings taking place, mostly with only a handful of people in each of them.

Finally, I noticed one particular meeting room was much larger than the others, and this was full of people sitting around a huge glass table. I presumed this was the meeting I was attending. I opened the glass door and entered the room. I had to squeeze past a number of people to reach a spare chair at the far end of the table. I sat down. The lady who was chairing the meeting paused what she was saying. From what I could tell, it had something to do with company pensions. She looked at her watch, then stared at me.

"Would you like to introduce yourself?" she asked.

I nodded sheepishly. I quickly recalled Nan's short briefing from the day before. It was one of her 'let's walk and talk' discussions. In the space of two minutes, she had given me the heads up on a couple of people to be on my guard against. One was Gladys Smart, a manager from the Derby branch. Nan explained that her and Gladys hadn't hit it off when they first met and have disliked each other ever since. The other person to be aware of was Charles Chunk. He was an American living in the UK and was currently managing the Norwich branch. She said he wasn't to be trusted, but she didn't say why. She said I would recognise him as he likes to wink at people. She also mentioned that he loved to use the word 'cynicism' and had done so at every meeting she had attended.

"I'll buy you a cup of coffee and a cake next time I see you if he doesn't use that word," she said as she finished briefing me and then left the building to join her husband, who was waiting in the car outside the staff entrance.

"Hello everyone, sorry I'm late. My name is Glen Finnan. I'm here representing the Nottingham branch on behalf of Nan Postlethwaite."

It crossed my mind to tell everyone that I was late because of the incident with the dog shit at the services but thought that might not be the wisest thing to do.

"I'm pleased you could join us Mr Finnan. Please pass on my best regards to Mrs Postlethwaite and tell her Gladys Smart was asking after her."

"I certainly will", I said.

After I had introduced myself, I couldn't help but notice that quite a few of the attendees continued to look inquisitively in my direction. Perhaps they hadn't seen anyone with front teeth as big as mine before. Or maybe they were mesmerised by my Liquorish Allsorts tie. Either way, I didn't think it was very professional to stare at people.

Sat next to Gladys Smart was a young-looking kid in a suit. Gladys informed everyone that the Derby branch was running a work experience programme and that Liam [the young guy in the suit] was part of that scheme. As the meeting progressed, I began to get the feeling that I had made an impression on young Liam. His reaction towards me every time I spoke was really encouraging. He seemed to laugh at everything I said. The more he laughed, the more it encouraged me to speak up at the meeting. I was feeding off his enthusiasm.

I updated attendees on the team building activity undertaken by staff from the Nottingham branch on their residential to the Lake District. I emphasised how it had positively impacted on interdepartmental collaboration. Liam was absolutely loving this feedback, but I could see Gladys Smart didn't approve. She didn't like it if there were any good news stories coming out of the other supermarket branches. She was only interested in the Derby branch. She slid her half-frame spectacles along the ridge of her nose closer to her face. Her brow furrowed, she lifted her chin and pressed together her lips in a mix of anger, disgust and contempt. She knew full well that the team-building initiative was organised by Nan Postlethwaite, and she didn't like it. She was keen to move on from this good news story. She had also clocked on, that Liam had taken a real shine to me.

"Are there any more updates from the Nottingham branch, or should I move on to the next agenda item?" asked Gladys impatiently, as she tried to deflect the attention away from me and move the meeting in a different direction.

I could see from Liam's enthusiastic expression he craved more feedback from the Nottingham branch, so I just went for it. I was on a roll.

"Yes, there is one more thing," I said.

I loved the attention, especially from Liam, who was on the verge of wetting himself.

"The Nottingham branch is developing a cutting-edge community support scheme whereby we will be delivering groceries to our vulnerable and elderly customers in the neighbourhood. We'll provide feedback on how this is developing at future meetings."

All of a sudden, there was a question from the far end of the table. The gentleman who spoke had a strong American accent. He sounded like he was from the American South, somewhere like Tennessee. His hair was blonde and shoulder-length. He wore a charcoal pinstriped double-breasted suit, a crisp white shirt with a red silk tie. When he lifted his coffee cup, it was possible to catch a glimpse of his yellow-gold cufflinks. It struck me that the rest of the males in the meeting room could learn a lesson from his cut.

"Mr Finnan," he said confidently. "I like the enthusiasm of you folks up there in Nottingham. But are you trying to tell me that some of your customers are going to receive groceries from your supermarket without leaving their apartment?"

I had a feeling that I knew who I was talking to, based on Nan's description, but thought I would double-check.

"Sorry, I didn't catch your name", I asked.

"My name is Charles……. Charles Chunk", he replied, giving me a huge wink as he slowly spelt out his surname for clarity.

"Yes, that is correct Mr Chunk."

This is where I embellished the truth a little bit. I added,

"The research we have undertaken in the communities around Nottingham indicates that this type of service would be in demand and has the potential to grow."

I didn't mention that the only people we had spoken to as part of this research were my gran and a few of her mates.

"We plan to start the service with one small van, but if our research is correct, we'll eventually need a suite of vans."

Mr Chunk started roaring with laughter, and then, as his laughter died down, he added,

"Ignore my cynicism Mr Finnan, but this grand scheme of yours in Nottingham will never catch on. I'll believe it when I see it."

My immediate reaction to his comment was that of disappointment. I wasn't disappointed because Charles Chunk didn't have any confidence in the proposed delivery scheme. It was that he said the word 'cynicism,' and that meant I hadn't won a free coffee and piece of cake from Nan.

Gladys Smart brought the meeting to a close soon after. You could tell from her face that she hadn't enjoyed it. She generally used this meeting to bang on about the brilliant things being delivered by the Derby branch. She certainly wasn't used to being outshone by a part-time student filling in for her arch-rival, Nan Postlethwaite. The last thing she announced was the location of the next meeting. It was to be in Nottingham!

The drive back to Nottingham was much smoother in comparison to what I had experienced earlier that morning. Much of the snow had succumbed to the impact of the traffic and turned to slush. As I drove, I reflected on how the meeting had unfolded. I was proud of my contribution, and I felt I had represented the Nottingham branch in a good light. I had certainly been the centre of attention. Young Liam had taken a real shine to me. Other attendees also seemed to be interested in what I had to say too. Some of them couldn't take their eyes off me. It must have been my choice of tie.

It was mid-afternoon by the time I reached Nottingham and parked up outside the flat. I didn't expect anybody to be in, but when I went inside, my flat mate, Steve, was in the kitchen making a cup of tea. I'd completely forgotten that he'd been for a job interview. Like me, he was a student. He already had a part time job. He worked in a take-away but he wasn't enjoying it. He couldn't stand the unsocial hours. He thought all the late nights were having a detrimental impact on the quality of his university assignments, so he was looking for something else. As I walked into the kitchen, he stopped drinking his tea and stared at me.

"What the hell has happened to you?" he asked.

"What do you mean?" I replied.

"It's your face. Something is wrong with it. You'd better go and look in the mirror!" he said.

I wandered out into the hallway and looked in the mirror on the wall. Oh my god. What the hell is going on? The right side of my face was a bronze colour, and the left side was just my normal complexion. How has this happened? Am I ill or something? Then the penny dropped. I rushed upstairs and into my room. I grabbed the moisturiser I had applied earlier that morning. Just as I had suspected, it was the fancy tanning moisturiser that I had been given. The writing on the packaging read: 'Instant face tanning moisturiser in less than 24 hours'. What a fool. Why didn't I spot this detail? Then, I remembered that I was interrupted by the car alarm when I was getting ready earlier that morning. I sat down on the edge of my bed. Now, it all made sense. No wonder young Liam was so enthusiastic towards me at the meeting and laughed at everything I'd said. I'd been his personal entertainment, and he knew it. If I hadn't shown up, the meeting would have been pretty dull for him.

As for all the other attendees, I thought it was my Liquorish Allsorts tie that had caught their attention. But no. They were all gawping at the side of my face, which was sporting a bronze glow. And probably trying to work out why I had decided to go for this look. God forbid, with the size of my teeth, I was hardly hiding a light under a bushel anyway. Why would I try to amplify a situation which already gave people enough reason to stare. I just wish somebody had said something to me. I suppose it isn't a British thing to do, though. It could have been interpreted as being ignorant or rude. Well, actually, in this case, it would have been really helpful if this had been pointed out. The only thing I could do about this now was try and remove the tan, so I resembled some form of normality. Hopefully, my appearance at this meeting would never be mentioned again. That was the hope, anyway.

A couple of days later, I decided it was no longer embarrassing to be seen in public and I ventured out to work my usual Saturday shift at the supermarket. The bronze glow on the right side of my face had all but vanished due to spending long periods of time in the shower equipped with a scrubbing brush and soap. Robin and I were busy working the yoghurts. He was his usual eccentric self and humming his customary tunes. The z-cars theme tune seemed to be his 'go to' melody that particular day. I knew he had a taste for craft beers and I think he had been out to his local pub the night before, as there was an odour of alcohol lingering around the aisle where we were working. I mentally compared Robin's discoloured white shirt, to the crisp white shirt worn by Charles Chunk a few days earlier. It was like chalk and cheese. I loved working alongside Robin though.

Our colleague, Ray, who was working the cheese section, sauntered towards us. He had just finished his mid-morning break.

"Glen, Nan wants a word with you. She is waiting for you in the staff canteen," he said.

I stopped what I was doing and wandered through to the staff canteen area. Nan was sitting at a corner table to the right of the entrance as I went in. I sat down opposite her, wondering what she wanted. On my side of the table was a cup of coffee and a giant piece of Victoria Sponge cake on a white plate.

"Hello, Glen Finnan," she said.

"A little dickie bird tells me that you played a blinder at the Regional Manager's meeting in Cambridge."

I looked at her nervously but carried on listening, nonetheless. The 'dickie bird' must have been Mavis Scallop, Nan's cousin, who was the Produce Manager at the Shrewsbury branch. She must have been in attendance, but as I was late to the meeting, I had missed the introductions.

"Apparently, you performed admirably and gave a very good account of the excellent service we provide here at the Nottingham branch. My sources tell me that my old sparring partner, Gladys Smart, couldn't compete with our initiatives. And I believe you had that little work experience chappy of hers, eating out of the palm of your hand."

There was a good reason for that, but I thought I wouldn't say anything and let her carry on.

"I'm due to speak to the Chief Executive next week about the delivery scheme. We need to show progress on that scheme by the time the next meeting takes place. Are you happy to get involved in the scheme, Glen Finnan?"

"Certainly, Nan, I'd love to", I replied.

"Right, here is a piece of cake and a coffee. I haven't bought you this because Charles Chunk 'didn't' say the word 'cynicism', because I have been reliably informed, he did. I have bought you this as a reward for standing in for me the other day and for doing a great job."

Then she got up and hobbled towards the exit. She was obviously still in pain from the procedure she'd had the other day to remove her ingrown toenail.

Sneaking about in the Bookies!

Back at University, the course seemed to be going really well as far as I could tell. At the end of year one, my average mark was 65 percent. I had proved to myself that I was academically capable of working at this level. I now needed to maintain this standard for years two and three, and I would leave university with a half-decent degree.

The most enjoyable aspect during year two was a module called Society Sport & Culture. It was about increasing the understanding of sociological theories, through examining sport and leisure. For the marked assessment element, we were instructed to work in pairs and carry out surveillance on groups of people undertaking sports or leisure activities. I paired up with my friend Tom, who had also signed up to do this module. The surveillance could be undertaken covertly if felt appropriate. We then had to write a 3000-word essay as to why we thought the individuals were partaking in this activity and displaying specific behaviours we uncovered. Any rationale and conclusions were required to be supported by sociological theory.

When it came to choosing what group of people to observe, the popular options were those groups of people partaking in sports or leisure on campus, such as the university's rugby or netball team. Another option was to observe students enjoying leisure time in the student bar. These, however, were never on my radar. I had other ideas.

"Let's do something different," I said to Tom.

"What have you got in mind?" he replied.

Without hesitation, I said, "Let's go and observe people gambling in a bookmakers."

He was unsure at first. Then, after a few minutes, he bought into the idea, especially as we couldn't come up with anything better.

A few days later, we entered the premises of the bookmakers we had chosen at random to complete our observations. It was tucked away down a side street, away from the main drag. It looked a little unkempt from the outside, but once inside, it seemed clean and well maintained. There was free tea, coffee and hot chocolate on tap, and always a plate of biscuits on the go for the punters.

With a constant supply of free snacks available, it was an ideal place for a couple of hungry students to hang out. Our initial dilemma was whether to inform the Manager of the bookmakers of our assignment and hope he would grant us permission; or whether to carry out our observations under cover. We decided to opt for the latter, as we wanted to observe the punters acting naturally. We felt if they knew what we were up to, they may behave in a different way and our research would be skewed.

What was clear on our first visit to the bookmakers was that it was an ideal environment for a covert operation such as ours. Writing on betting slips was the norm is these establishments, so this was the ideal way to make notes linked to our observations. We tested the process out, and nobody suspected anything.

Initially, we weren't entirely sure what kind of data to collect. We started making notes on random stuff, such as what the punters were wearing and how long they stayed in the bookmakers at any one time. However, on our third visit to the bookmakers, things changed, and our undercover operation took a different direction. We noticed that there was one particular group of guys who were in the bookmakers every time we visited. There were four of them. It didn't matter what time of day we went to the bookmakers; they were always there. This was gold dust to us, and this group gave us something specific to focus on.

We gave each of the group a name. This made it easier for us when we referred back to our notes at the end of each day. Tom decided on the names. He just picked them at random. He named them Chris, Harry, Hector and Mitch. We noticed there was a hierarchy in the group. Chris was definitely the leader of the pack. He was the one they respected and sought advice from. His knowledge of horse racing was second to none, and he would regularly communicate his viewpoint to other members of the group.

"Finegan's Lad last ran three weeks ago at Nottingham and was carrying nine stone three in a 7-furlong handicap. It came fifth and was beaten by 12 lengths. The handicapper has the measure of it, and the horse hasn't got a hope in hell", was one of many opinions Chris shared whilst we were in earshot.

Harry was second in command, probably with aspirations to be a leader himself one day. He was Chris's lookout man, and you would often see Chris and Harry tucked away in a quiet corner of the bookies, deep in conversation, which nobody else was privy too. Early interactions with Harry indicated to us he was the least friendly of the group. If anybody in the group suspected us of being in the bookies for reasons other than betting, it was him. The quietest member of the group was Hector. Hector wasn't very verbal. He wore the same pair of brown suede sneakers whenever we saw him. They suited him. He studied the horse racing form meticulously. He didn't engage too much with the other members of the group. From time to time, Chris would wander over to him, have a quiet word in his ear, and then move away again. We presumed this was vital knowledge that was being exchanged, but it was impossible to tell.

Although he was quiet, Hector was a valued member of the group. Mitch, or Mitch the Snitch, as we labelled him, was Chris's lackey. His greasy hair was combed over to try and minimise his bald patch. Chris would use him to run errands or to ask him to sneak around the bookies to find out information on his behalf, such as what the other punters were backing. We got the impression that he was a born loser, but that was only guess work on our part. Although he was part of the group, he was kept at arm's length and was only privy to certain information. If Chris or Harry had been provided with some inside information from one of their many contacts, he wouldn't be told about it. He had a loose tongue and couldn't be trusted. In the group, Mitch the Snitch, was at the bottom of the hierarchy. There was no question about that. He didn't seem to mind, though.

Now that we had this particular group to focus on, we next had to figure out why they were partaking in this activity and displaying the relevant behaviours we identified. Somehow, we needed to get closer to them without them knowing, but this wasn't going to be straightforward. They were really tight knit. Furthermore, we noticed they didn't seem to interact with other punters in the bookies. They only communicated amongst themselves. We experimented with different ways to befriend them. Tom tried sitting on the stool normally used by Harry. Harry wasn't very happy with this and made his feelings quite clear by shouting across to Chris,

"You can't even go to the toilet in this place without having your seat taken."

Tom had invaded Harry's space, and he didn't like it. He took the hint and gave up the stool. In another attempt to penetrate the group, I tried striking up a conversation with Hector.

"What do you fancy in the next race?" I asked.

Hector didn't even acknowledge my question and continued to stare at the newspapers containing the racing form pinned to the walls. He behaved as if I wasn't there. I decided not to push him any further and backed off. After several other unsuccessful attempts to infiltrate the group, Tom and I made the decision to collect our data from visual observation only rather than trying to glean information from verbal exchanges or befriend them.

Through earwigging their conversations and picking up the betting slips they had discarded, we noticed they all placed the same type of bet. It was called a Placepot. The Placepot is a very popular type of bet, as you can win big for a very small outlay. It's about selecting horses to be placed [they don't have to win] across the first six races of a race card. To increase their chances of winning, they each placed numerous Placepot bets at the same meeting, each with a different permutation. Effectively, they each adopted a spread betting approach.

Watching their behaviour during the live racing being shown on the big TV screens was fascinating. Chris was the most animated. As he stood there, with half-chewed betting pen tucked behind his ear, the top half of his body rocked backwards and forwards in tune with the galloping horses. Chris was also the most aggressive and he had no qualms in voicing his frustrations during and after races. Phases such as,

"Carson, you useless idiot."

"Cochrane, you should have retired years ago, you're past it" were comments aimed at the jockeys if the horse Chris had backed hadn't done the business.

Hector, on the other hand, behaved totally differently. When each race started, he would get up from his seat, and he would quietly manoeuvre himself so he had a better view of the race on the television screen. During the race, his demeanour remained the same. No matter how many times we observed him, he never showed any emotion whatsoever. We had no idea whether his horse had won or lost. Following each race, he returned to his seat and, took up the same posture [cross-legged] and continued to stare at the form guides pinned to the wall.

Overall, we visited the bookies on just over thirty occasions across a three-month period. We tried to call in at least three times a week if time allowed. Following our observations, we concluded that the most likely explanation for the group pursuing this leisure activity was financial gain. This was based on the type of bet [Placepot] they consistently placed. We also concluded that the buzz they experienced from placing bets and the personal challenge of beating the odds were other strong indicators for participating in this pastime. Other factors we considered were related to the pleasure gained from the social interaction and the feeling of safety of belonging to a closed group. We also concluded that habitual behaviour contributed to why they undertook this leisure pursuit, but evidencing this was more difficult.

We had observed the guys so intently over a number of weeks that we felt we had got to understand them, but without personally getting to know them. However, we did feel slightly guilty that they didn't know they had been under scrutiny for weeks. As we were about to leave bookies on our last visit, the group was engrossed in a three-mile hurdle race at Wetherby. Chris's horse was leading when it fell at the seventh fence. He went ballistic, and he hurled a tirade of abuse at the jockey and the horse. Another placepot had bit the dust. This wasn't the first time, and it was unlikely to be the last.

Surprise in the loft

The following day, I was working my usual Saturday shift at the supermarket. I had stocked up the milk, dairy & eggs section and was just about to start on the chilled meats section when Nan Postlethwaite came sauntering towards me. She was sporting a huge grin.

"I've got something to show you, Glen Finnan. Follow me."

I followed her off the shop floor, down the corridor past the canteen area and towards the staff entrance. As we opened the door and stepped outside into the car park, she gestured towards a vehicle parked a few yards way.

"What do you think of that Glen Finnan? It's brilliant, isn't it?"

I walked forward a few steps so I could get a better look. There in front of me was a brand new green and white van with the slogan 'A Retail Delivery Service you can count on' emblazoned down both sides. I couldn't believe what I was seeing. The bullshit I had spouted about 'older people's shopping habits' in the job interview all those months ago had now developed into this. The purchase of a brand new van and a new delivery service for elderly people in the community. Nan was still standing there, looking well-chuffed with herself, and I didn't want to spoil her moment.

"It's absolutely brilliant, Nan. I'm very impressed".

"So you should be," she said. "It took a lot of negotiation with the Chief Executive for him to agree to this deal. We are the first supermarket in the country to trial this kind of service. The research that you undertook was catalyst to the decision".

I shuddered as I cast my mind back to the conversation I had with my gran and her mates about whether they would use such a delivery service. Oh my god. It was hardly robust research. I think they only agreed to use it, so I would stop asking them questions, and they could continue with their game of bingo.

"Wait until Gladys Smart hears about this. She will be absolutely fizzing."

And off she turned, back towards the staff entrance, leaving me staring at the new purchase. She'd only walked a few paces when she stopped, turned to me again and then threw something towards me. A set of keys came hurtling through the air in my direction.

"You'll be needing these. You and Robin are on the first shift. The scheme is being launched this morning. Go and see Elsie Standhope at Customer Services. She has a list of customers who have placed orders. The phone hasn't stopped ringing since the new scheme was promoted on the local radio station last night."

She turned again towards the staff entrance, and as she walked away from me, I could hear her singing the lyrics from a pop song by the iconic pop group Queen, "we are…. the champions, no time for losers, cause we are the champions of the world". I guessed that somewhere in this short rendition, there was a reference to her arch-rival, Gladys Smart.

Robin was waiting for me at the Customers Services desk. So was Elsie Standhope. Elsie was one of Nan's friends from the church they went to. She was well past retirement age. She had worked at the supermarket for years and was really efficient at her job. She was also very direct and called a spade a spade.

"Where have you been dopey? Robin has been waiting here for ages. I have a list here, as long as my arm, of customers who have placed orders through our new delivery service. Chop, chop. You and Robin had better get a move on. The van is loaded up with bags of shopping and they have all been labelled. First stop is 17 Municipal Street."

I grabbed the list off her to have a look at it. Sure enough, there at the top of the list, it read 'Doris and Agatha Brown [the Brown twins], 17 Municipal Street'.

"How do you know they are twins?" I asked.

"Because I've known them for years," she replied. "They are good friends of mine."

I suspected foul play had taken place, and they had found themselves at the top of the pile due to Elsie's friendship.

Inside the delivery van was the smell of new interior. As Robin had never learned to drive, I was at the wheel. His job was to direct us to each house where we had a delivery to make. When he wasn't providing directions, he was humming. This particular day, his chosen melody was the theme tune to the British sitcom Dad's Army. When Robin was humming, I knew he was content. We'd made about six deliveries, including one to Elsie's pals, the Brown twins, when we arrived at a huge Victorian house with its own driveway and an overgrown garden full of conifers.

Robin handed me the bag of groceries and pointed at the label as he passed it across. The delivery was for someone called Jack Fish. Our routine was to double-check the contents of the bag against a checklist before handing them across to the recipient. This was to ensure there was no mix-up or that any groceries were missing. We noticed that this particular bag was full of fish-based items, including tins of tuna and salmon, jars of salmon paste and tins of pilchards and mackerel.

This has got to be a wind-up, or it's just a huge coincidence, I thought to myself. A bag full of fish related groceries for a guy with the surname Fish. Robin stopped humming. He was thinking exactly the same as me.

I knocked three times on the white wooden door using the black steel door knocker. A voice behind the door shouted he had heard us.

"I'm on my way. I'll only be a minute!" he bellowed.

As the door slowly opened, it revealed a man sitting in a wheelchair. He was wearing a light brown blazer jacket and matching pleated trousers. A dark brown handkerchief protruded from the top left pocket of his blazer. He resembled the actor Kenneth Williams, who was best known for his roles in the 'Carry On' films.

"Hello, Mr Fish, we have your grocery delivery from the supermarket. My name is Glen and this is my colleague, Robin."

"Oh yes, that'll be right. Do come in chaps," he said.

I quickly noted that although he looked like Kenneth Williams, he certainly didn't sound like him. His voice was quite gravelly.

"Do you mind taking the shopping through to the kitchen? I can't do a bloody thing sat in this chair. Would you like a cuppa, chaps? You must be parched. You could wash it down with piece of malt loaf if you like."

Interestingly, we had noted that a pattern had emerged during our first shift. At every house where we had made a delivery, we had been invited to go in for a chat and a cuppa. Our elderly customers were probably after a little bit of company for a few minutes or something. Nan and Elsie Standhope hadn't provided us with any guidance on how to deal with offers of hospitality from customers. Besides, we had so many deliveries to make that we kept declining the offers of free drinks and a chat, as we felt we didn't have time. By the time we'd reached Mr Fish's house, we had been working nearly two and a half hours, so it felt like a natural time for a break, especially as we were now standing in his kitchen.

"What did you say your name was again?" asked Mr Fish, as he looked in the direction of Robin.

Robin very rarely gave eye contact. That's just the way he was.

"It's Robin," he muttered.

"Put the kettle on, Robin, there's a good man!" shouted Mr Fish.

"You wouldn't have lasted five minutes in the military in my day with a whispering voice like yours. That shirt of yours looks like it could do with a damn good wash too. Is it supposed to be white?"

Robin was so busy rifling through Mr Fish's cupboards trying to find some cutlery for the tea and malt loaf that he was oblivious to the derogatory comments that were coming his way. As Mr Fish wasn't getting a reaction from Robin, he turned his attention to me. It crossed my mind whether now was the right moment to tackle the 'elephant in the room.' How was it that a guy with the surname 'Fish' had so many fish-related products in his shopping bag? In my mind, I was just starting to work through the different possible answers to this dilemma when I was asked a question.

"What did you say your name was again?" enquired Mr Fish.

"It's Glen," I said in a firm voice, ensuring I didn't fall into the same trap Robin fell into.

"Ah, yes," he said. "You'd make an excellent military man with a firm voice like that."

He looked me up and down before moving onto his next question.

"Would you do me a favour, old boy? I'm meeting the chaps down the club tomorrow evening, and I promised them I would take along some of my military memorabilia to show them. Would you mind taking a quick squint around the loft? I think that's where I last saw it. It's in a red and white shoe box labelled 'the good old days.' You can't miss it. There's a good chap."

Was this part of the service? I thought to myself. Rummaging around somebody's loft to help him find mementos from a bygone era? I thought we were there to deliver shopping. Then I looked across at Robin who was busy humming away whilst brewing the tea and buttering the malt loaf. I noticed he was now wearing a butcher's style apron, which he must have found in one of the drawers. He had made himself right at home. Seeing Robin in full flow without a care in the world pricked my conscience.

"Of course I will," I responded.

"Splendid!" bellowed Mr Fish.

"Go to the top of the stairs, along the landing, and there is another door on the right. Open that door, and there is another set of stairs that leads to the loft. I haven't been up there in years."

There was a musty smell to the house as I worked my way up the first set of stairs towards the landing. The impressive paintings that decorated the walls looked like they hadn't seen a duster for quite a while. This was the same for the red and green tartan carpet covering the landing and stairs. Goodness knows how long it had been since a vacuum had been run over it. I wasn't sure how long Mr Fish had been in a wheelchair, but it was clear the upper floor hadn't been lived in for quite a while.

I found the door on the landing Mr Fish had referred to. The steps leading to the loft were wooden and rickety. One step at a time, I treaded gingerly, as they didn't feel very safe. They led up to a sizeable rectangle loft hatch. There wasn't a hatch door at the top, although I suspected there may have been in years gone by. The second to last step was broken, probably due to people exerting pressure on it over the years to propel themselves forward into the loft.

The attic space was substantial. There were the common features you would find in an attic of a house of this age, such as exposed wooden beams, pipes, redundant wiring, cracks in the roof showing light and bits of airflow tubing. A musty smell hung in the air alongside the cobwebs that furnished the sagging roof.

A quick scan from a standing position, I could see boxes of old books, Christmas decorations, an old typewriter, an old computer, an old vacuum, bits of discarded furniture, bags of clothing and boxes of vinyl. I couldn't see the red and white box Mr Fish had specifically asked for, though. I began to explore further. The more I looked, the more I saw. I noticed a number of white-coloured archive boxes. There must have been about ten of them. They were all labelled up for someone called Geoffrey. I wondered who Geoffrey was. Maybe it was Mr Fish's son and these were things he'd left behind when he'd moved out.

In the top right corner of the attic, I could see a white sheet that looked to be covering some bulky items. I lifted the sheet too quickly and disturbed the layer of dust that covered it. Dust particles began swirling in the air, making viewing a little hazy for a few minutes until it settled down. Gotcha! At the back, next to the wall, was a red and white box. I could see from the writing on the side that it was an old shoe box that once contained a new pair of men's leather Brogue shoes. I reached over some other boxes to be able to grab it.

One of these boxes was open, so I could see the contents. I was flabbergasted by what I saw. I had never seen anything like this in my life! The box was full of magazines of naked men. I picked one up to have a flick through. There were penises everywhere. These were huge penises as well! On every page, there were photographs of well-endowed nude men in a variety of positions and poses, all looking invitingly at the camera. There must have been one hundred magazines in the box, at least.

Out of curiosity, I removed the lid of another box next to it. Same again. More magazines and more huge penises. Without looking in detail, these magazines appeared to be even more hardcore than the last pile. I carefully placed the lid back on the box. I suspected some of the adjacent boxes in that area of the loft also contained similar contents based on their shape and size, but I couldn't face looking inside.

I needed to get back downstairs. I was so preoccupied with what I had just witnessed that I completely overlooked what I was there to do. I stood up and was halfway across the dusty attic floor, then remembered about the red and white box. I retraced my steps, grabbed the box, and then worked my way back towards the loft hatch and back down the rickety steps towards the first-floor landing.

As I made the short journey downstairs, I struggled to get the images out of my head. Surely, these boxes were in the wrong house, I thought. In the short time I had known Mr Fish, he appeared to be an upstanding middle-class citizen, ex-military, and whose mobility had deteriorated, resulting in him spending his days in a wheelchair. Clearly, he must be storing the magazines for someone else. He had to be. Or was I completely naïve? It wouldn't be the first time, as I cast my mind back to the occasion when I drew a lamb joint instead of a marijuana joint in front of my fellow students at the University.

Mr Fish and Robin were sitting quietly in the kitchen area when I re-joined them. They were both tucking into buttered malt loaf and freshly brewed tea. Robin was still wearing his butchers style apron. For some reason, he'd also decided to take his shoes off. Goodness knows why he'd done that.

"Oh, there you are, old boy!" bellowed Mr Fish, when he noticed me enter the kitchen.

He spotted that I had the red and white box in my hand.

"Well done, old boy. I see you've located my box of military memorabilia."

"Yes, you've got a lot of stuff up there, but I found it," I said as I passed it across to him.

He flipped the lid off the box and started rummaging through the contents. As he did this, he asked flippantly,

"And did anything else catch your eye whilst you were up there?"

Now was my chance, I thought.

"Who's Geoffrey?" I asked as I bit into a piece of malt loaf. "There are quite a few boxes up there for someone by that name."

Mr Fish stopped rummaging through the red and white box and looked up. His voice dropped and was much gentler.

"Dear Geoffrey was a very good friend of mine. He used to spend a lot of time here at the house with me. Sadly, he passed away over five years ago. He was a lovely chap. He was a pescatarian, you know. I miss him terribly."

In the space of a few seconds, his demeanour had changed from a pompous former sergeant major [or rank similar to this] to a vulnerable and lonely old man who was grieving for someone dear to him. With this drop in mood, now wasn't the time to ask why he had ordered all the fish and why is loft was full of mucky porn mags. If I had to hazard a guess, though, I think Geoffrey was Mr Fish's long-term lover, and he was consuming piles of fish in memory of him. As we left the house, Mr Fish sat quietly in his wheelchair. He seemed to be in a trance as he clutched the red and white box closely to his midriff. We waved at him from the van as we gently drove down his driveway and onto our next delivery. He didn't acknowledge us. We weren't offended, as we knew his mind was elsewhere, and we respected that.

Ending the day sockless!

Nan was keen that the supermarket delivery service was a success. The next Regional Managers meeting was on the horizon, and we were hosting it. She wanted to show off our flagship project in all its glory to the likes of Gladys Smart and Charles Chunk. Robin and I seemed to be the nominated delivery team at the weekends. This suited me as the day seemed to go quicker than when working on the shop floor filling the refrigerators. After our experience at Mr Fish's house, we sought some guidance from Nan and Elsie Standhope on the boundaries of our remit. We weren't sure whether we had overstepped the mark and gone above and beyond the call of duty by doing a favour for the customer.

"As long as you deliver all the orders on the list and don't get into trouble, we don't care what you do," was Elsie Standhope's response.

Elsie and Nan were no spring chickens and had an old-fashioned approach towards workforce management. Their guidance and advice didn't seem to correlate with the management theories I was reading about linked to my course at university. In fact, they were exactly the opposite.

A couple of weeks after receiving this vague guidance, we had a chance to test it out. It was late one Sunday afternoon. It was our last delivery of the day. We arrived and parked outside the address highlighted on the delivery sheet, which was now crumpled and covered in the remnants of Robin's packed lunch. I had never been to this part of the city before. Most of the terraced houses on the street were run down and boarded up. Those properties still lived in, were poorly maintained and unloved. In days gone by, it was probably a street that was vibrant and full of life. It was easy to imagine it being a hive of activity. Neighbours popping into each other's houses, children playing outside, street parties and the like. I doubted it had experienced such scenes for many years. The pavements were deserted. It was soulless. It was silent. It was as if the street had given up the ghost and was awaiting the bulldozers moving in. Demolition was inevitable.

Robin knocked hard on the blue coloured door. Based on the indentations, the door had obviously taken a kicking or had been punched at some point during its lifetime. Nobody answered. Robin tried again. This time, he opted for a different rhythm to his knocking style; instead of the regular 'tap, tap, tap', he went for 'tap, tap, tap, tap, tap………tap tap'. The new rhythm worked a treat. We could hear some activity behind the door. It sounded like the unlocking of several door chains. Then we heard a woman's voice. The voice had a raspy tone to it, as if she had overdone it on the karaoke the night before.

"Who is it?" she asked.

"It's Glen and Robin from the supermarket. We are here with a shopping delivery. The delivery is for Connie Capstick. Is that you?" I shouted.

More chains were unlocked, and then the door opened slowly. A woman with blonde curly hair stood in front of us. She was wearing a dressing gown and looked like she had just woken up. Her dressing gown wasn't fastened properly, and she wasn't wearing anything underneath. Everything was on display. Either she didn't know, or she didn't seem to care. The situation was awkward. I'd never had a conversation under these circumstances before. The challenge was to avoid being distracted by her private parts and to maintain eye contact.

"Yes, I'm Connie," she said.

Her voice sounded huskier than ever; now she wasn't behind a wooden door.

"I don't feel very well. Would it be alright if you carried my shopping into the house?"

The words of advice from Elsie Standhope of "don't get into any trouble" were whirling around my head. What harm can be done, I thought? Just as I was about to answer, Robin handed me the delivery list and pointed to the address we were at. It read: 11 Victoria St – payment to be collected.

"Of course, we can, Mrs Capstick," I said tentatively. "Carrying your shopping into the house isn't a problem. We'll also need to collect the money for the shopping as it says on our delivery sheet that it hasn't been paid for."

Mrs Capstick, who, due to being practically naked, was now shivering by this point, nodded before turning to go back inside the house.

I followed behind her, whilst Robin brought up the rear, laden with two heavy bags of shopping, which he took through to the kitchen.

"I'll go upstairs and get you some money," she said before leaving the room.

I noticed that all her movements seemed to be in slow motion, as if she was under the influence of drugs or alcohol or something. She didn't seem quite fully in control of her actions. The other thing that crossed my mind was whether Mrs Capstick met the criteria for the delivery scheme. The scheme was meant to be for those over 60. Based on her facial features, [her face looked to have aged quicker than the other parts of the body we could see], she looked to be in her mid-forties. She was fifty years old, at tops. Somehow, she had managed to get through Elsie Standhope's rigorous assessment system though.

The living room we were standing in was unusual. Unusual, as it was very sparse. It was missing the customary things you may find in a living room, like a television, lamps, rugs, paintings and a coffee table. The only piece of furniture was a battered brown armchair, which looked like it had been rehomed numerous times. On the larger of the cream-coloured walls hung a wooden framed whiteboard. It was full of information about forthcoming medical appointments. The next appointment seemed to be at the Mental Health Inpatient Treatment and Support Unit at 10.00 am in a few days' time. The only other item was a silver portable radio on the floor in the corner of the room. It was switched on and making a strange chattering noise.

I eased myself into the battered armchair. It was comfy but gave off a dubious odour. The smell reminded me of something linked to my grandparents, but I couldn't place my finger on it. I noticed that Robin had decided to also take the weight off his feet. He was sat down cross-legged on the floor, revealing his burgundy coloured ankle socks with white trim. He was humming, but it wasn't one of his normal tunes. It was the theme song to the old movie, The Dam Busters. He refrained from imitating aeroplanes flying with his arms outstretched while singing it though.

We sat there waiting for Mrs Capstick to come back downstairs. Apart from Robin's humming, the only background noise was the chattering of the radio in the corner of the room. In my mind, I was willing Mrs Capstick to hurry up, as I needed to go to the toilet. I needed a number two. My mind drifted to when I was last in this position in somebody else's house, but I couldn't actually think of a specific situation where this had happened. But it did make me reminisce of the time when Laurie and I worked on the house by the canal and Laurie used Raymond Harrison's outside toilet. Suddenly, I snapped out of my daydream as the radio in the corner of the room, sprung into life. This switch in radio noise was also noticed by

Robin, who stopped humming immediately. The chattering was replaced by a male voice.

"Be on the lookout for a grey BMW"...... followed by intermittent radio chattering.

"Last seen, travelling south down Walter Street" was the next update.

"Ten – four ....copy that," said a second individual, again followed by intermittent radio chattering.

"Backup is en-route," continued the first individual.

"Ten – four" was again the response from the receiver of the call.

We were so engrossed in listening to the conversation coming from the radio that we hadn't noticed Mrs Capstick was now back in the room. I thought she might have slipped into some clothing when she was upstairs, but she hadn't bothered. Her dressing gown remained wide open with everything on display. As she thrust the shopping money into my hand, she broke wind. She wasn't embarrassed, though.

"Why is your radio tuned in to the police?" I enquired.

The pupils in her eyes were dilated, and she paused for a second before answering. She was fixated on my teeth. She probably couldn't comprehend why they were so big. I did have that effect on people.

"It's my husband. He's been released from prison today. He's trying to track me down," she answered.

"Why was he in prison?" I asked.

"He blinded someone. He hit them over the head with a baseball bat, and while they were unconscious, he removed their eyes with a razor blade. This was because he'd heard a rumour that this guy fancied me. He's a complete headcase. I'm really frightened. I've moved here from the south so he can't find me" she explained.

Listening to Mrs Capstick's tale of woe seemed to accelerate my need to go to the toilet, so much so that I didn't even ask permission to use the facilities. I just burst past her, through the door, and bolted up the uncarpeted stairs. At the top, I turned right. Luckily, the first door on the right led into a poky bathroom with a turquoise-coloured bathroom suite. My situation was so urgent I pulled down my trousers and threw my back end in the direction of the toilet seat.

The relief was immense. I sat there and absorbed my surroundings. Just like the living room downstairs, the bathroom was bare and didn't feel lived in. Patches of black mould had formed on the ceiling and walls. Fascinatingly, one of the patches on the ceiling was a distinct shape and resembled the country of Italy on a world map.

The satisfaction of probably being the first person to notice the Italian-shaped mould was cut short when I had a terrifying thought. What if Mrs Capstick's husband should turn up at the front door of the house in the next few minutes and find his missus half naked with two supermarket workers? How would we talk ourselves out of this situation? We wouldn't have a cat in hell's chance. This is the guy who blinded someone just because he'd heard a rumour! This situation would be totally different, as he would see it in the flesh, literally. As far as punishments go, he'd probably opt for something doled out in the Middle Ages, such as beheading or burning us at the stake. We had to get out of this house and fast. I was panicking.

In my panicked state, whilst still perched on the toilet seat, I started to look for the loo roll. There was a toilet roll holder attached to the wall, but it was empty. In my rush to get to the toilet, I hadn't considered looking to see if there was any loo roll. Apart from a sink, bath and toilet brush and holder, the bathroom was totally barren.

I sat for a moment and thought what to do. My concentration levels weren't great, though. I was imagining me and Robin chained to a giant stake with a bag of gunpowder hung around each of our necks, surrounded by gorse branches and faggots of wood. Mr Capstick stood there with his box of matches urging us to repent for encouraging Mrs Capstick to display her wares for all to see. I floated back into the real world. Suddenly, I had a moment of inspiration. I needed to sacrifice some clothing. Some clothing that if it went missing, nobody would notice. It had to be my socks.

Quickly, I removed my shoes and socks. The socks were nothing special, probably part of a multi-pack I'd received one Christmas or something. I used them to clean myself up. The next challenge was what to do with the soiled socks. I couldn't flush them down the loo. It would most certainly create a blockage. Mrs Capstick didn't deserve that. She had enough on her plate with her crazy husband on the rampage. The last thing she needed was the place covered in sewage and having to call out the plumber. There was only one other thing I could do. Hide them. Initially, I tried removing the bath panel, but to no avail. It was fixed on solid. There was only one other place, and that was inside the toilet brush holder. I removed the brush from the holder, carefully pushed in the soiled socks, and then returned the brush back to its rightful place before fleeing the scene of the crime and back down the stairs.

I burst into the living room. Mrs Capstick was sat in the brown armchair. She was munching on what looked like scrambled eggs. She must have rustled it up whilst I was upstairs. Her dressing gown was still not fastened. Robin was sat cross-legged, humming The Dam Busters theme tune. I noticed the tempo was quicker than when he hummed it initially. That's probably because he'd never hummed in front of so much naked flesh before. I turned towards Mrs Capstick. She was covered in eggs. Her hand-to-mouth coordination was all over the place.

"We have to go now. I hope things work out for you. Maybe we'll see you again sometime," I said.

This was a complete lie. She was the last person on earth I wanted to bump into again. Robin jumped to his feet. He also seemed relieved we were leaving. Within a couple of minutes, we were back in the van and on our way back to the supermarket.

Off to Thirsk………then sent to Coventry

I had become fond of Nan Postlethwaite. She had invested time and effort in me. She was also giving me every opportunity to develop myself professionally and gain new skills. She had spotted that inbuilt steely determination to do well that others hadn't. The fact that she had used one of my creative ideas [well, one that I had pinched from a magazine] to establish a flagship delivery scheme to help the business progress was a real boost to my confidence. She had even gone the extra mile by making me [and Robin] an integral part of the scheme.

Another character in my life who was supportive, was Patrick O'Hara. He was a Principal lecturer in the faculty of media at the university. He had been assigned to oversee my final-year dissertation. Patrick was a tall, dark-haired gentleman with bushy sideburns, which I often thought would benefit from a good trim. His cheap-looking charcoal grey suits seemed to hang off his wiry frame.

As part of his attire, he would mostly wear off-white shirts and floral ties. His off-white shirts would be of his own choice of colour, whereas Robin's off-white shirts were due to him being thrifty and too tight to go out and buy a new one. When he removed his suit jacket, which was pretty often during lectures, he always rolled his shirt sleeves up, giving me the impression he didn't want to look too smart. He had a lovely persona about him and was really easy-going. Not like some of the other lecturers who were uptight and stuffy. He would start every one-to-one meeting with the same sentence,

"I must get round to tidying up this office."

It was a mess. There were books, assignments, stationery, sports gear, unwashed coffee mugs and chocolate bar wrappers everywhere. Strategically placed around his computer monitor though, were numerous jars of unopened Marmalade. I recall he'd mentioned his liking for marmalade in a previous lecture. I was guessing these were gifts from former students who'd also appreciated his support.

We'd jointly agreed on the title of the dissertation towards the end of the second year. I was keen to increase my knowledge of sports marketing and was particularly keen to focus on the horse racing industry. He set some parameters to ensure the dissertation had a degree of focus to it. The agreed title was: 'How can marketing planning help increase the number of people attending horse racing meetings in the UK'?

Although the dissertation was officially a third-year module, Patrick strongly encouraged me to spend some time working on it over the summer period, if time allowed. He suggested I could perhaps develop some of the methodology I was going to use, such as questionnaires, and pilot test them on a small number of participants. He drilled into me the importance of well-structured questions that would enable simple analysis. The use of open questions was also encouraged.

In order to pilot test my questionnaire, I needed a day at the races. This wasn't going to be easy as I didn't have access to a car.

I did consider asking Nan if I could borrow the supermarket delivery van, but I knew what the answer would be to that question. It would be a firm 'no'.

Within a few days, though, this problem around transport issues to a racecourse was overcome, and it came via an unlikely source. My flatmate, Steve, had recently landed a new part-time job. He had left the job at the take-away and landed a cushy little number working behind the bar at a social club in the leafy suburbs of the city. He was much happier with this new arrangement as he worked fewer hours and wasn't rushed off his feet. The downside was that the unlimited supply of leftover pizzas, kebabs and burgers that used to appear every time he worked a shift suddenly stopped [for some reason, takeaways from the fast-food place Steve worked didn't trigger my phobia]. This wasn't ideal for a couple of hard-up students. We suddenly found ourselves spending more of the little money we had on groceries. Most of the meals we cooked seemed to comprise of mashed potato and gravy. Having something like sausage or chicken to accompany this combination was a rare treat.

On the occasional evening, I would join Steve at the social club. He would be busy on one side of the bar attending to customers whilst I was on the other side of the bar nursing a pint. I had a knack for being able to make my pint last most of the evening. This didn't go down too well with Gerald, the Club Steward. As the bar stock and takings are the steward's responsibility, Gerald soon realised that I wasn't really contributing to the profit margins. He knew I was taking the piss and took an instant dislike to me. I wasn't bothered, though.

I was propping up the bar one evening when I noticed an amateurish-looking poster on the Social Club notice board. The poster was surrounded by business cards detailing local taxi firms and takeaways. I wandered across the main bar area to have a closer look. In big black capital letters, the poster read: 'Trip to Thirsk races, Saturday 8 September. £20.00 for transport and entrance fee. Meet in the Social Club Car Park at 7:30 am. Minibus leaves at 7:45 am prompt. Contact Gerald McLean for further information. All Welcome'.

I rushed back to the bar and relayed the information to Steve. I was keen to go as I knew it was an opportunity to test out my pilot questionnaire. Steve was bang up for it, too. He loved horse racing. We just had to work out how we were going to fund the trip. This didn't take long. It just required a little bit of ingenuity. Steve sweet-talked Gerald into reserving him a couple of places. Steve agreed to work extra shifts behind the bar, but for no wages, until the cost of the trip had been paid off. Gerald agreed. All we needed to do then was source some money to place bets and for food and drink for the day. We jointly agreed that I could work extra shifts at the supermarket to offset those expenses.

The day of the race meeting soon arrived. We were both up early and enthusiastic with anticipation for the day ahead. I got stuck into a breakfast of Cornflakes and Weetabix combo with lashings of ice-cold milk. Steve was on his normal rounds of toast covered in cheap margarine and smothered in homemade raspberry jam, courtesy of his mother.

We arrived at the Social Club just before 7:30 am, as per the instructions on the poster. We were rather damp as the weather that morning was lousy. The weather forecast for the rest of the day in the Thirsk area wasn't looking great either. We clambered onboard the minibus. The driver of the bus was a guy called Syd. He had one of those moustaches that hadn't grown properly, and for some reason, he was wearing a cowboy hat. Maybe he thought it made him look cool.

The organiser of the trip, Gerald, took his rightful place on the seat at the front of the bus. He was equipped with a wireless microphone, clipboard and pen. He loved the responsibility of being the event organiser. He was wearing an olive-coloured blazer and a dark green and navy striped silk tie. His black and white striped umbrella was perched between his seat and the space allocated to store luggage. Rain droplets chased each other down the upright umbrella and formed a tiny puddle next to Gerald's foot. As Steve and I made our way towards the two vacant seats at the back of the bus, Gerald made a snide remark.

"I hope you've brought enough money to have more than one pint!" he shouted before laughing out loud.

I knew straight away that he was having a dig at me. I thought it would be best to ignore it rather than retaliate, so I just smiled at him, then took my seat.

The minibus was a 24 seater. Looking around the bus, the majority of those on board were middle aged couples. Making up the numbers was a couple of guys, who either didn't have partners, or if they were in a relationship, had decided not to invite their partners along. At 7:45 am prompt, Gerald stood up, and using his portable microphone, welcomed us all on board. He went on to give us some brief details of the day, including planned toilet stops [which he no doubt had meticulously researched] and estimated arrival time at the racecourse. He also provided some housekeeping rules about the bus. He was obviously relaying instructions that had been passed across by Syd. The main rule was that there was to be 'no drinking of alcohol' on the bus. Perhaps Syd had previously had a bad experience, where someone had got drunk and hurled all over his immaculate minibus interior, and he didn't fancy another deep clean. Gerald stressed that if anyone was seen drinking alcohol on the bus they would be removed. Gerald craved the power. He was in his element.

The minibus trundled out of the Social Club Car Park at 7:50 am. Outside, the rain was hammering down. The windscreen wipers on the minibus were on full speed and were just about coping. Despite the inclement weather, the atmosphere on the bus was really jovial. Talking to some of the other racegoers, it was apparent that they had never been to a race meeting before. They were complete novices when it came to the racecourse experience.

I was sat next to a guy called Ken. He was captain of the Social Club Bowling Team. His cousin, Jack, lived at Thirsk and he was hoping to bump into him. He didn't say whether anything had been officially organised though. During the journey he worked his way through a bag of Sarsaparilla tablets. He offered me one, but as I didn't know the source of the sweets, my eating phobia kicked in, and I declined.

The minibus pulled into a pub car park on the outskirts of Thirsk. It was 11:30 am. There were several other minibuses parked up. It was probably a regular pitstop for coaches due to its proximity to the racecourse and good parking. Before we left the minibus, Gerald made an announcement.

"The Golden Goose [name of the pub] is the last stop before Thirsk racecourse. It's renowned for its selection of craft ales and home cooked food. Make sure you are back on board by 12:25 pm as the minibus will depart at 12:30 pm prompt."

Rather than leave it at that, he decided to add in another phrase, which left all of us looking at each other in bemusement.

"Ladies and gentlemen.......start your engines!"

It was his way of letting us know that the pleasurable part of the trip started at this point in the proceedings. Into the pub, we went.

Just over an hour later, the minibus pulled into the parking area allocated for coaches at the racecourse. Basically, it was just a great big field. An old frail looking gentleman, wearing a flat cap, wellington boots and a Hi-Vis vest [with the word 'Steward' printed on the back] on top of his overcoat, provided directions to Syd on where we should park. The poor guy was absolutely drenched. We parked next to a coach displaying the name 'Bensons Travel of Sunderland' down either side. On the other side of us was a minibus displaying the name 'Helen's Luxury coaches of Wigan' in big gold lettering. Before we had a chance to leave the bus, Gerald stood up. Clutching the microphone, he announced,

"Take all your belongings onto the course and don't leave any valuables on the bus. The last race is at 5:30 pm. Please make your way back to the minibus as soon as you can, following this race. We aim to be back at the Social Club for 8:30 pm. Joyce Thompson is preparing us a pie and pea supper for when we return, at only £3.50 per head. Enjoy yourselves and be lucky."

It was just after 1:00 pm when we went through the turnstile and into the course. Steve and I were on a mission. We needed to test out the dissertation questionnaire to see if it was fit for purpose. I knew that racegoers would only welcome being interviewed at specific times, that is when they were not watching races or studying the form, placing bets or collecting winnings. Therefore, it was essential to conduct the questionnaires before racing proceeded. The first race was at 2:00 pm.

We needed to find somewhere dry to carry out the survey. By chance, we wandered into large covered bar area, packed with racegoers. We got chatting to a group of racegoers from Skipton. One of the group was a right miserable bastard but the remainder of them were happy to help out and were willing to be interviewed. We undertook five interviews each and were through them in half an hour. Following the questionnaires, we jointly agreed that one of the questions should be revamped as it failed to draw out detailed enough responses to support the research. Job done. Now we could relax and enjoy ourselves.

Despite the weather outside, people were having a good time. The bar we were in was buzzing. Everyone hoping they would finish the afternoon with their pockets full of cash after picking a few winners. Armed with pints of Yorkshire's finest ale, we began studying the form for the first race. I opted for a horse called Double Treble. Steve chose one called My Rosenior. He said that the name of the horse sounded similar to the surname of a player who played for his favourite football team, West Ham Utd. That was the only reason he backed it. Its form was shocking.

As it was still pissing down outside, we remained in the bar area and placed our bets on The Tote. The Tote is a system where punters pick their horses and put their money into a cumulative pool – everyone with a winning ticket shares a percentage of the pot. If fewer people backed your horse, you get a greater share if it wins. It was either this or go outside to the On-Course bookmaker and get completely soaked.

Steve, who was not renowned for being lucky cheered his horse home. He was so aminated during the race, he lost most of his pint of beer. There was a guy in front of us wearing a snorkel parker coat and the beer ended up inside his hood. He didn't know and we didn't care. Steve's horse had romped home at 33/1 so he had a healthy return on his five pound investment. We'd agreed beforehand that whatever we won on the horses, was equally shared, so I was also ecstatic when My Rosenior was rode to victory. I was quids in too.

After the third race finished and the mud-covered jockeys dismounted, an announcement came through the tannoy system.

"Due to the large amounts of rain, resulting in saturated ground, the difficult decision has been made to abandon the remainder of the meeting. We apologise for the inconvenience caused."

A chorus of boos echoed around the covered bar area we were in. As the boos subsided, they were replaced by the sound of hundreds of punters all in conversation about the decision they had just heard. Although slightly disappointed, the decision made by the racecourse hierarchy didn't concern me and Steve too much. Yes, the Thirsk meeting was off, but racing was still being broadcast on the television screens from other meetings around the country. We could still bet on The Tote at places like Leicester, Kempton, and Redcar, which, in effect, was what we were doing anyway.

Over the next two hours or so, Steve provided a complete masterclass of how to win at horse racing. Virtually, every horse he placed a bet on, went on to win. It was total luck too. He was choosing horses names at random, rather than reading the horse's form [Form is the record of a horse's previous performances]. He had the Midas touch alright! I wasn't complaining either, as I was benefitting from this fortuitous run of good luck he was experiencing. The more he won, the more beer we consumed. Eventually, we couldn't accommodate any more beer and moved onto the stronger stuff like rum and brandy. We were more than a little tipsy by this stage. It's fair to say we were inebriated. The day had panned out far better than we could ever imagined it would.

Immediately after the 5:15 pm televised race from Kempton finished, the crowded bar area started to empty. Of those still remaining, I didn't recognise anyone from our party. Come to think of it, I hadn't seen anyone from our party all afternoon. Speaking slowly and with my words all slurred, I just about mustered,

"Do you think we should make our way back to the bus?"

Steve just grinned.

I took that to mean yes. We left the dry and warm covered bar area and made our way out of the racecourse, across the road, and to the field where the minibus was parked. The rain hadn't eased off. It was hammering down and bouncing off the roofs of the coaches, still parked up. Due to the incessant downpour, the soggy field now resembled a mud bath. The coaches that could move were slipping and sliding all over the place. One coach, with the name 'Pickles Luxury Travel of Pickering' illustrated down its side, was motionless, except for its back wheels, which were spinning around in the sticky mud. That coach was going nowhere soon.

Steve and I trudged across the field in search of the minibus. Our footwear sunk into the mud with every step. We were that drunk, we couldn't walk in a straight line, never mind remember where the minibus was parked. All of a sudden, I heard a heavy squelching sound behind me. Steve had lost his balance and slipped. He was motionless for a few seconds. Then he slowly dragged himself to his feet. He was covered in brown mud. Because he fell face first, it looked like he was sporting a mud-coloured face pack.

In the distance, I could see a someone hanging outside one of the coaches, waving at us. He was wearing a cowboy hat. It was Syd. He was ushering us to hurry up. We moved as quickly as we could, taking into account the conditions under foot. As we approached him, he didn't look very pleased. In fact, he looked rather angry.

"Where the fuckin hell have you two muppets been?" he yelled at us. "This lot are baying for blood. They have been sat here for the last two and a half hours waiting for you. You have some explaining to do."

We staggered up the bus steps, leaving a trail of mud behind us. We were greeted with a deafening chorus of boos. Gerald then got out his portable microphone and, to the tune of, 'O Come all ye faithful', had everyone on the bus singing:

"Why are we waiting? Why are we waiting? Why are we waiting? O why? Why? Why?"

I vaguely remembered the song from my childhood, sung sitting round the dining table, knife and fork in hand, fists lightly drumming against the table in time with the music, while my mother slaved away in the kitchen. But I never ever imagined it to be sung by a group of slightly damp, pissed off adults, and under these circumstances. How were we to know that they didn't fully understand the protocol of going to a race meeting. If the live racing is abandoned, and there is still the opportunity to have a drink, watch racing and place bets, you should make the most of the opportunity. You don't have to automatically leave the course, jump on the bus and then go home!

In comparison to some of the buses, we made our way out of the boggy field relatively quickly. Luckily, the annoying song they were singing, petered out. Within five minutes, the combination of booze, and motion of the bus, had sent Steve to sleep. Ken, who was sat next to him, wrote the word 'twat' in the wet mud on his forehead. Ken had to keep himself amused somehow, now he was out of Sarsaparilla tablets. Although difficult, I was determined to stay awake. Someone had to keep an eye out for us. We were public enemy number one. The whole bus hated us for keeping them waiting. Syd hated us because the bus interior in Steve's vicinity was going to need a deep clean. The banter on the bus going back to the Social Club was exactly the opposite to the outward journey. It was now deathly silent. The only noise was coming from Syd's radio cassette. Ironically, one of the songs he played was The Gambler, by Kenny Rogers. You could cut the atmosphere with a knife. There was no doubt about it, they had all 'sent us to Coventry'. This was probably instigated by Gerald, the miserable bastard. The journey back took forever.

Within half an hour of reaching our destination, the journey back deteriorated even further. Ken, who was struggling with the silence, for some reason decided to forgive us. He leaned around Steve to direct his question towards me.

"So how did you get on at the races, then?" he asked.

Without thinking, I just blurted out,

"We're over £800.00 pounds up!".

The look of amazement on Ken's face was a picture. He then proceeded to jab Steve in the ribs, whilst at the same time questioning him.

"Is this right, you're over £800.00 pounds up?"

Steve woke up immediately. He was terribly confused. You could tell he didn't know where he was. He muttered something, but it was incomprehensible. Ken didn't have the patience to ask again. He took my word for it. He turned around to a middle aged couple sat behind him and Steve.

"They're over £800.00 pounds up"! he exclaimed.

This message was relayed to the back of the bus within seconds. It was like a Mexican wave of words, without any hands being raised. This news hadn't done us any favours. They were angry enough with us already because they had to sit on a bus in their damp clothing for two and half hours. Now they knew we were loaded from the races, this accentuated their animosity towards us. Things weren't looking good.

Whilst I was considering how we could get out of this mess, my thinking was interrupted by a strange noise. It was coming from Steve's vicinity. It was a retching noise followed by the sound of a semi-thick liquid hitting the floor from about two or three feet. Steve had hurled. The contents of his stomach had gone everywhere. This included all over Ken, who wasn't quick enough to get out of the way. He paused for a few seconds whilst the reality of the situation sunk in before shouting

"Jesus Christ, Steve's chundered!"

The Mexican wave of words started up again. The phrase 'Steve's chundered', was communicated around the bus in seconds. The news reached Syd, who without warning, slammed on the brakes. The minibus came to a grinding halt, on what was quite a busy road. He turned the hazard lights on, left his seat to come and investigate. He looked at Steve and Ken in disgust. Steve was covered in vomit and mud, whereas Ken had a pool of warm sick nestling in his lap.

"For fucks sake" he hissed.

It was obvious by his furrowed brow and reddening skin that he was furious. There were a few seconds of quietness before he pointed at Steve and me then screamed.

"Get off my bus now!".

Although it was Steve's fault the bus was going to have to be deep cleaned, he saw me as Steve's accomplice, and therefore my fate was sealed too. We couldn't be bothered to argue our case as we knew we wouldn't get a reprieve. We got to our feet and embarrassingly trudged down the centre aisle towards for the passenger front door. As we did so, Gerald picked up his microphone and started to bellow out a song, probably in honour of Syd. After all, he made the decision to boot us off the bus. The song went: "For he's a jolly good fellow, for he's a jolly good fellow, for he's a jolly good fellow, which nobody can deny. And so say all of us, and so say all of us, for he's a jolly good fellow, etc."

The bus pulled away, leaving us stranded on the side of the road. We were about five miles from home. We knew the way back, so we decided to walk. The walk helped to sober us up. We both thought we had been unfairly treated by Gerald and co. On principle, Steve decided he should quit is part time job at the Social Club. We used the winnings from the race trip as housekeeping to tide us over until he found another job.

Nottingham branch 2…….Derby branch 0…….

It was the day of Regional Managers meeting. Our branch [Nottingham] were hosting it. On the agenda was our new Supermarket Delivery scheme. Nan insisted on it. She also stipulated it was high up on the agenda. She was well aware that her nemesis, Gladys Smart, would be looking for any opportunity to criticise the scheme. She wasn't about to let that happen. Nan and Elsie had roped in me and Robin to cover this agenda item. We were the chosen ones. She was sending us into battle and we had to be at the top of our game.

Prior to the meeting, we'd been given a list of tasks to do by Nan, as a way of preparation. It read: 'clean supermarket delivery van [inside and out]; decorate van [use your imagination]; prepare presentation about scheme'. We were up for the challenge. We were desperate not to let the Nottingham branch down. We didn't want to let Nan down either.

Representatives from the other branches arrived at our store and entered the boardroom. Attendance was healthy and the board room was packed. Everybody knew of the rivalry between Nan Postlethwaite and Gladys Smart. There was always a chance of a lively debate when they were in the same meeting. This meeting had extra spice with Nottingham's new delivery scheme being on the agenda. Our facilities weren't a patch on Derby, and Gladys Smart knew it. Their store was only two years old and state of the art. She entered the building in her high heels, leopard skin dress, dyed black beehive hairdo and heavy red lipstick. She didn't have Liam, her work experience lackey, with her this time. He must have completed his stint and returned to education. She made a point of licking her finger and then checking for dust on various items of furniture in the boardroom, before tutting very loudly. She was oozing confidence and no doubt had a plan to undermine Nan.

The meeting commenced. Gladys Smart was chairperson and started proceedings with introductions, going around the table in an anticlockwise direction. Nottingham branch were strongly represented, with me, Nan, Elsie and Robin all in attendance. We also had an ally in the room. It was Nan's cousin, Mavis Scallop, who represented the Shrewsbury branch. Charles Chunk was at the far end of table. He was wearing a cream-coloured linen suit and pale blue shirt, which was most likely unbuttoned to give everyone a glimpse of his chest hair, whether they liked it, or not. From time to time, we got whiffs of his aftershave. It smelt expensive. Once the introductions were over, we moved onto the minutes from the last meeting. Gladys Smart was swiftly taking us through these, then suddenly she stopped.

"Who's humming?", she snapped, and looked in the direction of where it was coming from.

Robin, who had never been to a meeting like this before, and didn't know the protocol, was engrossed in the minutes. He was humming the tune to The Dam Busters movie, which was ironic, as it did feel like we were about to go into battle. I nudged him.

"Robin, the Chairperson of the meeting wants you to stop humming," I whispered to him, trying not to draw any attention to myself.

Robin was suddenly transported from whatever planet he was on, to being back into the real world. The humming stopped.

"Now we've dealt with that little issue, we'll move onto the next agenda item," she commented smugly, after embarrassing poor Robin.

She went on,

"The next agenda item is about a sales training course, that will be rolled out during Autumn across all our stores. It is mandatory that all members of staff attend. We have Kevin with us this morning, from our Mansfield branch. He is going to brief us about what is in store for us all".

"Excuse the pun," she said, then followed this up with a little giggle.

I looked across at Nan. Her face was like thunder.

"Excuse me Mrs Chairperson!" yelled Nan. She continued,

"I think you'll find you have skipped an agenda item. The next agenda item is 'Customer Delivery Scheme launched in Nottingham'. It's item number three on the agenda. When was the last time you had your eyes tested?" asked Nan.

"Oh, do excuse me, Mrs Postlethwaite, I'm getting carried away with myself; I didn't spot that particular agenda item. Now let me see……..", and she proceeded to push her half-moon spectacles upwards so they were closer to her face.

"I'm deeply sorry," she said, trying, but failing to sound sincere.

Nan knew too well that she had purposely made this blunder to wind her up. It had worked too. Nan was already hot under the collar after Gladys had humiliated a member of her team [Robin] only a few minutes earlier.

"I'm so sorry everyone. I'll try and improve my chairperson skills over this next term."

This was another dig at Nan. Gladys had been voted in as Chairperson for a third consecutive term [each term was 12 months]. Managers had cast their vote soon after the last regional meeting and she had narrowly defeated Doreen Higgins from the Birmingham East branch. According to Nan's cousin, Mavis, the rumour was, that the voting had been rigged, but nobody had any concrete evidence, so the decision couldn't be challenged.

"Now let me see. Ah yes. Agenda item number three is about the launch of a customer delivery scheme for the elderly residents of Nottingham. And here we have a Glen Finnan and a Robin Banks to talk to us about the scheme."

Robin and I got to our feet and made our way to the front of the room, where our overhead projector and screen were waiting. For a split second, I caught the eye of Nan and Elsie. Their expressions said it all. If the expression could talk, it would have said,

"Go on, Glen Finnan. Hit them with everything you have, son. We are relying on you."

Whilst Robin powered up the overhead projector, I beckoned those present to look out of the huge Board Room window onto the car park. Our colleague, Ray, slowly drove the delivery van and positioned it in front of the window. The van was decorated with silver balloons and a huge golden bow supported by gilded ribbons. It looked immaculate.

I was about to start delivering the speech when Gladys Smart chirped up,

"Are you feeling ok, Mr Finnan? You look quite pale."

She'd obviously remembered my bronzed complexion at the last meeting, and this was her way of trying to put me off my stride. It didn't work, though. I launched into the presentation with gusto. I used phrases like maintaining independence, improving quality of life, alleviating loneliness and isolation, and positive social interaction. I included photographs and quotes from satisfied customers [the Brown twins and my gran's mates]. I included delivery statistics, income growth and forecast for future deliveries. I stated that if the service was to grow at a similar rate, a second delivery van would be required within three months. I even included details of how the scheme was supporting the environment.

Gladys Smart was twitching and shuffling about in her seat. This was uncomfortable listening for her, and she'd had enough. Derby branch was being blown away by this flagship scheme, and she couldn't cope with this.

Like an excellent relay team, I passed the baton across to Robin. Normally, Robin didn't say much, but he did on this occasion. He was wearing a crisp white shirt that was slightly too big for him. Nan had borrowed one from the clothing aisle, especially for the meeting. She wanted him to look smart. His normal attire [the shirt that had lost its original colour and turned grey] wasn't appropriate for this occasion. In his own unique way, he shared details of a competition we had launched. The store was giving away a free bag of shopping to one lucky customer on the delivery list, each week. The competition was the brainchild of Elsie Standhope. Surprise, surprise, the Brown twins were victorious on the first week the competition was launched.

He also gave attendees sample uniforms to scrutinize that were to be trialled by the delivery drivers. Amusingly, he'd drafted his presentation notes on a piece of cardboard that obviously used to be a Cornflake packet. Goodness knows why he hadn't used a sheet of paper or crib card like anybody else would do. As he read off his script, all eyes were on the Cockerel on the packet rather than Robin himself. Maybe this was a clever tactic of his to draw the attention away from himself. Neither of us mentioned Mr Fish's porno collection or our escapades at Mrs Capstick's house. We kept it all positive. We concluded the presentation by saying the last sentence in unison:

"This is a retail delivery service you can count on."

Nan and Elsie were beaming from ear to ear, as was Mavis Scallop. Gladys Smart on the other hand was furiously mopping her brow with an embroidered pink handkerchief and complaining she felt faint. Patricia Peabody from Nuneaton branch had to help her out of the Board room and escort her to the First Aid room so she could lie down.

Charles Chunk took it upon himself to act as interim chair whilst Gladys was indisposed.

"You good folks up here in Nottingham sure have got a 'whizz' of scheme going on", he said in his strong American accent.

"I was very sceptical of young Mr Finnan's grand plan when he briefed us at the last meeting, but I take it all back. I'm blown away. As they say in my home town, back in Tennessee, this scheme is 'Sexier than socks on a rooster'!"

After a huge slurp of coffee, he looked in the direction of Nan.

"Mrs Postlethwaite, surely young Mr Finnan deserves promotion following his marvellous achievements? I'm hoping you are going to tell us all gathered here today, that this is your intention".

He had certainly put Nan on the spot. Nan looked at me, and I looked back at Nan. Then she turned her attention back to Charles Chunk.

"This is certainly something I will be seriously considering. Glen Finnan has inbuilt steely determination to do well. Others might not be able to see it but I spotted this the moment I clapped eyes on him."

Chapter 3: Daphne Dapper

This is me

My name is Daphne Dapper. I'm fifty-five years old and live in a bustling market town in County Durham. For the record, I'm not overkeen on the name Daphne. Since I was a young girl, I've always been besotted by the name Philippa. Not sure why, though. I used to pester my parents to change my name, but they were having none of it. In fact, they seemed to get quite upset with me when I broached the subject, which I did many times. I live alone in a charming three-bedroom semi-detached house on the outskirts of town. When I say, 'I live alone,' I mean I don't live with any other human beings. I do, however, share the house with my six-year-old cat, Columbus.

Most of the neighbourhood knows Columbus, as he has a distinctive look. His tail is missing! He wasn't in an accident or anything like that. He has always been tailless. I acquired Columbus from my next-door neighbour, Tony Mathew [more about him later]. He was the last of the litter to be rehomed after his cat Suki, gave birth to eight kittens. The obvious question when most people clap their eyes on Columbus is: is he a Manx cat? If you didn't know, the Manx cat is an ancient breed from the Isle of Man and is best known for its lack of a tail. I did wonder whether it was possible for a litter of 'Heinz 57' kittens to include a Manx cat amongst them, but the vet soon put the record straight on that. She explained that cats who are born with no tail [or a short tail] usually have this feature due to a random genetic mutation. The only cat breed that is truly tailless is the Manx, but there are many other types of felines with extremely short tails.

In 2021, I inherited the property I live in when my parents passed away. They were involved in a tragic accident whilst on holiday in Kenya. They had booked a luxury safari to celebrate their 50th wedding anniversary. It was something they had always wanted to do. They could only afford to go on the trip because Dad's cousin, Alice, had left him a few quid in her will, so they decided to treat themselves. My mother must have sent a postcard the day before the accident. It didn't arrive until two weeks after the double funeral took place. It was really weird as it felt like I was being contacted from beyond the grave. In my mum's neatest handwriting, she had written:

"Hi Daphne, having a lovely time here in Samburu National Reserve. Yesterday, we spotted wildebeest, antelope, leopard and speckled pink flamingos. Today, our guide, Wilson, thinks we will see elephants and rhinos, so we are very excited. The safari is everything we imagined it to be. The weather is sweltering, and your father has come out in a heat rash. See you when we get back. Mum & Dad."

I liaised with the Kenyan authorities over many months to try to understand how mum and dad died. However, I was never able to establish the truth. All I know is that they somehow got separated from the rest of the group on the safari. In the Coroner's report, it states my dad lost his new binoculars and wandered into the bush to find them. There is a presumption that when he didn't emerge from the bush, my mum must have panicked and decided to look for him. Screams could be heard and then it went all silent. It was thought they were crushed by a crash of aggressive black Rhinos who mistook mum and dad for predators. They were pronounced dead at the scene. At the funeral, Lisa Holiday, the lady from the travel agent, who booked their vacation, explained she recalled a conversation, whilst they were booking the safari.

"They wanted to get up close and personal to the wildlife," she explained.

How ironic was that?

Today is the 10th July 2023. My cousin, Deirdre has organised a weekend away. I don't exactly know why she has organised the trip, or exactly where we are going. Normally we don't keep anything from each other, so this behaviour on her part is a bit odd. Whatever she has planned, I'm confident she will have my best interests at heart. She always has. Deirdre is my closest friend and has been for as long as I can remember. She is 58 years old but has the complexion of someone much younger. She was recently chatted up by a bloke in the pub and mistaken for someone in her late thirties!

She cringes when others describe her as 'tomboy'. With her short cropped dark hair, loose fitting neutral clothing and lack of make-up, she certainly fits the mould. Activities such as football, rugby and hockey have always been her preferred pastimes, as is camping, and spending time in the great outdoors. Deirdre is a member of a local hiking, outdoors and social group, so is often away for a few days at a time. Sometimes these excursions can include wild camps. Some of the other women in the group don't sign up to these, as there are no toilet and washing facilities. This doesn't faze Deirdre. She will quite happily use a trowel to dig a makeshift toilet in the middle of nowhere and have a number two. She just gets on with it.

Another thing you need to know about Deirdre is that she is tech savvy and has always loved gadgets. Whatever the era, she is always the first person I know to have the latest technology on the market. Not that she wants to show off, or anything. She is just fascinated and enthusiastic about technology and loves to understand how it works.

The Sony Walkman was the first gadget I ever recall her owning. Over the years this has been followed by gadgets such as Nintendo entertainment systems, handheld game console's such as Gameboy, flip phones, remote control robots, PlayStations, MP3 players, video cameras and so on. Nowadays, it's her Smart phone which she is never without. She tells me that her phone helps her 'manage her life effectively'. Apart from the obvious phone calls, the phone reminds her when she has appointments, it helps her to navigate and get to different locations and helps her manage her fitness by showing how many calories she is burning. She even uses the phone to do her banking and manage her finances. It is always in her back right pocket of her jeans or combat trousers. She is never without it.

I love Deirdre dearly. She keeps me organised. Well, her smart phone does anyway! She also does her best to keep me out of trouble. This is no easy task. Even when mum and dad were alive, Deirdre was the person I turned to for comfort, knowledge and advice. Although I rubbed along with my parents ok, I didn't feel a bond or strong connection between us. That fundamental basic emotional support just didn't seem to be there. It was weird really. I remember watching Deirdre regularly being hugged by her mum and dad, [my Aunty Anthea and Uncle Roger], and being encouraged to do well at whatever challenges she faced. I can't remember this happening to me. Although I lived in a household of three, I felt alone. I suppose this can happen sometimes. Maybe it depends on the personalities of the parents and the learned behaviour from their own childhoods, who knows?

Not only was there a lack of emotional connection between me and my parents, we didn't particularly look like each another other, either. Characteristics such as eye colour, hair colour, skin tone, dimples and freckles, that are often passed down from parent to child, just weren't apparent. The most striking visible difference between me and my parents was hair and eye colour, and skin tone. They were both dark haired with brown eyes and a darker skin tone, whereas I'm a redhead with green eyes and a pasty complexion. They both loved the warm weather and for those rare occasions when we holidayed abroad, to places like Majorca or Benidorm, they would both be sprawled out all day in the sun, whereas I was encouraged to stay in the shade, as I would just freckle up or burn.

On the theme of family resemblance, I noticed that Deirdre and Uncle Roger shared the same eye colour and shape of nose. She also inherited similar features to Aunty Anthea too. They shared the same gait and temperament. Without thinking about it too deeply, maybe I'm just similar to Columbus, in that I don't resemble the rest of my family. I think genetics is a weird and complex area.

I've been told by some people who I meet, that I'm 'unique' or a 'rare breed'. They don't mean any harm by it. It's just an observation on their part. I'm guessing this is down to my dress sense and character. Well, I hope it is, anyway. With my unmistakable thick fringe, butterfly shaped framed spectacles and brightly coloured outfits, I probably stand out in a crowd. The double wardrobe in my bedroom is full of outfits made up of my favourite colours, which are yellow and light pink. I also have twenty-six pairs of shoes. All my shoes are various shades of red. I'm very rarely seen without oversized bows [the bigger the better] and side plaited pigtails in my hair.

I'm also obsessed by earrings, but only purchase them if they are wacky. Earrings replicating things like shrimps, watermelons, parrots and fake teeth are all part of my collection. At the last count, my collection consisted of 84 pairs. The record for the largest collection of earrings belonged to a lady in the USA, who owned 37,706 different pair of earrings, or it was, last time I researched it. In the past, people have laughed at me because I'm different. This doesn't bother me. I laugh at them back because they're all the same.

I think being different and going against the grain of society is the greatest thing in the world.

I recall a conversation with Aunty Anthea when I was about ten years old. I was being teased by a girl about my clothes. I was wearing a brown corduroy skirt with embroidered iron-on patches of bees. I loved that skirt. Aunty Anthea sat me on her knee and said to me,

"Daphne, just wear what you feel comfortable in."

I've never forgotten those words of advice ever since. My other obsession is mints! I've loved them since I was a little girl. I don't know why though. Mintoes, Everton Mints, Mint Humbugs, Polos or Peppermint Creams, I've always got a packet of something on the go. Mint Imperials are easily my favourite though. I could work my way through a 200g bag in one afternoon, no problem. The amazing thing is that I still have all my own teeth even after the number of mints I consume on a weekly basis.

I'm a happy go lucky type of person. I'm cheerful about most things and have a positive view on life. I don't take anything seriously. Even if I try to take things seriously, I am unable to. I continually laugh at myself and the escapades I get up to. 'Whatever happens, happens', is my motto. This drives Deirdre mad. She is so serious and organised. I've told her, because she is caught up in the seriousness of it all, she will miss out on the joyful and happy aspects of life. She just replies;

"Ugh, I wouldn't get through the day if I had an outlook like yours!"

Inked-up

Deirdre can't understand or cope with my impulsiveness. She never knows what I'm going to do next. I'm unpredictable and it unnerves her. I once set off into town to buy some cat food for Columbus. As I strolled down the high street towards the supermarket, a shop called 'Mythical Passions', caught my eye. The window was packed with gifts ranging from beautiful fairies and mythical unicorns to gothic, steampunk and dark legend dragons. I spotted they also stocked a large range of incense, aromatherapy and fragrance oils.

The thing that really caught my attention was the fact this was an award-winning tattoo studio. Without hesitation I marched towards the shop entrance and opened the door. A bell rung inside the shop to make staff aware every time the door opened. It was one of those noises that might begin to get on your nerves over time. A young woman appeared from another part of the shop and made her way to behind the counter. She was wearing a sleeveless top and was covered in multicoloured tattoos. Her tattoo choice was definitely based on a reptile theme. Brightly coloured lizards, snakes and geckos made up her sleeve. She also had numerous piercings too. Her nose, eyebrows and tongue were all sporting different styles of jewellery. I admired her for her individuality and alternative style.

"How can I help you today?" she asked in a soft Geordie accent.

Her warm smile put me at ease. Without any hesitation, I replied, "I'd like to get a tattoo, please."

"Have you thought about what type of tattoo you want and whereabouts on your body you would like it?" she asked. "If you are unsure, we have lots of artwork examples you can look through." She pointed at a pile of lever arch files on a battered oak table next to an adjustable leather couch. Without any consideration whatsoever, I blurted out,

"I'd like a tortoise wearing a Fez please, and I'd like it on my bum!"

Holy moly! Where did that come from? Had I been influenced by the tattoos of the reptiles on the assistant's arm? A tortoise would certainly fall into the reptile category, wouldn't it? And why a Fez? As far as I know, I didn't have any links to Morocco. I recalled that the Fez derived its name from the place where it was first manufactured - the holy city of Fez. Nor was I a particular fan of comedian Tommy Cooper or the pop group Madness. Last, but not least, why had I chosen my bum of all places to have a tattoo? I'd not even stopped to consider whether I had clean underwear on. The last thing the tattoo artist would want to clap eyes on is manky undergarments! That might affect her concentration levels.

I suppose the most likely rationale for choosing my backside was because it would be out of sight of everyone. I knew full well that mum and dad wouldn't approve; I once heard them have a discussion about tattoos. They both expressed strong views, especially about the types of people who had them. I remember my father describing people who had tattoos as "dangerous and rebellious and not to be trusted". This discussion may have subconsciously triggered my choice of body part to be tatted. I suppose this was the compromise. I could have the satisfaction of knowing I had a tattoo, whilst they wouldn't have the foggiest, unless they somehow caught sight of me in the nude, which was an unlikely scenario. Little did I know at that time that I would only need to hide the tattoo for a few months, as my parent's trip to Kenya was just round the corner.

The tattooist was a petite lady who whiffed of Patchouli oil and roll-up cigarettes. Her premature facial wrinkling was probably caused by the nicotine addiction she obviously had. I lost count of how many times she said,

"Just popping out for a puff, love. I'll only be a few minutes."

I didn't find this frustrating. It was a relief. The pain caused by the constant pricking sensation nearly had me blubbering, even though she was being gentle with me, as she knew it was my first time in the tattoo chair. She explained,

"I'm not hammering in the ink like some tattooists would".

To try and distract me she made small talk. I was in that much pain that I listened, rather than talked. She told me about her lifestyle choices; how she avoided buying groceries and preferred to live off the land. She talked of her love of pagan and polytheist traditions. She spoke of other tattoo artists she was influenced by. American artists such as Don Ed Hardy and Jacci Gresham. Tattooing people was not her only interest. She was currently studying for a Norwegian Language Degree. She taught me that the word 'tortoise' in Norwegian, was landskilpadde. After just over two hours of excruciating pain, I emerged from the tattoo shop with my inked-up bottom and with strict aftercare instructions to keep my new addition well moisturised. As I made my way home, I felt a great sense of achievement. I was also convinced that I was the first ever member of the Dapper family to have a tattoo. How cool was that?

I stopped off at Deirdre's on my way back home. She was sat in her conservatory reading a manual for the latest gadget she had bought. It was called a Segway S-Pod, and she was fascinated by it.

"I've got something to show you" I said.

Deirdre stopped concentrating on the Segway S-Pod and looked up. She had a worried expression on her face. Rightly so.

"Oh no, what've you gone and done now?" she asked.

I was smiling like a Cheshire Cat. I dropped my trousers, turned around and bent over.

"I went into town to buy some cat food for Columbus and came back with this. It's great, isn't it?"

Deirdre dropped her Segway S-Pod Manual on the floor in horror and took a step forward to get a closer look.

"Bloody hell Daphne, what the hell is that?" she gasped.

"It's a tortoise wearing a Fez," I replied.

Deirdre couldn't take her eyes of it.

"I know it's a tortoise wearing a Fez. I can see that. But it's tattooed on your arse."

Deirdre stared at it from every angle.

"What possessed you? You've never mentioned getting a tattoo before. Your mum and dad are going to go bananas with you. They are also going to go bananas with me, as they expect me to try and keep you on the straight and narrow. Oh Daphne, this is a disaster!"

"Well, I don't think it's a disaster" I said. "I think it's rather nice. It was a spontaneous decision, and I don't regret it."

Deirdre headed off towards the kitchen and mumbled to herself,

"I need a cup of tea."

She returned carrying a circular tin tray. On it, was two mugs of tea and a small plate, packed high with fig roll biscuits. She seemed to have calmed down a bit. She knew there was no going back, and what was done, was done. Deirdre sat down on the settee. She stared into space as she popped one fig roll into her mouth after another. Understanding how to use her Segway S-Pod was no longer a priority. Ensuring the tattoo remained hidden, was. Suddenly, Deirdre stood up. She dashed off in the direction of the kitchen. When she returned, she was clutching a white tin. On the front of the tin were the words 'First Aid' and it was decorated with a distinctive red cross.

"I've got an idea," she said, flipping open the lid, and rummaging through the contents of the tin. "Gotcha!" she said, holding up a packet of extra-large Elastoplast plasters.

"Now listen to me Daphne. As a precautionary measure, you'll need to cover up the tattoo every day with one of these Elastoplasts.

If you are ever in a position where you have to explain to anybody [especially your mum and dad] why you have an Elastoplast on your bum, just say you have a painful infected boil and you are trying to stop it becoming any worse. Have you got that, Daphne? Have I made myself loud and clear?"

"Yes, I think so," I said, as I giggled to myself.

"Right, that's sorted then," said Deirdre. "I can sleep easy knowing that a solution to the problem has been found. There's just one more thing Daphne. Where is the cat food that you were supposed to buy in town?"

The expression on my face said it all. She knew I had completely forgotten about the cat food and that I had got distracted by the whole tattoo thing.

"Poor Columbus will be starving" I said in a sympathetic tone.

"Listen," Deirdre said sharply, "I'll pick up some cat food for Columbus and drop it off later. You've had an eventful enough day already, and what's more, I can't trust you go back into town without getting another tattoo!"

Technophobe

Whereas Deirdre is a whizz with technology, I'm exactly the opposite. I'm rubbish with all that technology stuff. I'm a stereotypical technophobe if there is such a thing. I avoid technology like the plague. I keep explaining to Deirdre [who continues to try to introduce me to different forms of technology], that I just 'don't get it' and that when it comes to understanding technology, my brain must be wired differently to most of the population. Maybe I was born without this 'technology wire' or if it is there, it's probably become so frustrated, it has given up the ghost! Downed tools and gone on strike. Forever.

It can't be easy managing a technophobe. Deirdre does her best though. She has the patience of a saint. I didn't even know how to use the remote control for the television, properly. She resorted to covering up all the buttons that she didn't think I would use, with pink card and Sellotape. The only buttons I can now press are on/off, volume and those so I could switch channels. I hope we have more success with the mobile phone I have just bought. I've avoided having one for nearly thirty years, but on the insistence of Deirdre I've recently succumbed, and have agreed to have one. Deirdre looked into it for me, and identified a model that even I may be able to get the hang of. It's black, with big buttons. She tells me it's simple to use and 'idiot proof'. I think it may have been designed for the more 'senior' members of society. It hasn't got any fancy additional features, like being able to connect to the interweb, if that's what it's called? That might not be the right terminology. I just tend to make things up if I don't understand them.

I remember the time when she turned up at my house with a computer.

"We've got some new computers at work. This one was surplus to requirements, and I thought of you" she said in a confident voice.

I'd only had the computer a few days and I couldn't get it to work properly. I called Deirdre to tell her about the problem and she said she would call in on her way home from work. When she arrived, she couldn't believe what I was doing. I was blasting the computer with my hair dryer.

"What the hell are you doing that for, Daphne?" she asked.

"I was chatting to Mr Kovac in the corner shop and told him I had just been given a second-hand computer, but it didn't work. His diagnosis was that he thought my computer might be 'frozen'. So, I'm trying to defrost it with my hair dryer"!

Deirdre, who doesn't often crack a smile, burst out laughing. In fact, she was in hysterics. I joined in laughing too, once she'd explained things to me. That the word 'frozen' has a different meaning when it comes to the world of computing, and it's nothing at all like the fish fingers in the freezer. We still laugh about that incident to this day.

Job interviews aren't easy

Deirdre isn't the only one in the family who tries to keep me on the straight and narrow. Her dad, Uncle Roger, does too. It was Uncle Roger who gave me my first job. Roger owns a Mystery Shopper business. I think he took me on as a favour to mum and dad. I was in my mid-twenties, and I was struggling to land a job. Even lousy jobs which nobody else wanted to do. Every application I made was generally followed up by a letter in the post a few days later, which, more or less, all started with a similar tone:

"Dear Ms Dapper, thank you for your application for the role of [named position]. We've had an overwhelming number of applicants, and unfortunately your application was unsuccessful."

Managing to get an interview wasn't easy. On the odd occasions this happened, I think the panel had often made their mind up about me within minutes of me entering the room. Maybe they didn't take me seriously because of my appearance or dress sense. Perhaps they thought I was peculiar, or worse still, I would bring down the tone of their organisation. Who knows? Although I didn't conform to the normal standard, I didn't think I should be penalised for this.

Because of my lack of success in gaining employment, Deirdre suggested I should ask for feedback from interviews. She was always coming up with nuggets of wisdom like this. By doing this, it would highlight the things in the interview I did well and the things that I didn't. It would also paint a picture of how I come across and what I could do differently, or the same, next time.

The feedback I received was varied. It included standard phrases such as: lack of experience; lack of effort in preparing for the interview; displayed a lack of knowledge when asked about the company; lacked depth and clarity with responses.

I also received feedback which was a bit more personal. This included being told by one employer that I wasn't dressed appropriately for the interview. This was probably the day when I chose to wear my wacky wabbit troll earrings. Another employer explained it was my 'appearance' that had contributed to me being unsuccessful. I presumed the reason for this that I been sunbathing in the garden the day before and turned up for the interview with a badly burned face. I was as red as a tomato.

The most unusual reason for not landing a role was when I went for a job interview at the local greyhound track. The feedback was straight to the point. It read: "the candidate made inappropriate noises [unspecified] throughout the interview". I guess this was in relation to me constantly sniffing because I had a streaming cold. It had clearly got on the nerves of one of the interviewers on the panel and he/she had taken umbrage.

Twenty-five years later, I'm still working for Uncle Roger. He's stuck with me through thick and thin, even when the business has been going through some difficult times. Uncle Roger reminds me of a giant teddy bear in appearance. Deep down, he's kind-hearted, dependable, and always there to listen and support. Unlike when I was younger, these days, he has rather a large stomach. He's five feet six and weighs in at 20 stone. No matter which pair of trousers he chooses to wear, they are always bursting at the waistline. Goodness knows how his trouser buttons remain intact. His inactive lifestyle has contributed to his rapid weight gain. He also loves his grub. His Achillies heel is pudding. Particularly puddings with custard. He's tried them all. If Uncle Roger ever went on the television show Mastermind, I reckon British puddings would be his specialised subject. Jam roly-poly, syrup sponge, spotted dick, apple & blackberry crumble and sticky toffee pudding definitely make it into his top 10.

Aunty Anthea always makes the custard from scratch, too. None of this packet or tinned stuff. She makes custard to die for. She's renowned for it. His numero uno, however, is homemade rice pudding. His eyes light up when he knows this is on the menu. He's even been known to do a little jig as Aunty Anthea carefully carries through the rice pudding from the kitchen to the dining room. He will always finish off his rice pudding by picking up the empty rice pudding dish and saying:

"Anthea......... Ambrosia don't half make a mighty fine rice pudding.......but it isn't a patch on yours!" before roaring with laughter at his own joke.

The first assignment

My first assignment working for the 'Quiet Customer' [this is the name of Uncle Roger's business] was at a Berni Inn on the other side of town. I didn't have a clue what a Mystery Shopper was, so Uncle Roger had to brief me shortly before setting off.

"Daphne, a Mystery Shopper is a person who poses as a real customer whilst assessing the customer service provided by a company or organisation they are asked to visit. A mystery shopping assignment might be a quick visit to the bank to make a general enquiry, or it might be an overnight stay at a hotel. In your case, it's a trip to the Berni Inn on Newcastle Road. Mystery Shoppers are responsible for determining the quality of products, customer service, and store environments while posing as ordinary customers and then they are required to submit reports on their findings soon after their visit. Tonight's visit to the Berni Inn is a good one to get you started."

He then went on to explain the key characteristics to be an awesome mystery shopper.

"Mystery Shoppers: need to have an eye for detail; to be able to follow the directions of the client; to dress appropriately and act as a normal shopper; be reliable; be honest; have good memory skills; be good at writing and be organised. You are made for this role Daphne. I can't understand why I haven't thought about employing you earlier. Don't worry about anything. You'll be fine."

Had Uncle Roger lost the plot? Did he really want to employ me? Am I really Mystery Shopper material? He's known me all my life, and he knows full well what I'm like. No way am I organised. I'm scatty and airy-fairy. As for dressing appropriately, I don't dress naturally like the average consumer. I'll stand out like a sore thumb. I'm not sure he's thought this through properly. And why wasn't I given a proper interview? I just seemed to have walked into the job automatically – no questions asked. Somewhere along the line, I'm guessing my parents must be involved. They both seem a lot chirpier since the chat at the dinner table the other night. My father said,

"Daphne, your Uncle Roger needs some help with the business. He is going to put some work your way. As you don't have any other irons in the fire, you might as well give him a hand and see how you get on."

Uncle Roger had booked me a table at the Berni Inn for 6:00 pm. The bus to that part of town was late, so I didn't get there until ten past six. For most people, being late for the first day in a new job would have been a disaster. It didn't concern me, though. Timeliness has never been my strong point, so why should I worry about it now. My outfit for the evening was my pink V-neck swing dress, spotted leggings and white sandals. I also dug out a pair of knife and fork earrings from my earring collection, as I thought they were apt for this type of occasion.

On entering the premises, I was shown to my table by a female assistant. She had short hair and reminded me a little bit of Deirdre, apart from the fact that this girl smiled much more than Deirdre. She was wearing an immaculate uniform consisting of a red shirt and black skirt. Pinned to the shirt was a silver-coloured name badge. She was called Carly. She seemed to have a natural pleasantness about her. Not something drummed into her through attending a Customer Service course. I sat myself down on a high-backed wooden dining chair with a leather seat pad.

"By all means, take a look at the menu."

Her eyes hinted towards the centre of the table, where the menu was located in a wooden block menu holder.

"Someone will be across shortly to take your order."

She then turned 180 degrees before making her way back towards the entrance to greet more diners. I had a few moments to take in my surroundings. Tudor-looking false oak beams, deep red furnishings, parquet floor, the smell of steaks sizzling in the kitchen and a pleasant ambience as a result of chattering diners and the clinking of cutlery. Whilst absorbing the atmosphere I remembered the conversation I'd had with Deirdre before leaving the house earlier that evening. She'd been on Mystery Shopper assignments herself as a favour to her dad when he was short staffed, so she knew the ropes. As it wasn't protocol to undertake assignments armed with notepads and pens, Deirdre had written out some instructions as she knew there was every danger I would get sidetracked. She scribed the instructions on the palms of my hands, using a blue biro. I rolled over my left hand and it read; don't daydream, don't get distracted, and don't forget why you are there. I glanced at my right hand, and it read: quality of customer service, quality of food and drink, and atmosphere inside the venue. I was as prepared as I could be.

Suddenly, I felt a presence beside me. I quickly turned over my biro-covered hands.

"Hello, my name is Brian," said a voice.

I looked up, and there was a gangly-looking young man with shoulder-length black hair. He was armed with a notepad and pen. He looked panicky. Aside from his ill-fitting uniform, the first thing I noted was his screechy voice. I wondered whether he always talked like that or whether nerves were affecting his vocal cords. He was staring at me intensely. I think he was taking in my unique appearance. I'm not sure he had ever come across anybody like me before. With my thick fringe, butterfly-shaped framed spectacles and knife and fork earrings, I think I came as a bit of a shock.

As he stood analysing me, I was analysing him at the same time. Then I spotted it. Lodged inside his left nostril was a huge bogie. It looked like it could escape at any minute. As I contemplated whether I should point out this unwanted bit of mucus, the screechy voice burst into life again.

"Err, would you like to order a drink, Miss?"

Still staring at the bogie, I got distracted and said,

"I'll have a large glass of Spanish wine, please."

Goodness knows why I ordered a glass of Spanish wine, as I'm a lightweight when it comes to alcohol. I've only ever had the odd

Babycham at Christmas and I feel lightheaded after drinking that. I must have been preoccupied by the bogie.

"Err, OK then," he said. "I'll take your food order when I return."

And off he trotted towards the bar area. As I waited for my drink, I casually turned over my right hand and looked at the bullet points written by Deirdre. Bugger! I've already broken one of the rules, I was thinking to myself. I've been distracted by Brian's nasal mucus. I need to concentrate more. A couple of minutes later, Brian returned, carrying a small silver tray, on which was a large glass of Spanish wine.

"Here you are, Miss. Are you ready for me to take your food order now?" he screeched.

His visit to the bar hadn't changed anything. Brian's bogie was still on display for all to see.

"I'll have the Prawn Cocktail for my starter, please, followed by the Prime Rump Steak as my main course."

"How would you like your steak, Miss"?

I was now starting to get used to the screechy voice. Not covered in your nasal mucus would be a good start, I was thinking to myself.

"I'd like it well done, please. Oh, and can you ask the chef to give me extra onion rings because I really like them" I said, before giggling nervously.

The expression on Brian's face changed from nervousness to confusion.

"I'll have a word with the chef and see what he can do," he screeched before heading towards the kitchen.

I'd only managed one gulp of wine before Brian was back.

"Your Prawn Cocktail, Miss."

There in front of me was a cocktail glass containing a gloopy mix of defrosted prawns and sweet Marie Rose sauce balanced on a nest of iceberg lettuce. Based on the speed of his service, I presumed the Prawn Cocktail was pre-prepared and stored in a fridge. I could see he was no longer staring at me so intensely. Maybe he'd now become familiar with my appearance. I wasn't such a freak anymore. He must have warmed to me.

"Thank you," I replied, then took another gulp of Spanish wine.

He smiled uncertainly. Hang on, I thought to myself. Where's Brian's bogie? It's gone. Somewhere between him going to the kitchen and returning to my table, the bogie had disembarked his left nostril. Where the hell was it? Holy moly, I had a sneaking suspicion it was hiding in my Prawn Cocktail!! The thing is, I couldn't prove it. Bloody hell. I was really looking forward to that Prawn Cocktail, and now I couldn't risk it. I started poking at it with my spoon, but it was no good. I'd have had to go through it with a fine-tooth comb and this wasn't the time or place.

I took another gulp of Spanish wine. It created a sensation of warmth in my body. The wine was starting to make me tipsy. I was on the fringe of breaking another rule that was written on my left hand, the one that said, 'don't daydream,' when I was interrupted by a familiar screechy voice.

"Is everything ok, Miss. You've hardly touched that."

I didn't have the guts to tell him the truth, especially as he was trying his best to provide a high-quality service; that I suspected my Prawn Cocktail had probably been infiltrated by the contents of his left nostril and I didn't fancy rolling the dice. I tittered and just said the first thing that came into my mind.

"I forgot the Prawn Cocktail included lettuce, and unfortunately, I'm allergic to it."

To add more colour to my lie, I elaborated further.

"By mistake, I once ate a tuna and lettuce sandwich, and my symptoms were once so severe, I suffered anaphylaxis."

Brian looked at me in a confused state. Then I could see he'd had a lightbulb moment.

"Would you like me to ask the chef if he will make you a Prawn Cocktail minus the lettuce?" he said enthusiastically.

"No thanks, I think I'll move on to my main course if that's ok."

I could see a tinge of disappointment in Brian's face that he didn't quite manage to 'pull off' his grand idea and restore equilibrium.

"I'll have another glass of Spanish wine, please. I'm starting to feel a little bit drunk. But you only live once, don't you, Brian?"

"Yes, of course, Miss," he replied,

As he set off in the direction of the bar area once again, I blurted, "Make this one an extra big glass of wine."

But I may have been speaking to his back and I'm not sure if he heard me. Whilst waiting for Brian I took a moment to absorb the atmosphere inside the Berni Inn. Diners of all ages were chatting and laughing in between courses. Background music added to the atmosphere. The music was generated by a 1950's American Retro style Diner Juke Box to the right of the bar. Based on the type of music being played, I presumed the room full of diners comprised of Northern Soul fanatics. I quite happily tapped my feet to a catchy tune by the Velvelettes called 'Needle in a Haystack', joining in with the bit that went,

'She-doop, she-doop, la la….She-doop, she-doop, la la'.

Just as the next northern soul track was getting into full swing – it was 'Do I love you [Indeed I do]', by Frank Wilson, Brian arrived at the table. He was ladened with food and drink. For the first time in the evening, there was an air of confidence about him. His vibes of uncertainty and stress had dispersed. And I was about to understand why.

"Your extra-large glass of wine, Miss."

And then he slowly lowered a large oval white plate containing rump steak, chips, mushrooms, an extra-large portion of onion rings and a side salad. Then Brian confidently explained,

"I've had a word with the head-chef, and he has specially prepared you a 'lettuce-free' side salad, as we don't want you to suffer from any allergic reactions, do we?"

Remembering my porky pie from a few minutes earlier, I now had to play along with it. But being half-cut made me feel less guilty.

"Ahhh, how sweet of you, Brian. That was a lovely thing to do," I said before standing up, flinging my arms around him and giving him a tight squeeze.

Brian was taken aback to say the least. The expression on his face said it all. He was probably only hugged by close family or on special occasions, not by some punter he barely knew.

"My pleasure, Miss," he said unconvincingly. "Now, can I get you any sauces to go with your meal?" he added after composing himself.

"No thanks, everything is great," I said.

As Brian stepped away back towards the kitchen, I took another big gulp of wine before looking down to peruse the contents of my plate. Just a minute, I don't recall Brian bringing two plates of food to my table. Oh no, due to the alcohol I had consumed, I now had double vision. Things were becoming a little hazy!

The next thing I knew, it was the following morning.

"Wakey wakey, Daphne," a voice said.

I tried opening my eyes but failed miserably. I heard the voice again.

"Wake up, Daphne, it's 9 o' clock, and I should have set off for work by now."

The voice sounded very much like Deirdre. I managed to open my eyes the second time around. There was Deirdre leaning over me. Her face was about 6 inches from mine.

"Good morning, Daphne. You're back in the land of the living."

Her breath reeked of coffee. It made my stomach churn. I felt absolutely dreadful.

"Where am I?" I asked in a croaky voice.

"You're at my place. You've been on the settee all night. I got a call from the Berni Inn at about 11:00 pm last night. I had to drive there and collect you. You were totally smashed out of your head, Daphne. I couldn't take you home in that state. Your mum and dad would have had a right strop. What the hell happened? It's not like you to have a bevvy. I've known you all my life, and I've never seen you drink alcohol before, apart from the odd snowball at Christmas."

Deirdre's coffee breath wasn't helping matters.

"Oohhh, I don't feel well at all. And I'm really thirsty," I moaned.

"By all accounts, you had a hell of a thirst last night, too!" ranted Deirdre. "Do you realise you drank two bottles of Spanish wine? It's not pop, that stuff, Daphne. It's 11% alcohol. What came over you?"

I closed my eyes and grimaced as Deirdre gave me an account of last night's proceedings. She'd obviously got the lowdown from the staff at the Berni Inn when she'd picked me up. I couldn't remember anything. For me, last night was just a blur.

"Apparently, you were the star act last night. You kept selecting a song on the Jukebox, called Saturday Night by Whigfield. Then you proceeded to try to teach all the other diners and staff the dance moves. At one point you even got on the table itself and started strutting your stuff. I didn't know you liked Whigfield. You kept that to yourself. And when you weren't dancing, you were causing havoc elsewhere in the place!

"Thanks to you Daphne, the Berni Inn on Newcastle Road no longer has any tropical fish left in its fish tank. You lost your balance during one of your dancing routines and fell into it, dragging it off its stand and onto the floor." Deirdre paused to catch her breath, before continuing. "The floor was full of neon tetra, guppy and siamese fighting fish flapping about helplessly! And who the hell is Brian? That's all you were going on about on the way back in the car last night. Brian this…and Brian that. Is he your new fella or something?

"Anyway, I apologised to the manager last night and explained that you don't normally drink, and your behaviour was totally out of character and that it won't happen again. I also slipped them a few quid so they can buy a new fish tank. I have also let my dad know that you were unwell and that you had to abandon the assignment. He knows not to expect a mystery shopper report later on today. I didn't tell him why you were unwell, though. Basically, I've covered your arse Daphne, and you owe me big time."

I covered my face under the duvet. My head was pounding, and I felt nauseas. I couldn't bear listening to the antics I had got up to, the night before. It was so embarrassing. Just when I thought things couldn't get any worse, Deirdre chirped up once more.

"Oh, and one more thing. You chundered all over my front doorstep last night, so you can clean that up later. I've got to go to work now. Make sure you lock up before you go."

My career as a Mystery Shopper hadn't got off to the best of starts. However, I persevered. Uncle Roger described me as a 'work in progress'. He knew what my weaknesses were, and he tried to mentor me. He was mostly concerned about my lack of reliability and my inability to be organised.

"These types of traits are incompatible in the workplace, Daphne," he once told me.

To try to help me address these shortfalls, he asked me to attend various training courses paid for by the company. One of the courses covered Eisenhower's Urgent/Important Principle and was designed to teach me to become a more organised person. When I returned from each course, Uncle Roger would ask in a jokey tone,

"Did the trainer lick you into shape, Daphne? I expect you are the finished article now, and all my problems are solved?" before chuckling to himself.

When he wasn't sending me on courses, he would constantly remind me to focus on what was important.

"Make lists," he would say.

"Make daily, weekly and monthly to-do lists of important tasks. Manage your time well. Use calendars and planners. Manage your mail and phone calls. Stay organised."

All this advice went in one ear and out of the other. After all, it was me, Daphne Dapper, he was talking to.

Dougie's Driving School

"Daphne, I need you to learn to drive," Uncle Roger blurted out one day.

I didn't quite hear him as he was munching on one of Aunty Anthea's homemade ginger biscuits at the time.

"What was that, Uncle Roger?" I asked.

He leaned forward whilst brushing the biscuit crumbs onto his giant mahogany desk before casually sweeping them into his hand and then discarding them into a plastic bin.

"I need you to learn to drive," he said again, only this time more clearly.

"So far, I've restricted you to assignments locally, but I need to send you to assignments that are further afield. At the moment, you are relying on public transport and all and sundry to ferry you around, including our Deirdre. I'd like you to be a little bit more independent. It will be good for you and good for business. This morning, Gloria Peach [he paused and put his finger on his cheek as he thought], you've met Gloria, haven't you?"

I didn't have time to answer.

"Well, she had to give backword on an assignment, as her husband, Frank, has a bad back and is bed-bound for the foreseeable. If you'd been mobile and had your own wheels, you could have covered that assignment at short notice. This is why I need you to learn to drive. What do you think Daphne? Fancy it?"

I was too busy daydreaming about spinning around town in a pink and white convertible VW beetle to even acknowledge his question.

"Daphne," he said again, but in a more forceful manner. "What do you think?"

I didn't give it too much thought; I just nodded enthusiastically.

"Excellent," said Uncle Roger. "I'll have a word with my mate Dougie Parsons. He's the driving instructor who taught Deirdre. We'll get your first driving lesson booked in. I'll pay for the lessons through the company's account. A dozen lessons should do you."

Little did Uncle Roger know the scale of the task that lay ahead!

Within a couple of weeks of my conversation with Uncle Roger, I found myself sitting next to Dougie Parsons in his red Mini Metro. Each side of the car was proudly emblazoned with the wording, 'Dougie's Driving School'. My parents were gawping at me through the living room window. They had never encouraged me to take driving lessons, probably because they thought I was incapable, but suddenly, they were now taking an interest. When Dougie wasn't looking, I ushered at them to move away from the window, but they just ignored me. In fact, it had the opposite effect. My mother decided to put on her glasses so she could get a better view. It was so humiliating. After all, I was 26 years old, not an adolescent.

Dougie had a full head of dark brown curly hair and was clean-shaven. He wore a red V-neck sweater, navy and white checked shirt and navy-blue cotton trousers. Inside the car, the interior was immaculate. There was a combination of smells going on, too. The overpowering scent of Dougie's Blue Stratos aftershave was going head-to-head with the aroma being released from the Feu Orange Traffic Light Car Air Freshener hanging from the interior rear-view mirror. His car was his office. There was no doubt about it.

With Dougie at the wheel, he explained we were heading to a quiet industrial estate on the edge of town. It was where he took all his first timers. As we drove into the estate, it was obvious it was pretty run down. Based on the graffiti, litter and burned-out Ford Fiesta, it wasn't the type of place you would want to be at night. Apart from the odd parked car and transit van, there was no other traffic about. Once the car was at a standstill, and we safely parked up, Dougie announced that we should change seats. It was now my turn to be in the driver's seat. Dougie was looking calm and relaxed, whereas my stomach was in knots.

"Right then Daphne," he said.

"This is your first lesson, and nerves are natural, so don't worry. I'm going to take you through some of the basics."

He explained to me how to position my seat and mirrors; secure and manoeuvre the car using the handbrake, gears, and clutch control. He then progressed to the basics about 'moving off'. These instructions focused on getting ready to use your gears; checking your mirrors and blind spot; and clutch control, including finding the biting point. As you can imagine, with the way my mind operates, the phrase 'biting point' was very confusing. I had to quickly get to grips with the fact it was nothing to do with food!

I'd only been in the car for fifteen minutes or so when I realised why Dougie was dowsed in Blue Stratos. It was to compensate for his bad breath. It was awful. It smelt like he had just eaten a Scotch egg. What could I do? Should I tell him? Maybe he had a medical condition and couldn't help it. I recalled once reading in a magazine [whilst at the doctor's surgery] that certain medical conditions can cause bad breath. I felt sorry for his wife. Mrs Parsons must have completely lost her sense of smell to be able to tolerate that. I decided not to confront him as it might be embarrassing. I needed to do something, though. I knew I wouldn't be able to cope with this unpleasant odour for another forty-five minutes. Thinking on my feet, I said,

"Is there any chance I can wind my window down, Dougie? It's very warm in here."

"That's fine Daphne, it's probably because you feel anxious. If I'd have had a pound for every learner who'd asked to wind their windows down, I'd be a very rich man," he said and chuckled to himself.

Well, that's a surprise, I thought to myself. It looks like I'm not the only student driver to have found myself in a contaminated tin can on wheels, with no way out. Then I hatched a cunning plan. As I was never without mints, I delved into the pocket of my cardigan and pulled out a couple of Everton mints.

"Sucking on one of these should help with my nerves," I said hopefully. "Would you like one Dougie?"

He smiled and accepted the mint, before carefully removing the wrapper and popping it into his mouth.

"If I'd have had a pound for every learner who'd given me a mint, I'd be a very rich man" he said, as he tried to manoeuvre the sweet around his mouth and speak at the same time. "You are now going to practice driving in a straight line, using the clutch, accelerator and brake," instructed Dougie, in a confident manner.

He seemed to have every confidence in me that I could pull this off.

"Holy moly," I said quietly to myself.

This was the bit I was dreading. Nobody had mentioned to Dougie that I was a technophobe and that I had an irrational fear of technology, especially computers and other digital devices. To me, learning to drive Dougie's Mini Metro, was like learning to master a huge digital device. And it put the fear of God into me. Here I was, with all these buttons, lights, pedals, and knobs in front of me, and I didn't know what they all did, let alone, which to touch first. This wasn't like trying to work a TV remote control. It was far worse. I couldn't ask Deirdre to climb into the car and start sellotaping over all the controls or functions I didn't need, like she'd done with the remote control at home. This time, I was on my own.

"Place your right foot to the accelerator pedal and hold it steady," Dougie commanded.

"As you slowly start to lift your left foot off the clutch, you'll feel the engine and wheels starting to engage. Continue to slowly release the clutch pedal until you feel a slight 'bump' or 'grab'. This is the biting point, and it indicates that the engine and the wheels are perfectly matched. At this point, the car should start to move forward as you release the handbrake. Right, Daphne, let's give it a go."

"Ok then," I said. And giggled nervously.

I pressed the clutch with my left shoe. Then started to apply pressure on the accelerator. 'Vroom', made the noise of the car. The dial on the rev counter flew beyond the 1500rpm recommended by Dougie. In fact, the dial flew past the 2000rpm marker, generally required for a hill start.

"Easy does it, Daphne!" shouted Dougie,

He tried to raise his voice above that of the 'vroom' noise made by the car.

"Now, begin to raise your left foot off the clutch."

I tried to follow his instructions, but the car juddered to a stop. It all went very quiet in the car. The quietness was interrupted as I burst out laughing.

"That wasn't supposed to happen, was it, Dougie?"

"No Daphne, it wasn't, but it was your first attempt. Let's give it another try, only this time, give it less gas and remove your foot from the clutch slightly slower. You removed it far too quickly last time."

Over the next forty minutes or so, we repeated the process twenty-five times, with exactly the same outcome; that is, the car stalled, and then I burst out laughing. On the hour mark, I noticed that Dougie was no longer as easy going and relaxed as he had been at the start of the lesson. As a matter of fact, he seemed to be getting a little hot under the collar. Probably because he'd never been in this situation before, most of his students learn from their mistakes and begin to make progress. They also probably get frustrated, embarrassed, or disheartened if they continue to do things wrong. Here, he had someone who was wetting herself every time the car stalled.

"I'm not sure you are taking this seriously, Daphne", he said, in a disgruntled voice.

"Oh, I am Dougie, you'll just have to get used to me, that's all." Dougie looked confused.

"It looks like I will, doesn't it. Now let's swap seats and I'll drive you back home."

Dougie seemed deep in thought on the drive back. He may have been wondering whether he had bitten off more than he could chew with his new recruit. He pulled up outside the house. I was relieved to see my parents were no longer staring out of the window.

"See you at the same time next week," he confirmed, before driving off for his next appointment.

Getting the hang of it

A couple of days later, I was asked by Uncle Roger to call into his office. It was based in a three-storey building, located on the high street. Uncle Roger's office was on the first floor and was directly above a menswear outfitter, called Green & Sons. This was handy if he needed to pick up any attire for work. Through the odd purchases here and there, he knew the owner, Sidney Slack. From time to time, Sidney commissioned the Quiet Customer to undertake some mystery shopping assignments on the performance of his business.

"Aahh, Daphne, nice to see you," he said as I entered the room.

Uncle Roger's green jumper was covered in crumbs, probably the remnants of another one of Aunty Anthea's homemade ginger biscuits.

"Pull up a chair," he said.

He leaned back and put his hands behind his head. His jumper rose upwards a couple of inches to reveal his large belly, a proportion of which was hanging over his trousers.

"I see you are getting the hang of writing and submitting the Mystery Shopper reports," he commented. "The one you wrote the other day, about the assignment at the bank, was really clear and specific. You have a real eye for detail Daphne. Just one thing though. I know you were there to interact with bank representatives, evaluate customer service and experience various banking services first hand, but it wasn't necessary to remark on what the cashier was wearing or her choice in perfume. Nor was it necessary to comment on the fact that you thought the lady in front of you in the queue had broken wind. These are external factors that the client isn't particularly interested in. Overall, you are making good progress. Before long, you'll be challenging for 'Employee of the Month' Award."

This was Uncle Roger's way of motivating staff within the team. A gold coloured resin trophy, measuring 15cm in height, was up for grabs each month, with the successful employee taking it home to display. The problem was that everyone knew that Alison Armitage won the award every month. And that if she didn't win it, she would make Uncle Roger's life hell. One month, he made the mistake of giving the award to Julie Tinker. This news didn't go down at all well with Alison Armitage. Within 24 hours, she went off sick with stress [allegedly], leaving poor Uncle Roger having to ring round other members of staff at very short notice to fill assignments. Alison also removed Uncle Roger from her Christmas card list. It's business as usual now though. The trophy is back on Alison's mantlepiece, and everything is calm once again.

"Daphne, a new assignment has come in at short notice and I'm giving you first option. How do you fancy spending a night or two in a luxury hotel, sipping drinks by the pool and eating at the exclusive hotel restaurant? Are you up for it?" he asked.

I was genuinely interested, but also, equally suspicious.

"Where's the catch?" I enquired.

"I'll come to that in a minute," he said casually, then continued to sell the idea to me.

"Daphne, it's just like any other assignment, but this one is at a hotel. Once you arrive at the hotel, you'll have a long list of requirements to complete the assignment. You'll need to make full use of the facilities such as pool, bar, restaurant, health spa, and so forth, to gain an all-round experience of the venue, to be able to complete a review. What's not to like?"

Uncle Roger knew I was interested. The daft grin on my face was a giveaway. Something wasn't right though.

"Come on Uncle Roger. Out with it. What's the catch?"

"OK", he said reluctantly. "There are two things Daphne. The first thing is that the assignment is in the North of Scotland. The Scottish Highlands to be precise. So, you would need to get yourself there. And the second thing is, that I need you to take someone with you. If you are in a pair, you will blend in more and nobody will suspect you of being a Mystery Shopper. Oh, and the final thing is that the assignment is this weekend. Still keen?"

The advantage of having a personality like mine was that I didn't think too deeply about things. I was happy to jump into situations with both feet and deal with problems as I came across them. When I encountered problems or got myself in sticky situations I generally ended up in hysterics and saying to myself, 'that's another fine mess you've got yourself into Daphne'.

"Yes, Uncle Roger, I'm still keen" I confirmed.

"Any idea who could tag along with you? What about that chappy our Deirdre mentioned the other week. Apparently, you were raving on about some fella, weren't you? He was called Billy or something."

"What....do you mean Brian the bogie from the Berni Inn on Newcastle Road?"

"Yes, that's the fella" he confirmed. "Why is he called Brian the bogie?" Uncle Roger enquired.

"You don't want to know Uncle Roger," I grinned. "Let's leave it at that shall we. No, Brian the bogie isn't in the running for this trip. Leave it with me. I think I know someone who might be though."

Coastal escapades…. a one-legged Scotsman….and his furry friend

Tony Mathew was my next-door neighbour. He'd lived next door for quite a few years and had developed a close relationship with the family. He was particularly supportive to me following my parents' accident in Kenya, where they were tragically killed. Tony had moved to the area from Scotland as a young man. He'd always wanted to train as a nurse. He'd responded to a recruitment advert in the Scotland Express which read, 'Would you like to work in the NHS?' Tony applied and landed a role working as a nurse assistant. His placement was in an institution at the north side of town, that looked after patients who were intellectually disabled. He'd only been in the job a matter of weeks when he was called into Royston Spark's office.

Royston Spark was the senior tutor. He was a wiry fella with a well-groomed ginger beard. Royston was a fella who was not to be messed with. Tony thought he was being summoned to Royston's office for his appraisal. He didn't know he was being interviewed for a job. He went into Royston's office as a nursing assistant and came out as a trainee nurse. A condition of the new job role was that he had to commit to three years training, so he could become registered with the regulatory body. Tony was happy to sign up to this contractual arrangement.

Tony's appearance made him easily distinguishable and different from others. Firstly, there was his large protruding ears. On a windy day, they did him no favours when walking down the street, especially when walking against the wind. He once looked into a procedure for having protruding ears corrected, but didn't go through with it, due to it not being accessible on the NHS. He did however experiment for a short period and glued his ears to the side of his head using a strong adhesive. Although he thought this improved his look somewhat, it was never going to be a long-term solution. Since then, he's just let his ears do their own thing.

Secondly, Tony is hairy. Super hairy is probably a better description. He has hairs growing out of every orifice and would probably give an orangutang a run for its money in the body hair department. To curtail the hairs on his ears, he once tried to master the art of Turkish singeing. When done professionally, this dramatic technique sees a lit taper or wand being brought into contact with the hair. The result is the excess hair is literally smouldered away. Unfortunately, Tony didn't have a taper or wand, so attempted the procedure with a box of Swan Vestas. As you can imagine, the outcome wasn't great. The next few days were spent with his left ear smothered in gooey, thick liquid from the flesh of his Aloe vera plant.

The third and most obvious distinguishable feature was that Tony only has one leg. Shark attacks, or swimming with alligators are yarns he will spin, about why his left leg was missing, but truth be told, he had a leg defect at birth, and after a number of unsuccessful operations, at the age of seven it required amputation. In addition to these visual differences, you can throw into the mix, attributes such as lack of observation skills, dyspraxia and partial deafness. The latter resulting in Tony cranking up the volume when speaking mainly because he has difficulty in hearing his own voice.

None of these characteristics have held Tony back though. He has a happy go lucky attitude and a positive outlook on life. He also sees the funny side of things and often pokes fun at himself despite the challenges he faces. He is really good fun to be with. There is one major problem though. Because Tony and I are similar in many ways, our trips out together have always tended to be unpredictable, with something not going to plan or us finding ourselves in unusual predicaments.

Our last trip out was a couple of months ago. Tony was looking after Mrs Peterson's dog, Jasper, whilst she was on holiday. Mrs Peterson lived next door-but-one to Tony and she was a great neighbour. The type of neighbour who would always be popping round for a chat, often with gift in hand such as a freshly baked apple pie or a jar of homemade marmalade. Tony was fond of her. Jasper was one of those snappy Jack Russell types who needed plenty of exercise to wear him out. Tony planned to take him to the coast and give him a run on the beach. He asked me if I would like to join him.

Normally we would travel by Tony's motorbike and sidecar, but as we had Jasper with us, we decided to take the bus. The journey took just over an hour, and we arrived at the coast early afternoon. It was breezy, but not cold enough for coats. We casually wandered along the promenade exchanging tales from the previous week. I was bringing Tony up to speed regarding my latest mystery shopper assignments, whilst he would tell me about some of the characters he looked after where he worked. He was telling me about a new patient called Arthur Macdonald.

Arthur, Tony explained, was a lovely guy, with a deformed hand. He was the mischievous type, with a wee twinkle in his eye. He had been admitted after having a stroke. He didn't do much, he just sat on his bed all day. Arthur barely spoke, but when he did say something, it was the same catchphrase each time.

"My balls, my balls, are as big as St Pauls!", he would announce at the top of his voice.

Nobody was quite sure where this phrase came from, but as Tony said with a kind smile,

"It made for good entertainment during a long shift."

We'd been at the coast for about an hour. So far, things had been pretty uneventful, and we hadn't gotten into any scrapes or predicaments like we normally did when we were together on a trip out. However, that soon changed. There was a mobile ice cream van called Bob's Ices parked up on the promenade. The pink and white van was sporting a strapline that said, 'Cream of the Crop,' which we both agreed was a clever 'play on words.' Tony treated us each to a large '99' with raspberry sauce.

We headed across to a brightly coloured green bench so we could sit down and eat them at our leisure. The ice cream was delicious. Jasper was pestering us to throw his red rubber ball and kept nudging Tony's prosthetic leg with his nose. Tony picked up the ball and threw it in the direction of the seafront. It flew over a small wall.

Jasper approached the wall at some speed. He leapt forward, hurdling the wall and disappeared out of sight. We didn't think anything of it and continued licking our '99s' furiously. A few minutes passed, and then Tony asked,

"Have you seen Jasper?"

"No, not for a while," I answered.

"I'd better go and look for him," said Tony.

He slowly levered himself up off the bench.

"Oh no. This fuckin bench is covered in wet paint," he moaned.

I took a closer look. Sure enough, we had been sitting on a freshly painted bench for the last twenty minutes and we didn't have a clue. How had both of us missed the 'Wet Paint' signs, dotted around the place? It's fair to say that our observational ability had certainly let us down again on this occasion. My normal reaction kicked in and I burst into laughter. So did Tony. We both now had green stripes plastered across our backsides.

Tony wandered towards the small wall that Jasper had hurdled a few minutes earlier. He turned towards me and shouted,

"Bloody hell Daphne! You better come over here and see this."

I was still laughing at Tony's stripey chinos as I approached him. We both peered over the wall together. There was a drop of about twenty feet, onto some uncut grass and bushes which ran parallel with the lower promenade. We both looked at each other, then back down towards the grassy area again.

"Blimey, I didn't realise there was such a long drop the other side of the wall, when I threw his ball. Poor Jasper must have had a hell of a fright when he found himself in mid-air. The question is, where is he now?" Tony enquired.

There was a combination of concern and panic in his voice. As quickly as we could, we made our way down to the grassy area, to begin to look for him. This took a few minutes as we had to walk along the promenade for a couple of hundred metres in a northerly direction, down some stone steps to the lower promenade and then double back on ourselves. We then proceeded to search for Jasper, whilst calling out his name in the hope he would respond to our calls.

Passers-by informed us they hadn't seen him when we provided his description. He was a regular looking Jack Russell really, white with black and brown patches and a brown face. It was hopeless. There was no sign of Jasper and no sign of Jasper's ball either. After about half an hour we decided to have a break from looking and stepped across the road to a seafront café that sold fish and chips. We needed to think what our next move was. We were also quite exhausted and peckish.

Once inside the café, Tony needed to go to the toilet, so made a beeline for the gents. It was mid-afternoon, so there were plenty of tables to choose from. I sat down close to the toilet door, so Tony could see me when he came out. As I started to peruse the menu, I noticed the familiar aroma of fish & chips seemed to be in competition with something else. Something unpleasant, but I couldn't put my finger on it. Suddenly, I got a tap on the shoulder and there was an angry looking fella wearing a white apron. The words 'Battersby's Fish & Chips' donned his apron pocket. He obviously had a connection to the place. He had his hands on his hips, and he was scowling at me.

"Do you mind asking your friend to leave the premises" he growled.

I was on the verge of asking him why he wanted Tony to leave, when I realised what the problem was. There was a trail of dog muck left by footsteps, from the café entrance to the entrance of the toilets. It was stinking the place out.

Tony appeared from the toilet and wondered towards the table where I was seated. He was oblivious to everything that was going on.

"Don't take your coat off. We're leaving" I said.

"What do you mean, we're leaving" said Tony, in a confused state.

The angry looking guy arrived with his mop and bucket. He looked directly at me.

"I thought I told you that your friend had to leave."

He was now looking angrier than ever, as he plunged his mop into the disinfected hot water, before pressing it down into the wringer and twisting it with force to get rid of the excess water. Tony was still looking baffled.

"Look at the state of your shoes mate and look at the state of my café floor. As you have just been in there [and he pointed to the toilet door], no doubt the floor in there is covered too" he fumed.

Tony looked down. His shoes were caked in dog muck.

"Oh shit" he said ironically. "I must have stepped in the stuff when we were looking for Jasper in the grassy area, below the wall. How the hell have I managed to stand in it with both feet though?"

This wasn't the time or place to delve into the intricacies of how this had happened. We had to get off the premises sharpish. We left the café and trundled off towards the bus stop. Tony spotted a litter bin and decided to sacrifice his footwear and go home in his socks. He was concerned he would upset other passengers on the bus with his pongy shoes. He clambered on the bus looking a little dejected. He received some puzzling looks from the other passengers. They probably wondering why an amputee was travelling in just his socks. Two hours earlier, he'd arrived at the coast, fully clothed, with a canine companion, and was now leaving without his shoes and without his dog. Also, the clothes he was wearing were covered in green paint. Tony had some serious explaining to do when Mrs Peterson returned from her holiday.

Scottish Highlands….here we come

"Ring, ring…... ring, ring…… ring, ring."

It was Uncle Roger on the other end of the phone.

"Daphne, have you found someone to pair up with for the assignment to the hotel in the Highlands? If not, I'll need to make a few phone calls."

"Yes, it's all sorted, Uncle Roger. Tony Mathew, my next-door neighbour, has agreed to come with me."

"Excellent stuff. Err, is that the fella with one leg who dumped his shoes in a bin at the seaside, because he trod in the dog shit?" Uncle Roger asked.

"Yes, that's him," I said, before giggling like a schoolgirl.

"I thought so. Our Deirdre mentioned something about that. Have you got your transport sorted?" was Uncle Roger's next question.

"Yes, we're using Tony's motorbike and sidecar to get up there."

"Rather you than me," Uncle Roger chuckled. "I doubt I would even squeeze into a sidecar these days. Make sure you wear a motorcycle helmet, won't you?" Then he became serious. "Remember, Daphne, this isn't a jolly you are going on. Try to blend in and be just like any other hotel guest on vacation — the only difference is that you'll be getting paid. Make sure Mathew or Tony, or whatever he is called, knows we'll cover his expenses.

"Don't forget, it's crucial to the shopping process that you remain covert in your actions and not give up the secret that you're a Mystery Shopper. This means no spilling the beans to other hotel guests in the lobby, talking about your assignment near the pool, or behaving strangely enough to warrant suspicion." There was a short pause to let this sink in, before he continued. "This could be a bumper contract with this hotel chain if we play our cards right. I'm relying on you, Daphne. Our Deirdre will call round to your place later, with the assignment details. Oh, and one more thing, I presume you've informed your parents you'll be away for the weekend?"

"Yes, Uncle Roger. They are cool with it all. See you when I get back."

It was a very early start the following morning. We were away by 6:00 am. Tony had estimated it would take about six hours to reach the hotel in the Scottish Highlands. Throw in a couple of pitstops and it would be closer to seven hours. He had been working the previous day and had not finished work until 10:00 pm. His normal shift pattern was two consecutive thirteen hour shifts, followed by two days off. He could also have as much overtime as he wanted, but seldom took up this option. Looking after forty intellectually disabled patients for thirteen hours, was quite taxing. He was generally run off his feet at the end of a shift, or in Tony's case, his foot. He was in good spirits and looking forward to the trip despite being bleary eyed and tired.

The journey north was relatively smooth. There was only one mishap along the way and we both saw the funny side of it. It happened when we were about an hour from our destination and travelling along a single-track road. Either side of the road the rolling highland landscape was covered with iconic Scottish heather. The scenery was stunning. It was just about as rural as you could get. Suddenly, Tony slowed down the motorbike and sidecar and we came to a halt. We had reached a wooden gate in the road. Post and wire fencing was attached to both sides of the gate and span off across the heather landscape as far as the eye could see. We presumed it was a boundary fence to separate out land from different landowners.

Tony gave me the nod to go and open the gate. I appreciated this, as it gave me a chance to get out of the sidecar and stretch my legs. I opened the gate, Tony drove through, then I closed the gate behind us. I returned to the sidecar. I had one leg back inside the sidecar, when I saw a vehicle approaching in the distance. It was the first vehicle we had seen in a while. To be helpful, I decided to delay getting into the sidecar and to open the gate for the oncoming car. There was probably an unwritten rule for situations like this. It just felt the right thing to do. I closed the sidecar door and walked towards the gate.

The car came to a standstill a few yards from the gate. I was useless when it came to car makes and models, but I knew this one as mum and dad had a similar car many years ago. It was a classic car. A scarlet and violet Morris Minor Traveller. The driver wound down his window. He was small and hunched over the wheel. Maybe he had a curvature of the spine or something. He looked to be in his late forties, and his dark hair was balding.

"Good day" he said loudly. "It's a fine day for the race", he added.

"Err.... race....what race would that be?" I asked. I was totally confused.

"The Human Race" he confirmed, then burst out laughing.

I chuckled at his eccentricity. The dark haired lady next to him didn't see the funny side of his quip. She'd probably heard it before. She was straight faced with rosy cheeks. I got the feeling she had a no-nonsense approach. I presumed she was his wife. On the back seat were two children. The girl was plain looking with short dark hair. She wore a sullen expression like the lady. It was the boy that caught my attention though. He stood out from the rest of them, and his appearance was markedly different. He had ginger hair and looked quite sad. He wore a short sleeved blue shirt, decorated with embroidered badges. If this was a family outing, he didn't look like the rest of them. This reminded me of my own situation. I didn't resemble my parents either.

I opened the gate, and the car slowly went through. The driver showed his appreciation by papping his horn a couple times. The little boy with the ginger hair turned and looked at me out of the back window as they drove away. I stared back and waved frantically at him, hoping it would maybe make him smile. For some strange reason, I felt we had a connection. I don't know why I thought this way. I'd never had this feeling with anyone before. I was mesmerised by him. It seemed like I stood there for ages, but it was probably only a matter of seconds. The car got smaller and smaller before evaporating into the beautiful Scottish landscape.

The last couple of minutes had felt surreal, even trancelike. I snapped out of it and turned to return to the sidecar. I let out a high pitch shriek. Tony and the motorbike and sidecar had gone. What had happened? Surely, he hadn't driven off and left me deliberately? He must have thought I had climbed back into the sidecar, but not looked properly and then set off without me. That's the only conclusion I could come up with. I would just need to wait and hope it didn't take him too long before he noticed the sidecar was empty. I sat on a big boulder by the side of the road. Someone had carved their name on the boulder. "Jim woz here, 1976". Maybe Jim was in a similar scenario to me, or maybe he was rambler who just needed a rest and decided to leave his mark.

Thirty minutes went by and there was no sign of Tony. The only indication of civilisation was a farmer who sped past in his Land Rover, and a few inquisitive blackface sheep. On the hour mark, I could see a speck on the road in the far distance. It was heading in my direction. As the speck got bigger, I recognised Tony's white motorcycle helmet. He was driving like the clappers. As he got closer, he eased the bike down before drawing up alongside me. I could see on Tony's face, that he was relieved to see me.

"I'm ever so sorry Daphne", he blurted out. "I thought you'd climbed inside the sidecar earlier. I must not have been concentrating and just set off. I stopped up the road there, for a pee, and noticed you weren't there. I nearly had a heart attack. I thought you might have fallen out of the sidecar or something. Then I remembered about you opening the gate for the Morris Traveller and have ridden back as fast as I can. Have you been OK?"

"I'm absolutely fine, Tony" I replied.

I could see the funny side and started laughing. He soon sensed that I had found the incident to be amusing and calmed down. Before long, he soon started to roar with laughter himself. In between bouts of laughter, Tony yelled,

"This could only happen to us, Daphne!" before resuming his laughter rhythm.

"You could be right Tony……. you could be right!" I shrieked, as I squeezed into the sidecar, being careful not to squash our luggage. This time, Tony ensured I was on board and gave me a 'thumbs up' sign before continuing the journey.

Hotel Shenanigans

The location of the hotel was spectacular. It was set in 36 acres of gardens and woodland, nestling next to the shores of a large loch. Leading up to the hotel entrance we navigated a long-wooded drive snaking past the emotive ruins of a medieval castle. The hotel itself was Victorian. Parts of it had been modified as it moved with the times to keep up with the demands of leisure and tourism visitors in the twentieth century. This involved the addition of a swimming pool and a nine-hole golf course. Both were on our radar to explore.

Inside the hotel was equally as impressive. The hotel brochure's description of the interior was spot on: 'drawing rooms filled with deep sofas, fireplaces and huge oak bookcases brimming with books of all genres. The main restaurant is Scot's pine panelled and includes a conservatory with magnificent panoramic views over the loch. Upstairs, the deliciously pretty bedrooms are all elegantly decorated in soft pastel colours and deep velvet, with classic reproduction furniture, voluptuous curtains, polished wood floors and oriental rugs'. I just thought the place was cool. There was even a complimentary miniature dram and a packet of shortbread biscuits awaiting us, for when we reached our twin room. We appreciated this as we were both ravenous.

The brief for the hotel assignment was pretty standard. Key areas to assess were things like customer service, quality of product and cleanliness of the hotel facilities. We also had to assess whether the hotel lived up to its five-star rating. The visit got off to a positive start. A young lady at reception greeted us with a warm smile upon arrival. She also gave excellent eye contact. She was wearing a smart tweed uniform, made up of bright bursts of colour that married perfectly with the hotel's luxury interior. The lobby area was clean, warm and well lit. Soft Highland bagpipe music radiated from wall mounted speakers, creating a gentle ambiance. The staff had registered that Tony had a prosthetic leg and explained that if he needed any additional assistance during his stay, he should ask a member of staff, immediately. I tittered with excitement. I couldn't believe I was staying at such a lavish facility. I was also getting paid for it.

There was a specific request in the assignment brief that included: testing each faucet in the bathroom, flushing the toilets, checking the lights and even measuring the distance between wall paintings to see if they're up to scratch. We weren't restricted to what was on the checklist either. There was an instruction to elicit fake problems to test time, crisis management and problem-solving skills of employees of the hotel to see how they responded to these situations. Tony agreed to be in charge of creating the fictional complaints, mainly because he could keep a straight face in these situations, whereas I would just burst out laughing. He was also more mischievous than me.

The first fictional complaint he made was about a 'so-called' broken table lamp in the room. He removed a light bulb from the lamp and reported it to staff working on the front desk. Once he'd called to complain, he made a note of how long we waited before getting a response, the tone the employee took when replying to the complaint, and how quickly the problem was resolved.

Tony, who was now getting the hang of mystery shopping, decided to test the staff further on efficiency and politeness. He phoned reception and made a complaint that the pillows on his bed weren't 'fluffed up' enough. The hotel sent up one of their front-of-house crew, a burly Highlander called Angus.

Angus was very cordial and willingly fluffed up Tony's pillows. Tony decided to push his luck and made several other calls to reception, asking for his pillows to be fluffed up. This didn't faze Angus and he continued to deal with the request whilst remaining friendly and amicable. By the fifth phone call, Tony was unquestionably taking the piss. He realised he had pushed his luck too far when Angus faced up to him, squeezed Tony's meat and two veg with his huge Highland hand, and sarcastically said,

"Is there anything else you would like me to fluff up for you sir?"

Tony didn't make any further calls to reception after that. For the next 24 hours, he fluffed up his own pillows!

Later that day, we ventured into the restaurant for our evening meal. So not to raise any suspicions that we were Mystery Shoppers, we tried behaving like a couple who were romantically involved. I'm not sure how convincing we were though as neither of us had much experience when it came to romance. The menu included classy dishes such as roasted pork belly, creamed cabbage and pommes anna. Tony wasn't used to such swanky cuisine. His diet mainly consisted of beans on toast, especially when he was at work. He often reminisced about being a student nurse when he would devour plates of the stuff twice a shift, all made by canteen assistant, Harry.

Harry's role seemed to be 24/7. It didn't seem to matter which shift Tony was working. Every time he frequented the canteen, Harry would be there, running the show. He didn't need to ask Tony what he wanted. He knew. Within seconds Tony would be presented with four rounds of toast, lashings of butter [courtesy of the EU butter mountain] and as many beans as the plate could accommodate, all for the princely sum of ten pence. Although times had changed, Tony hadn't and he still loved beans.

The member of staff assigned to our table was a young Scottish girl called Morag. She clarified this during her introduction.

"Hi, I'm Morag; I'll be your server for tonight," she said in a soft Gaelic accent.

Further dialogue with her revealed that she lived in a small hamlet one-mile north east of the hotel. Some other members of her family were also employed at the hotel, but she didn't go into detail. She was really efficient at her job, and her manners were excellent. Her knowledge of the menu was first-class. This wasn't like being at the Berni Inn with bogie Brian. The Berni Inn was good, but this was in a different league.

When it came to choosing our meal, I opted for crispy lamb shoulder, aubergine and roasted cauliflower. Tony deliberated over his choice before finally opting for pan-fried duck breast, pumpkin and cheesy garlic roasted asparagus. He was slightly wary about having the asparagus as greens didn't always agree with him. But he decided to go with it anyway. Ultimately, this turned out to be a big mistake. A catastrophic mistake, even.

The meals were lovely, but as soon as we got back to our hotel room, the asparagus started to work its magic. Tony was emitting so much gas, as a result of the asparagus, that we had to sleep with the bedroom windows open. The situation was so bad that we considered calling a doctor to see if anything could be prescribed for his flatulence problem. Tony decided against it, as he was adamant the situation would improve once he dropped off to sleep. It didn't. It continued, even whilst he was snoring heavily. The pong in the room was so rank that I had to ring down to reception and ask Angus if he would kindly bring up a peg so I could put it on my nose. He offered a pair of earplugs, too, once he fully understood my dilemma with Tony's snoring. He'd encountered some unusual requests over the years, but nothing like that. As fast as Tony released the gas, he then breathed it back in again. He was basically inhaling his own farts. It was a vicious circle.

The following morning, Tony was still suffering from wind. To add to this, he also had belly cramps. Although not feeling one hundred percent, he decided to go for a dip in the hotel swimming pool before breakfast. He felt it would invigorate him for the day ahead. The pool was also one of the hotel areas that had to be checked out as part of the mystery shopper assignment. In the changing room, he slipped into his red knee length swim shorts. They were decorated with blue starfish. He carefully placed all his personal items in his chosen locker, inserted his hotel token, removed the locker key and pinned it to his shorts. He then walked the short distance towards the side of the pool, took off his prosthetic leg and leaned it against an artificial palm tree by the side of pool, before easing himself into the water.

A grumpy looking lifeguard sat on a freestanding chair watching him. He was high up and had a perfect view of the pool. Other hotel guests must have had the same thought as Tony as there were about eight others all working their way up and down the thirty-metre pool. Tony started clocking up a few lengths of his own. His preferred stroke was freestyle. Being an amputee, this was the style that suited him and helped him move through the water relatively quickly.

After a dozen lengths or so, Tony stopped to catch his breath. He held on to the side of the pool until his breathing eased. He could feel his stomach churning. He wondered whether farting would help, so he let one go. His red swim shorts inflated like a balloon. Amused by his underwater fart, Tony set off swimming again. A few minutes later, he decided to let one go whilst mid swim. He sensed it propelled him through the water so continued to release his gas at regular intervals. Other swimmers seemed oblivious to his secret antics.

Suddenly, Tony heard the noise of a loud whistle being blown repeatedly. He stopped swimming to see what was going on. He had to tread water as it was too deep for him to stand up and reach the bottom of the pool. The grumpy looking lifeguard had climbed down from his raised chair and was at the side of the pool blowing his whistle and waving his arms about frantically. He didn't look happy. Tony was confused and in disarray. He could see other swimmers begrudgingly getting out of the pool. They were also confused as to what was happening. Tony tried to get the lifeguard's attention, which wasn't easy, whilst treading water.

"What's going on?" Tony shouted at the top of voice.

The lifeguard stopped blowing his whistle for a moment and shouted back,

"Someone has shit in the pool. You need to get out".

Sure enough, he turned around to see a small area of the pool contaminated by discoloured water. It resembled a mini oil slick, only this was brown and yellow in colour. Yuk, he thought to himself. How disgusting. He made his way to the side of the pool. He yanked his body on to the poolside, put on his prosthetic leg, then trundled towards the changing room. The lifeguard gave Tony a stern look, as he walked past him. His face was red with anger. Tony knew there was a chance he was in the frame for the 'poolsgate' incident, but he wasn't 100% sure.

By lunch time, Tony's stomach problem had cleared up. We were aware we would need to leave the hotel by about 3:00 pm that afternoon, as we had a long journey back. We were both keen to try out the nine-hole golf course before we had to leave. Neither of us had played golf before. We knew we were going to be hopeless, but as it was part of the assignment to check out as many hotel amenities as possible and were keen to give it a go. When we had pre-booked the round of golf at the start of the weekend, we had been asked by the young lady at reception whether we had any special requirements. She was aware Tony had a prosthetic leg, so the question was geared towards him rather than me. Tony had agreed with her that if there was anything that could support his mobility getting around the golf course, he would be grateful.

Adjacent to the tee-off area for the first hole, was a sizeable wooden structure, used to store the hotel's golf equipment. Angus was there to greet us. He recognised Tony instantly.

"Ah, we meet again", he shouted as we walked towards him.

"I hope you slept well last night with those fluffed up pillows of yours", he said, then laughed jovially.

Tony saw the funny side and smiled back.

"Are you both ready for your round of golf?" he asked.

We both nodded eagerly.

"Ok, I'll go and get everything you need," said Angus before disappearing into the wooden facility.

It wasn't too long before he appeared again. He was driving a fancy white golf cart loaded with two black bags, full of golf clubs.

"This is your transport for the afternoon," he said, gesturing towards the golf cart. "You wouldn't think it has the ability to reach 0-60 mph in just 6 seconds, would you?"

There was a moment's silence as he waited for our response. Tony looked at Angus in a puzzled manner and was just about to respond when Angus started to roar with laughter. His open mouth revealing several gold fillings in the back cavity.

"Only joking" he said, still amused by his own remark.

This was obviously a joke he rolled out to hotel customers on a regular basis.

"Its top speed is 10mph" he stressed. "Don't try and go any faster than that."

He then moved on to give us some pointers on which golf clubs to use, for each shot. It was all a little bit technical for me and the only thing I remembered was that we should use the stick with the big wooden end [the Driver] each time we teed off. The rest of the information, especially the bit about low numbered irons and high numbered irons was all gobbledygook. It was still all very exciting though.

"One last thing," Angus explained, "try not to create any divots on the course, especially on the greens, as Frazer will go crazy."

He didn't go into detail who Frazer was, but we quickly worked out Frazer's job was probably linked to the upkeep of the golf course. He also sounded like a guy who was pretty strict and took his job very seriously.

Tony was keen to drive the golf cart, which was fine by me. He couldn't wait and was soon sat in the driver's seat and ready to zip us up the fairway. To say we were useless at golf was an understatement. We were mega useless. As much as we tried, we weren't capable of hitting the ball any considerable distance. Therefore, it took several shots to reach the green on each hole. On the third hole, it took me 23 shots to get my ball onto the green. It must have been hilarious for any passers-by who were watching us. A proficient golfer would have reached the green in three shots. Frazer wouldn't have been too happy if he'd have seen us in action. We were making divots all over the fairway. We weren't doing this deliberately. It was accidental, due to us being golfing novices. But the bottom line was that there were clumps of turf flying everywhere.

To reach the tee-off area for the seventh hole, we decided to travel up a gentle incline across a stretch of bank adjacent to the fairway. We weren't sure if this was the correct route, but we were pretty confident we were heading in the right direction. As we approached the top of the incline Tony started fidgeting. He seemed to be having trouble with his prosthetic leg.

"You ok Tony?" I enquired nervously.

As I asked the question, I noticed we were getting dangerously close to the top of the incline. It was difficult to see the lay of land beyond this. Tony didn't appear to be slowing down.

"Put your brakes on!" I yelled.

"My foot is jammmmmmm!!!!"

He didn't quite finish his sentence. The bank petered out, and the golf cart flew forwards into the abyss. Unfortunately for us, it wasn't designed to fly, like something you might see in a James Bond Film. The cart somehow twisted in mid-air. This was probably influenced by Tony's heavier body mass. I made a high-pitched screaming noise. Tony made a noise, too. But it was more of an "aaaah!" sound.

The golf cart landed on its front right wheel, then rolled onto its side. Surprisingly, it was a quiet landing. We had landed on something soft, too. On closer inspection, we were nestled in a sandy bunker. All was quiet, apart from the noise of the back wheels of the cart, which were still spinning. I was a bit dazed, but other than that, I think I was OK. I wasn't in any pain or anything, I was just relieved I was still in one piece after the experience. I now knew how Jasper must have felt when he leapt over the wall at the coast. It's pretty scary when you are in freefall and don't know what you are going to land on.

I turned to see if Tony was ok. He was nowhere to be seen. Somewhere between launching off the top of the bank and landing into the bunker, Tony had vacated the vehicle. Well, the majority of him had anyway. His prosthetic leg was there next to me. The foot of his prosthetic was still jammed in the footwell of the golf cart. The rest of him must have been catapulted away from the cart during the incident.

There was a groaning noise coming from somewhere nearby. I peered around the front wheel of the golf cart to get a better view. There were golf clubs scattered everywhere. Tony was laying face down in the sand about twenty feet away. I clambered out of the wrecked golf cart and made my way to him. I crouched down by his side. I was praying he wasn't about to die.

"Are you ok Tony? Are you in pain?" I asked tentatively.

Tony raised his face from the bunker. Grains of sand completely covered his face. He groaned once more, then spluttered,

"This could only happen to me and you, Daphne."

Then he proceeded to spit out the grains of sand that had found their way inside his mouth. Thankfully, he seemed ok.

By this stage, other golfers had spotted something had happened and were on top of the bank, gawping down at us. One of the onlookers fainted. He saw Tony lying face down in the sand, with only one leg, and concluded it had been severed in the accident. Tony hung on to me as he pulled himself up. The imprint of his body was left in the sand. Typically, we both started laughing. This was generally our default position to when we found ourselves in a pickle. In this instance, it was probably a reaction to the general craziness of the situation, not to mention the comedown from the adrenalin rush we had both just experienced.

Word got back to Angus quickly and it wasn't long before he arrived at the scene. To say we had just wrote-off one of the hotel's fancy golf carts, he handled it pretty well. He checked we hadn't suffered any injuries then gave us a ride on his golf cart back to the hotel. He offered us both a shot of whisky to calm our nerves. Although it was a lovely gesture, we both declined. Tony didn't want any alcohol in his system before the long drive back home. Before he departed, he gave me a big hug and then shook Tony's hand. I sensed Angus had a strong grip as Tony seemed to grimace during the exchange.

"Safe journey back, and hope to see you both again soon," he said before hopping back onto the golf cart and driving off.

Our assignment at the hotel had come to an end. It was time to head back home. Tony turned the key and the motorbike and sidecar started first time. He had a quick look to see if I was in position, before driving down the long-wooded drive and away from the main hotel building. I was sad to leave such a tranquil place. I delved into my pocket and pulled out a couple of mint humbugs. I removed the crinkly wrapper, popped one in my mouth and relaxed back into the leather seat. Staring at the dramatic Scottish highland scenery sent me into daydream mode. I smiled to myself as I reflected on the last twenty-four hours. We'd completed the assignment, but in doing so, we'd caused havoc. We were responsible for polluting the hotel swimming pool and we'd wrecked the golf course. It now had so many divots and mini craters; it resembled the surface of the planet Venus. We'd also smashed up a golf cart and damaged two sets of golf clubs. We had certainly left our mark!

Driving Dougie Barking Mad

It was my 30th driving lesson. Not that I was counting or anything. My parents were once again stood at the living room window, ready to wave me off. So far, all the lessons had taken place at the run-down industrial estate, on the edge of town. For the first 30 weeks, I'd been trying to master the basics of 'moving off and stopping'. Today was different. Dougie had decided not to return to the industrial estate. He had instead opted to introduce me to roads where traffic was likelier to be busier. I don't think he had taken the decision lightly, but he had probably come to the conclusion that I couldn't continue on the industrial estate for ever.

He was wearing a branded yellow polo neck jumper. I'd thought I'd seen most of his jumper collection by now, but this one was a new one on me. The jumper had a green crocodile in the left breast area. Maybe it was a recent gift from Mrs Parsons or perhaps he'd treated himself, or something. I also noticed something else. Dougie's hair. It had changed colour. On my first lesson over 6 months ago, Dougie had a full head of dark brown curly hair. Now he resembled a Silver Fox. How was this possible? I thought to myself. And how come I hadn't spotted this earlier? This was typical of me. Most of the time I'm away with the fairies and don't always notice the obvious. Anyway, now I was aware of it, I thought I'd better keep schtum. I didn't want to draw attention to it.

"Right, Daphne, your next challenge is to conquer the 'mirror, signal, manoeuvre' routine," said Dougie sternly.

He seemed agitated. Thinking about it, he'd been like this for a while now. What happened to the Dougie from my first driving lesson who was chilled out, friendly and calm? He had been replaced by an uptight, grumpy man. Maybe he was behaving like this because he'd turned grey overnight, or perhaps it was because he was about to spend another hour with me, the worst learner driver in history.

"We are going to have a little drive around the outer edge of town," he said. "As we do this, I want you to use your mirrors to check the position of traffic around and behind you, and act on what you see. When appropriate you will need to use your indicators to show other vehicles what you intend to do. I also want you to consider adjusting the speed and position of the car, so it's safe for any manoeuvre you want to make. Hopefully everything will fall into place once you set off, Daphne."

I was under no illusion that this latest lesson was going to be a step up from tootling backwards and forwards on the industrial estate. I was surrounded by an abundance of buttons, levers, pedals, dials, switches and knobs, which all needed to be somehow managed in a particular order whilst travelling at speed. If Dougie didn't know I was a technophobe by now, he was going to know it in the next few minutes. He was also going to know that I couldn't multitask either.

Over the next forty-five minutes or so, Dougie's patience was stretched to the limit as I made one mistake after another. First of all, I failed to stop at a zebra crossing. This was because I was too busy checking my mirror and caught sight of my own reflection. I noticed my fringe was wonky and was starting to adjust it when Dougie screamed,

"PEDESTRIAN AHEAD!!"

Thankfully, Dougie's reflexes kicked in and using the dual controls, he anchored on to save the day. We just avoided mowing down an elderly lollipop lady, but it was only by inches.

Throughout the lesson, I had difficulty finding the right speed. I was going slow when I should have been going fast and I was going fast when I should have been going slow. Also, despite Dougie always reminding me, I constantly forgot to signal when approaching junctions and roundabouts or turning left and right. Dougie got particularly annoyed with me when I spotted Deirdre walking down the street and shouted "whoo hoo" at her, through the car window.

"Easy does it, Daphne!" shouted Dougie, as the car stalled for the fourth time consecutively at some traffic lights.

Some of the drivers in the vehicles behind us were becoming annoyed and demonstrated this by sounding their horns. Dougie put his left arm out of the passenger window to acknowledge the other drivers, and to try and appease them.

"Daphne, you're releasing the clutch far too quickly. Remember what I told you. You need to listen for the biting point."

"Ok, Dougie" I said, whilst crunching into another mint imperial.

He was sucking mint imperials too. The problem with his bad breath hadn't resolved.

As the lesson was drawing to a close, Dougie instructed me to indicate and take the next right off the main road. We entered a small shopping complex. In front of the shops was a number of clearly marked parking spaces. Dougie pointed at the space he wanted me to park in. I think he deliberately chose a space without any cars either side, so there would be no chance of any collisions with other vehicles.

"Easy does it, Daphne" said Dougie, as I began to turn into the bay.

We were moving far quicker than we should have been.

"BRAKE!!" shouted Dougie.

Instead of braking, I hit the accelerator by mistake. Luckily the dual controls came to our rescue again as Dougie pressed sharpish on the brake pedal. We both flew forward, only to be caught by our seatbelts. But for Dougie's intervention his mini metro would have ended up inside a Chinese restaurant situated in front of the parking bay. Dougie sat there in silence. He was lost for words. I think he was at breaking point. He just stared at the neon sign in the window of the restaurant. It was promoting an 'all you can eat oriental buffet'. Suddenly, he burst back into life.

"I'm just nipping into that store over there," he announced, pointing towards a pet supplies store. "I need to pick something up.

You might want to get out of the car Daphne, get some fresh air and stretch your legs."

We had been driving around for the last hour with the windows down due to Dougie's bad breath, so I didn't need any fresh air, but I was ok with the idea of stretching my legs.

Dougie was in the pet store longer than I anticipated. I stretched my legs for a short while, then got back in the car because it was quite chilly. Different thoughts were going through my mind. I was playing out the conversation I would no doubt have with my parents when I got home:

"How has your driving lesson gone, Daphne?" [them].

"It's not gone that well, if I'm honest. I don't think the driving instructor is impressed with my progress. Hopefully I'll put in a better performance next week" [me].

"Well, me and your father passed first time and consider ourselves to be very competent drivers. In fact, your father's driving instructor once told him that he was the best learner driver he had ever taught" [my mother].

This wasn't the first time my mother had pointed out their excellent driving capabilities. Talk about rubbing it in. I'd obviously not inherited their genes when it came to mastering the art of driving. I suppose this was something else that could be added to the list when it came to lack of traits between me and my parents.

Dougie opened the rear door of the car and placed several bags on the back seat. The bags were bursting at the seams with cans of dog food.

"If you don't mind, Daphne, we'll swap seats, and I'll drive you back home. We've had an hour, and I'm afraid my nerves are shot to pieces."

"That's fine Dougie. If you are sure," I replied.

To be honest, it suited me to be back in the passenger seat.

"You've never mentioned that you have a dog, Dougie," I enquired, as we drove steadily along the main road.

"Yes, we've had him a few weeks now. Mrs Parsons has always wanted a dog. She thought it would be good company for us and taking it for a walk every day would help to keep us fit. We got it from the dog rescue centre. It's based out near the coast. We've called the dog 'Rocket'. The rescue centre was struggling to re-home him. He'd been there a number of weeks. Apparently, he had been abandoned by his previous owner and was found wandering around the promenade area."

My ears pricked up. The description of this canine sounded very familiar. It couldn't be……. could it?

"What sort of dog is he, Dougie?" I enquired tentatively.

Dougie smiled.

"He's a Jack Russell Terrier," he replied.

I sensed from his response that he and Rocket had formed a strong bond since he had been adopted into the family. Oh my god,

I thought to myself. There can't have been too many Jack Russell Terriers that have gone astray from their owners in that location over the last few weeks. Surely, this has got to be Jasper. I needed to probe further. In order not to give the game away, I chose not to be too direct. I wasn't into lying, but on this occasion, I felt it best to conceal the reasoning for my questioning.

"My grandparents used to have a Jack Russell Terrier called Joe [this was a complete lie]. He had brown fur with a patch of white fur on his chest. What colour is your dog Dougie?"

"He's white with black and brown patches and a brown face," replied Dougie.

"Oh, that's lovely," I said.

In my own mind, this was enough to confirm, well 99% anyway, that Dougie's new addition, was in fact the dog me and Tony lost, when we went to the coast a few months ago. This was an amazing coincidence that it was now the family pet of my driving instructor. I was in no doubt that Tony should be made aware of what I have discovered as soon as possible. Mrs Peterson had never fully forgiven him since he broke the news that Jasper had disappeared. Maybe there was a chance Jasper could be reunited with his rightful owner. But how?

Later that evening, I popped next door to see Tony. He had just finished one of his gruelling 13-hour shifts at the institution. He was sat in his armchair working his way through his evening meal. It was omelette, baked beans, two slices of bread and butter and a cup of tea. He had removed his prosthetic to give his stump some respite. It was aching. Being on his feet most of the day had taken its toll. Between mouthfuls of food, he chatted enthusiastically about his day at work and about what his patients had been up to. This time, he was recounting a tale about one of his longer-term patients, called Pete Jacket. He was a tall, unassuming guy who said very little. Tony explained that every time Pete visited the toilet to open his bowels, he would return with a poo in his hand, present it to Tony, then say, "Cheesy Pie Daddy." Tony burst out laughing, then muttered the phrase "Cheesy Pie Daddy" to himself, several times, as if he was in a daydream state, before snapping back out of it and refocusing on his meal. He would recount stories like this most weeks. He was really fond of the patients he looked after and would move hell and high water, so they had as comfortable life as possible.

Tony was slurping the last dregs of his cup of tea when I delivered my news.

"Tony, I think I may have found Jasper," I said eagerly. "I think he now lives with my driving instructor, Dougie Parsons and his wife Patricia. They've renamed him and he's now called Rocket."

Tony put down his empty mug of tea. His exhausted face suddenly had some life in it.

"Honestly, Daphne? How have you managed to discover this?" He asked excitedly.

I recounted the conversation I'd had with Dougie earlier that day.

"What do you think, Tony? It has to be Jasper, doesn't it?"

Tony pondered my question for a couple of seconds.

"I agree, Daphne. A Jack Russell Terrier found wandering on the promenade at the coast. The timeline fits too. It just has to be Jasper. This is super exciting. We have to get him back."

The demeanour of his face then shifted from that of delight to troubled.

"Mrs Peterson hasn't been the same since he went missing. I feel it's affected our relationship too. She has stopped calling round. She used to come here at least twice a week with a tub of homemade baking and we'd have a cup of coffee and a natter. I feel that she blames me for his disappearance. I'd do anything to rewind the clock and return to those days."

Tony stared at the mantelpiece in front of him. He was deep in thought. I knew not to interrupt him. He then turned to look at me and was grinning like a Cheshire Cat.

"I have a plan to get Jasper back, Daphne. Everything is going to be ok. I'm going to need your help, though. We are also going to need Deirdre's help too. Leave it with me, and we'll go through the finer details tomorrow."

This wasn't the only good news that evening. As I walked through the door, my father handed me the telephone.

"It's your Uncle Roger. He wants a quick word with you. Don't be long as your tea is almost ready."

I put the phone to my ear.

"Is that the Kangaroo Queen?" Uncle Roger asked, then started laughing.

"I bumped into Dougie Parsons earlier, and he was telling me all about your driving lessons. Keep at it, Daphne. I'm sure you'll get there in the end."

I wasn't impressed that Dougie was blabbing about my abilities [or lack of them] behind the wheel. Uncle Roger continued,

"Anyway, the reason for ringing is that I have some good news. Firstly, we have secured a contract with the hotel chain who owns the hotel in the Scottish Highlands that you visited recently. They were impressed with the report from the assignment you completed. So was I, Daphne. As a result, you have won the employee of the month award. You know what I'm going to say next, don't you Daphne?"

"I think so, Uncle Roger."

"Yes, Alison Armitage has gone off sick, which means I have an assignment to cover at short notice. It's for a new supermarket that has opened in town. The company originates from Germany, and their prices are very reasonable. Are you up for it, Daphne?"

"Yes, I suppose so, Uncle Roger."

"Marvellous. That's what I like to hear. Staff who are committed to the cause. I need to keep the money rolling in to pay for all those bloody driving lessons of yours," said Roger as he chuckled to himself before signing off.

Operation Jasper

The following evening, Deirdre and I were huddled around Tony's kitchen table to discuss 'Operation Jasper'. Tony was taking this operation very seriously. He'd obviously given it some thought over the course of the day. Notepads and pens were supplied for recording purposes and mugs of coffee and digestive chocolate biscuits were supplied to maintain energy levels. He explained that 'Operation Jasper' was to be carried out across three stages. There was to be: an information gathering stage; a surveillance stage; and the implementation stage. He then went on to allocate our roles. We listened intently.

Tony's main role was to source a replica dog. This wasn't going to be easy, but it was crucial that this was right for the overall operation to be successful. Luckily, Tony had a trump card up his sleeve. Pedro. Tony had known Pedro for years. They grew up together in Scotland. Pedro was one of those guys who could lay his hands on things. It was best not to ask him where he got things from though. Although Pedro sounded Italian, he was as Glaswegian as they come. He was no stranger to the odd deep fried mars bar and a pint of heavy, that's for sure.

To assist Pedro in sourcing a replica dog, he would need to be supplied with as much detail as possible, including photos and lots of them. This was where surveillance was going to play an important role in proceedings. An understanding of Jasper's daily walking routine was really important to the success of the mission. Deirdre was asked to take on the role of surveillance, mainly because she had the latest hi-tech camera to capture those all-important snaps.

My role was to pump Dougie for as much information about Jasper as I could. For example, we would need to understand Jasper's size, weight, eye colour and teeth condition. We would also need the brand of dog collar to purchase the exact same one. Getting these minor details wrong could jeopardise the whole operation.

Meetings to discuss Operation Jasper took place every Tuesday evening at Tony's house. Information was shared, notes were drafted, and photos were scrutinised. Following every meeting, a bundle of information was then posted up to an address in Glasgow for the attention of Pedro Connelly. Word that was coming back in the other direction, was that he was having difficulty in sourcing a Jasper lookalike. Tony wasn't too concerned about the delay. It was giving us more time to gather in-depth data at our end.

Out of the blue, one Sunday evening, an emergency meeting was called by Tony. We knew he had some important news to share as we had strayed away from the regular Tuesday night slot. We sat around his kitchen table as normal. The digestive biscuits had been replaced by a Victoria Sponge cake. He was also grinning from ear to ear. Deirdre was more impatient than me.

"Come on, Tony, out with it. We don't normally meet on Sunday evenings. What's happened?"

"Some important news has come through from Pedro," Tony announced. "He has found a match for Jasper. The dog is identical in appearance. He couldn't find one in the UK, so he had to broaden his search. He's sourced the dog from Spain. We've struck the jackpot."

I couldn't contain my excitement and let out several whoops of delight. Deirdre, on the other hand, was more reserved about the news she had just heard. Tony sensed this.

"What's going through your mind Deirdre?" he asked.

As ever, Deirdre had her sensible head on.

"If the dog is coming across from Spain, there are things we are going to have to take into consideration. The dog may need to be vaccinated. It may need certain treatments and be put in quarantine. Not to mention the additional cost and potential delays to the operation."

Deirdre was right to raise these concerns. She was intelligent and shrewd. Unlike me, who was the dippy one in the Operation Jasper team. Tony soon put us all in the picture.

"Don't worry; Pedro will ensure that the correct process is followed and that the dog is cared for until I can travel to Glasgow to collect him."

Deirdre's looked a little bit more at ease after Tony had responded to her query.

"You haven't told us how much this is going to cost, Tony", she said casually as she reached for another slice of Victoria Sponge.

"Don't ask," responded Tony.

"It will be worth every penny just to see Mrs Peterson's face light up when we get her beloved Jasper back. Trust me."

Approximately five weeks later, the day had come for Operation Jasper to be implemented. I found myself with Tony, camped out in thick Rhododendron bushes in the local park. We were wearing army-style camouflage jackets and trousers. Tony had gone the whole hog and applied camouflage makeup to his face, too. We were equipped with binoculars, walkie-talkies, a contraption on a stick that resembled a net to catch butterflies, sandwiches and a flask of coffee. Next to us, on the ground, in a small cage, was Diego. There was no doubt about it, Diego was the spitting image of Jasper. It's as if they were twins. Fair play to Pedro. He had fully delivered against the brief he had been given.

Nearby, Deirdre was casually perched on a park bench, pretending to read a book. Suddenly, Tony's walkie-talkie stopped crackling and sprung into life.

"Do you copy?" [Deirdre].

"Affirmative". [Tony]

"Target approaching. Prepare to implement Operation Jasper." [Deirdre]

"Copy." [Tony]

"Over and out." [Deirdre]

The tension in the Rhododendron bushes rose to another level. It was up to Deirdre now. Her role was crucial. If anyone could pull this off, she could. She was ice cool. Deirdre lowered her book as

312

Dougie and Jasper approached the bench. Jasper was off the lead and carrying a stick in his mouth.

"Good morning!" shouted Deirdre as Dougie got closer. "It's Dougie, isn't it?"

Dougie turned to look at Deirdre. He didn't recognise her immediately.

"It's Deirdre Dapper. You taught me to drive a few years ago."

Eventually, the penny dropped with Dougie.

"Ah yes, Deirdre, I remember you now. How are you doing? Are you still a dab hand at 'three-point turns'?" Dougie enquired.

Deirdre smiled. "I'm doing well, thanks. Life is good. I've not seen you in the park before" [this was a blatant lie, as Deirdre had had Dougie under surveillance for the last month as part of Operation Jasper].

"I'm in here most days with the dog," Dougie answered.

To maintain the conversation, Deirdre enquired, "I think you might know my dad, Roger?"

"Ah, that's right, you're Roger's daughter, aren't you. In fact, I bumped into your dad the other day, and we had a catch-up. He's a nice guy."

Jasper was stood patiently on the footpath, waiting for his stick to be thrown.

"What's your dog called?" Deirdre asked, knowing full well what his name was.

"He's called Rocket," Dougie confirmed. "We called him that because he is super-fast. He would chase sticks and balls all day long if we let him. He's great company."

"Do you want me to throw the stick for Rocket?" Deirdre asked.

"Be my guest," replied Dougie.

Deirdre picked up the stick. She held it in the throwing position. Before launching it, at the top of her voice, she started to count backwards, starting from ten. Dougie laughed. He didn't know this was a planned signal to the other members of the Operation Jasper team.

"Brace yourself, Daphne…. brace yourself," whispered Tony.

Suddenly, a stick came clattering into the Rhododendron bushes. We could hear it. We just couldn't see it. The stick got lodged in amongst the large evergreen shrubs rather than dropping to the ground. Seconds later, Jasper appeared. He was just a few yards away from us at the back of the bush. But he didn't seem keen on venturing into the undergrowth.

As soon as Tony gave the signal, I threw a handful of chicken-flavoured dog treats in his direction. Jasper didn't waste any time and began to hoover them up. Whilst he was distracted, Tony made his move and quickly placed the butterfly net over the top of him and then yanked him towards us. He let out a little yelping noise, probably triggered by the surprise. Tony then held onto Jasper tightly whilst I unlocked the cage and pulled out Diego. Whilst the cage door was open, Tony then bundled Jasper in and locked it.

"ROCKET……ROCKET!" shouted Deirdre.

A few seconds passed, then she tried again.

"ROCKET….HERE BOY!" she shouted.

It seemed louder this time. We couldn't see Deirdre but could hear footsteps making their way down the side of the bush. We were praying that these were Deirdre's footsteps rather than Dougie's. Otherwise, Operation Jasper was in jeopardy. Out of nowhere, Deirdre appeared at the back of the bush. She was on her own. She whispered, "Dougie is waiting on the footpath. He didn't want to get his shoes dirty."

Tony carefully handed over Diego to Deirdre. As he did this, Deirdre shouted, at the top of her voice, "OH, THERE YOU ARE ROCKET. YOU NAUGHTY LITTLE DOG. STOP CHASING THOSE SQUIRRELS."

Tony gave Deirdre the thumbs-up signal and then ushered her away. I was bursting with excitement, but knew I had to remain silent. Carrying Diego, Deirdre made her way back to the footpath where Dougie was waiting. This was the crunch moment. Would Diego 'be passed off' as Rocket, or would we be rumbled?

Six weeks of meticulous preparation had gone into planning Operation Jasper. The anticipation was unbearable. From our hiding place in the bush, we could just about hear Deirdre's conversation with Dougie. She explained that Rocket had been distracted by a red squirrel at the back of the bush and was trying to chase it. She also thought that it was probably a good idea to put Rocket on the lead for the remainder of the walk. Her explanation was very convincing.

Thankfully, Dougie didn't seem to question anything Deirdre suggested. This was a huge relief. Deirdre explained she was heading in the same direction as Dougie and offered to walk with him towards the park exit. He was quite happy to do this, and they set off together, with the new Rocket walking with them on his lead.

As soon as their voices faded away, I couldn't contain my joy any longer and whooped with delight and did a jig on the spot. Tony was more wary. As lead of Operation Jasper, he knew we weren't out of the woods yet. Hastily, he put his index finger to his lips. It was my cue to be quiet. I duly did so. Fifteen minutes later, we were all back at Tony's house for a debrief. Tony and I were anxious to see if Deirdre had any feedback. She confirmed that Dougie seemed none the wiser that the two dogs had been swapped. She said he was more interested in talking about parallel parking and reversing around corners, than paying any attention to the dog.

On the face of it, it seemed like Operation Jasper had been successfully implemented. The only thing left to do was to safely deliver Jasper back to his rightful owner, Mrs Peterson. Tony was keen to fulfil this task alone. He knew he may need to bend the truth a little when explaining to Mrs Peterson how he had managed to find Jasper. He was ok with that though. The main thing was that Mrs Peterson and Jasper were about to be reunited.

Reflection and Reminiscing

2021 hadn't been my best year. The passing of mum and dad had been a challenging time for me personally. Life up until that point had been pretty stable. This was a major bump in the road, and it affected my rhythm. For some strange reason, though, I wasn't suffering from overwhelming distress that they had been taken away from me. Truth be told, we never felt that close anyway. This might sound like a weird thing for a daughter to say about her own parents. But it was true. We didn't have that special bond in place where we shared feelings and sought to understand each other. I don't recall having in-depth conversations with them and being my authentic self.

Maybe it was my fault. Someone like me, with an 'airy fairy' personality, may not deserve this kind of relationship and to be taken seriously. Showing compassion, talking about my vulnerability and feeling equally supported was picked up by Deirdre most of the time. As I spent so much time with her, she seemed the obvious choice. However, this kind of support didn't come naturally to her. Saying that, she was more than a capable stand-in for my parents.

What the death of my parents clearly demonstrated, was my lack of independence. I didn't realise how much I relied on them. It was those everyday things like my morning wake up call, cooking meals, paying bills and ironing. It wasn't that I was lazy, I just didn't think about these things or understand how important they were until they were gone. I shouldn't have needed to rely on them really. Not at my age. I was now in my early fifties. I wasn't like Deirdre, an independent woman with her own place, who could deal with everything life threw at her. I was clueless. I hadn't changed or matured, despite being in my early fifties. My only asset, as far as I could see, was that I had become a half decent Mystery Shopper. This was through the ongoing guidance over many years of Uncle Roger. He had persevered with me, and I was really grateful to him for that.

By 2021, both Jasper and Diego had long since died. Jasper went on to outlive Mrs Peterson in the end. Sadly, she died of dementia. Towards the end of Jasper's life, he had trouble breathing, and generally getting around. The reason for this was because he was HUGE. Mrs Peterson's illness meant she kept forgetting that she had fed him, so she was constantly filling up his bowl with dog meat.

Jasper was not one for refusing food, so would devour each meal that was presented to him. At two stone, Jasper was so obese, he had to sleep on a blanket on the living room floor as he could no longer jump on to the sofa. Diego lived out his days with Mr and Mrs Parsons. They never did discover that the two dogs had been switched that day in the park. Also, they could never quite understand why Rocket went from being supersonic to medium paced overnight, and why he started to have a siesta every afternoon!

At the start of 2022, I failed my driving test. It wasn't the first time, either. It was my thirteenth attempt! I was averaging a driving test every two years. I parted company with Dougie after the 'roundabout incident'. Or should I say, Dougie parted company with me. We were coming towards the end of one of my Tuesday afternoon lessons, when we approached a roundabout at the east side of town. It was a roundabout that I had tackled many times previously. As I approached, Dougie gave me a clear instruction to "Go straight over the roundabout."

He was then distracted by something in his Highway Code Manual, and he took his eye off the ball. I thought the advice was a little bit odd, but thought I should do as he had asked, and drove at the roundabout head on, mounted the kerb before landing the car in the flowerbeds in the roundabout's central island. It took three hours to remove the car from the roundabout and the incident made the front page of the local press. Dougie was very embarrassed and too ashamed to show his face at the North of England Driving Instructor's annual awards that particular year!

Since then, I've worked my way through most of the reputable driving instructors in the district, including Vernon's Driving Academy and Topcat School of Driving. Down the years there has been varied reasons for failing my test. The first time I failed my test, I drove out of the test centre on the wrong side of the road [to be fair, it was a very narrow road]. I told the examiner that I had just got back from France, where I had become so immersed in the culture that I'd forgotten which side of the road to drive on. He didn't buy it and it was an instant failure.

Another time I failed my test, I thought a line of parked cars was a line of traffic waiting for the traffic lights to change. After seven excruciating minutes of waiting, the instructor asked me to drive around the parked cars. Again, it was an instant failure. The most bizarre reason for failing my test was when I was distracted by an attractive motorcyclist. A good-looking man on a motorbike caught my attention while I was driving and, without realising, I started to drive directly towards him. The instructor had to enforce an emergency stop as I nearly hit the man on the motorbike. I then blamed the move on my bad eyesight! Some people may refer to this as a 'dizzy blonde moment'. I would refer to it as a 'me' moment. Lacking concentration and being unpredictable is part of who I am.

I'm currently with Patsy's School of Motoring. I thought I was bonkers until I met Patsy Dixon. She's as mad as a box of frogs. Out of all the driving instructors I've spent time with, she is the most fun. Patsy sees me as a challenge and is confident that when it comes to taking my next driving test, it will be fourteenth time lucky!

Decluttering

In March 2022, both Aunty Anthea and Deirdre persuaded Uncle Roger to retire from running the business. They eventually wore him down, after weeks of constant nagging. He should have retired much sooner, but he couldn't seem to let go. He just loved the hustle and bustle of day-to-day business operations. The 'Quiet Customer' was his baby and that's all he had known for the last forty years or so. He was worried that he wouldn't have anything to 'live for' if he stepped down. He didn't have any specific hobbies or pastimes away from work, and that concerned him. Especially as he'd recently read a magazine article, stating that on average, a newly retired person has 14 hours of leisure time to fill each day. This filled him with horror.

The burning question was, who could manage the business if Uncle Roger wasn't at the helm. Someone who thought she might be in the running was Alison Armitage. She had been biding her time and waiting for this day to come along. She thought highly of herself and saw this as an opportunity for promotion. Nobody could touch her when it came to winning employee of the month awards. But was she capable of managing the business itself? And did she have the experience in areas such as negotiating, strategic planning, accounting, legal and marketing? That's what it would take to make a success of it.

To celebrate his retirement, Aunty Anthea booked a holiday in Portugal for herself, Uncle Roger and Deirdre. It would give Uncle Roger a chance to wind down and begin to get used to living a life of leisure. It would also give Uncle Roger a chance to mull over the possible contenders to manage the business, prior to finishing, he had received some job applications, including one from Alison Armitage and planned to assess these applications from the luxury of his sunbed.

It was now nearly nine months since my parents' accident. I hadn't done anything about clearing out mum and dad's personal belongings. Everything was just how they had left it. The wardrobes in the bedroom and spare room were still choc-a-block with their clothes. Their toiletries still took over the entire bathroom cabinets and countertops. The Victorian bookcase, full of dad's encyclopaedias, was gathering dust in the back room. Even the Jane Austen novel my mum was reading was still on the table by the window along with her reading glasses.

Deirdre had offered to help with going through everything, but we could never find the time when we were both available. This kind of task would be right up her street because she was so organised. For me though, the thought of clearing their personal belongings was overwhelming, and I knew I would get sidetracked.

Leading up to the family trip to Portugal, Deirdre convinced me that I should make a start on the clearance and distribution of items whilst she was away. She promised to draft some instructions that would make the task less cumbersome and keep me focused. It made sense to make a start on the task as my Mystery Shopper rota was pretty light the week Uncle Roger was away, and I had some time on my hands.

Deirdre kept to her promise and wrote out a set of instructions that aimed to make the decluttering task easier. She didn't do things by halves, our Deirdre, and the instructions spanned to two pages of A4 notepad paper. I made a cup of tea, sat down in the armchair and started to read through the instructions. My poor concentration levels meant I didn't get to the bottom of the second page. The bits I did remember were that I should aim to work through one room at a time and that I should designate zones for items to donate, sell and throw out. I also had to be kind to myself and take regular breaks, especially if things became too emotional.

With a pocket full of mint imperials to boost my energy levels, the first room I decided to tackle was mum and dad's bedroom. I'd only ventured into the bedroom a couple of times since their passing, and one of those times was to select outfits for their funeral. That wasn't an easy task, and after consulting with Deirdre we agreed on dad's favourite pin stripe suit, and for mum, it was her favourite powder blue floral dress. Now it was time to empty the contents of the wardrobe they shared. The wardrobe was dark brown polished oak with brass swan neck drop handles. Apart from the odd scratch here and there, it was in reasonable condition in view of its age. They'd bought it in the 1970's soon after they were married.

A concoction of aromas hit me as I opened the wardrobe doors. Floral scents of hyacinth, jasmine and white lily combined with the musky scents of sandalwood and vanilla of mum's Charlie Blue perfume competing against the distinctive clean smell of dad's

Brylcreem. The musty smell of a storage space rarely opened was also part of the equation.

The contents inside the wardrobe were methodically organised. That would probably be mum's influence. Everything had its place. Mum's garments to the right of the hanging rail and dads to the left. Some items that were carefully placed onto the bed triggered fond memories, particularly key events or family occasions. Mum's long burgundy sleeve dress generated thoughts of Aunty Anthea's seventieth birthday meal at the plush Manor House Hotel on the banks of the River Wear. She spilled some mushroom soup on the outfit during the first course, then fretted everyone would comment on it for the rest of the meal, particularly Anthea's sister Cynthia. Dad's blue and yellow checked shirt was the one he was wearing on the photo on the mantelpiece downstairs. On the photo, he was looking ever so smug with himself at the summit of Scafell Pike, after conquering it for the first time.

The lower level of the wardrobe was split. On my father's side of the wardrobe, it comprised two drawers, where on my mother's side, it was an open compartment. I needed to crouch down to empty the open compartment properly. Based on the contents, it looked like my mother had commandeered this space in the wardrobe. It was a heap of random items such as dress belts, summer footwear, scarves, swimwear, and hats, some of which, I'd never seen before.

Just when I thought I had retrieved all the items, I could feel there was something else at the back of the compartment. This didn't feel like clothing or clothing accessories. It was rectangle shaped and felt like it was made of wood. I struggled to get my fingers underneath it, so slid it towards me so I could get a better view of it. I lifted the item out and there in my hands I was gazing at a hand painted hinged box. The box lid was made up of a gorgeous design and intricate carvings inspired from traditional oriental culture. I'd never seen the box before. What was it? Initially, I thought it might be a container my mother used to store her heirloom jewellery. How wrong I was. It's contents shocked me to core.

Who am I?

I opened the box lid carefully. A small number of items were cushioned by the box's velvet interior. Staring up at me was a photo of a baby. I picked it up to inspect it closer. The style and condition of the photo gave me the impression it wasn't recent. It was creased around the edges and looked like it had been handled many times.

The baby in the photo was wrapped in a white shawl. There was a strong resemblance to me. I turned over the photo. There was a date on the back. 16th June 1968. That was the same date as my birthday. Something wasn't right and I could feel my body temperature begin to rise. In the quietness of the bedroom, I could hear my heartbeat bumping along.

I picked up the second item. It was a turquoise and white coloured cot card. Something that may have been used to identify newborns on a hospital labour ward. The card included the following details: first name, last name, date and time of birth, gender and birth weight. The infant's name was Philippa Price. The date, time of birth, and birth weight written on the card were identical to mine. I had always known my birth time was 12 noon and that my birth weight was 6lb 6oz, as they were so easy to remember. Here I was sat on the floor of the bedroom holding a photo of a baby, with the baby's identification details identical to mine, except for the baby's name.

My mind was racing. One question after another. Was this baby me? If it wasn't me, who was it? How was it, that nobody had ever mentioned a Philippa Price before? None of what was before me made sense.

The final two items were neatly folded into thirds. They were discoloured due to age and were now an off-white shade. I unfolded the first document and began to absorb the information in front of me. It was a birth certificate. My eyes darted from side to side, skimming the content as I went. I started to talk out the words quietly, as I read them. I didn't consciously do this, it just happened.

"Name: Philippa Daphne Price. Date of birth: 16th June 1968 at Bolton District General Hospital Farnworth. Name and surname of father: Jack Raymond Jones, a trainee mechanic of 67 Duckworth Street, Atherton. Name and surname of mother: Pauline Ann Price, a factory worker of 67 Duckworth Street, Atherton".

I didn't hesitate and quickly moved to the final document in the box. I found myself talking out the words quietly to myself again, starting with the title of the document.

"Certified copy of an entry in the Adopted Children Register. Date and country of birth of child; 16th June 1968, Farnworth, Townleys. Name and surname of child: Daphne Carmel Dapper. Name and surname, address and occupation of adopter or adoptees: John Sheridan Dapper, 246 Swingpump Road, Stanhope, County Durham, Local Government Officer and Brenda Dapper, his wife. Date of adoption order: 18 December 1968. Date of entry: 8th January 1969".

I sat down on the floor in an ungainly heap. I didn't really do crying. But a teardrop rolled slowly down my right cheek and onto the document in my hand. Even someone as scatty as me, could work out what the contents of the box meant. I was ADOPTED! There was no doubt about it. It was there in black and white. But I had never been told. Here I was at the grand old age of 54 finding it out for the first time. I was completely stunned.

I had no inclination that my parents weren't my biological parents. I stared at the document again. The words began to fade out and were replaced by a powerful mental image. The image was of the little boy with ginger hair in the back of the Morris Traveller on the isolated road in the Scottish Highlands. We'd locked eyes that day. We had a connexion. He looked so different to the rest of his family. I think he must have been adopted too. I just didn't know it at the time. His image faded and I found myself once again staring at the document I was clutching. It had only been a matter of seconds, but it had been enough time for more teardrops to roll down my face. That urge to declutter at the start of the day, no longer seemed important. It was time to halt proceedings and absorb the information I had just accidentally stumbled across.

A few minutes later, I was downstairs. I was sat in the armchair clutching a cup of tea. I couldn't stop staring at a photograph on the mantelpiece. The photo was of my parents on their wedding day. I put my tea down on the pine coffee table next to me, stood up and walked towards it. I lifted the photograph up, tilted it back and began to bombard them with questions, as if they were physically in the room and could hear me.

"Why didn't you tell me that you had adopted me?" I cried.

"Had you just not found the right moment?"

"Surely you were going to tell me one day?" I asked softly.

"Well, I know now. I suppose I'd just better get on with my life then, as if nothing has happened, hadn't I? That's not going to be as easy as you think."

And I carefully put the photo back in its place and sat down. By now, my tea was a reasonable temperature to drink, and took a couple of decent sized slurps. I contemplated what I should do next. I needed to talk this through with someone. The obvious choice was Deirdre. I always talked to Deirdre about important issues. And this issue was massive. But she was away in Portugal with Uncle Roger and Aunty Anthea. They had only been there a couple of days and didn't want to disturb their holiday. I know I wasn't one for thinking things through too deeply, but even I knew it wouldn't be fair to drop this bombshell on them whilst on vacation. Following his retirement, Uncle Roger deserved a stress-free holiday, despite my newfound information that his niece was an adopted person.

Tony, next door was the other option, but he had mentioned he had been asked to cover somebody else's hours and was working night shifts. He didn't particularly enjoy working nights. It tended to make him grumpy and wasn't much fun to be around, so I thought it best not to bother him. For the time being, I decided it was best to keep the information to myself.

Over the next few days, I pondered, then pondered some more, about the fact I had accidentally discovered I was an adoptee. My thoughts were only interrupted when I attended mystery shopping assignments that were in the diary. One assignment was a visit to a well-established family-run bakery business, and the other to the independent cinema, in town. Both assignments provided a welcome distraction to the ever-growing list of questions that were slowly filling up my brain and making it feel foggy. Apart from the obvious question [why didn't my parents tell me I was adopted?], others soon followed. It was not too dissimilar to conveyor belts that are used on production lines. Only these weren't manufactured products that were continuously travelling towards me one after another; they were questions, none of which I knew the answers to. Questions on my imaginary conveyor belt included things like:

Why did my parents choose to adopt?

Was it not possible to have children of their own?

What happened to me during the period [6 months] of being born and arriving with my new family?

Who were my biological parents?

What were they like?

Why did they decide to give me up?

Are they still alive?

If they are still alive, should I search for them?

Have they ever tried searching for me?

What would they think about me if we met?

What would I think about them?

The questions were endless.

A few days later, on the Friday evening, I received a call from Deirdre. I was surprised she was ringing as they were due to fly back from Portugal the following evening. She felt the call couldn't wait until she got back. During our daily exchange of text messages, she sensed I wasn't myself and wanted to know if I was OK. Although I was still clueless with technology, I could just about manage to send text messages and Deirdre had picked up that my messages weren't as rambling and scatty as normal. I'd usually witter on about unimportant stuff such as the price of cat food or the contents of my fruit bowl. She was very astute and had spotted something that concerned her.

I lied during the call and pretended everything was fine, when obviously it wasn't. Still, I didn't reveal the shattering news I'd uncovered about the adoption. At the end of the call, Deirdre made a promise to call round to the house as soon as she got back to the UK.

Later that evening, I was flicking through a family photo album. I'd come across it when I was beginning to declutter the bedroom a few days earlier. I'd seen it several times before, but not for some time. The album had some age to it and showed signs of wear and tear. It contained mainly black and white family photographs from years ago.

Mum had written descriptions under some of the photos, as a reminder. 'A day trip to South Shields – 1971', 'Dad sunbathing on holiday – Benidorm 1980' and 'Opening presents on Christmas day – 1974' were some of the captions she'd scrawled in that familiar handwriting of hers. One particular photo caught my attention though. It was labelled 'Holidaying with Roger, Anthea & Deirdre – Scarboro 1971'. The photo was of both families posing for a photo on the promenade at the popular seaside destination. I was in a pram holding what looked to be the remains of an ice cream cornet. My face was plastered in the stuff. I'd probably be about two or three years of age, depending on whether the photo was taken pre or post June of that year. Deirdre was in the photo too. She was wearing sunglasses and holding a black and white football under her arm. She 'd only be about six years old but looked so grown up. Dad must have asked a passer-by to take the photo as he was on it too.

Analysing the photo, the difference in family dynamics stood out like a sore thumb. Uncle Roger, Aunty Anthea and Deirdre were huddled together and were openly expressing their affection for each other. There wasn't that touchy-feely vibe radiating from mum, dad and me. We were very much posing without any bodily contact. Maybe that lack of bond or strong connection between us, that I'd experienced as I moved through adolescence into adulthood, could have been prevalent during childhood too. For a split second, I felt totally dejected.

The feeling of dejection soon lifted when I looked at the photo again. This time I was looking at Uncle Roger. He looked so slim back in the day. Not carrying all that weight like he is now. He scrubbed up quite well. No wonder Aunty Anthea was swept off her feet by him.

Spilling the Beans

Something then happened that doesn't happen that often. It was a lightbulb moment. A moment of realisation. I could have kicked myself for it not coming to me sooner. Uncle Roger and Aunty Anthea will know I'm adopted. They must do. They hung out together with my parents all the time. They went out as a foursome when they were courting. Dad and Uncle Roger were brothers for god's sake. If anybody could shed any light about this adoption, then it had to be them. This lifted my spirits. I went to bed that evening in a positive frame of mind.

The next day I popped into town for some cat food for Columbus. These days, he was eating cat food specially designed for senior cats aged 7 years plus. I should really have bought in bulk, but as I was travelling back home by bus, I was limited in how much I could carry.

On the way back to the bus stop, I stopped outside a tattoo shop and gazed through the window. It was the same tattoo shop I had frequented a few years earlier for my own tattoo. A likeable-looking guy with greyish hair was sprawled face down across the black leather couch. He was wearing a grey t-shirt and black shorts. His choice of tattoo looked to be some sort of coat of arms incorporating a greyhound type dog, three hares and the word 'Fideliter.' Unless he had tattoos hidden by his clothing, this tattoo appeared to be his first. It was fascinating to watch the tattoo artist in action as she meticulously dragged the needles across his skin. I was mesmerised.

Suddenly, the tattoo artist stood up, reached for her tin of baccy on the table next to her, then stepped outside the shop and stood next to me on the pavement. It was the same tattooist who'd done my tattoo, a petite lady who whiffed of Patchouli oil and roll-up cigarettes. She didn't make eye contact and didn't seem to mind me gawping through the shop window. A few moments passed as she went through the process of rolling herself a cigarette. You could tell by the precision; she had done it thousands of times before.

"Are you still liking your landskilpadde?" she asked.

I was taken aback by the question.

"Ooh yes, definitely," I answered, without really considering the question and understanding what she was referring to.

She'd sussed I didn't have a clue what she was talking about.

"It's Norwegian for Tortoise," she said confidently. "If I recall, you have one tattooed on your backend."

Gosh, she'd remembered me. I was very impressed. There must have been hundreds of customers she's tattooed since I was last in her shop. She had a couple more drags on her roll-up, then re-entered the shop to attend to her customer. It was time for me to go home and feed Columbus.

I wasn't home long when I heard a familiar voice.

"OK, out with it Daphne Dapper. Spill the beans; tell me what's going on."

Deirdre had called round after returning from holiday, and she demanded answers.

"You can't fool me, Daphne; I've known you too long. Why were you acting weird when we were in Portugal and sending very curt text messages. Has something happened? This had better be good because I haven't even unpacked my suitcases. I just left them in the hallway at home and came here straight away."

"You'd better sit down," I said.

She looked at me with those big hazel-brown eyes. I think she sensed something was amiss. She slowly sat down on the two-seater settee. I handed her the hand-painted box.

"I found this at the back of the wardrobe when I started to declutter mum and dad's bedroom. I think you had better take a look inside it."

Deirdre half-heartedly inspected the box before adding,

"And this is the reason you've been acting weird. Because of the contents inside this box?" she asked.

I nodded furiously.

Deirdre lifted the lid gently. Just like I had done almost a week earlier. Firstly, she picked up the photo of the baby. She stared at it intensely. Then she casually turned it over. I don't think she expected to see anything on the other side, but it revealed the date: 16th June 1968. She didn't say anything, but she was smart and no doubt she'd clocked the date was my birthday. She next picked up the turquoise and white coloured cot card. She scrutinised it closely. Her face was emotionless. She looked towards me.

"Your birth weight was 6lb 6oz wasn't it, Daphne?"

I nodded. The third item she picked up was the birth certificate. Her eyes darted back and forth as she analysed every word. Her eyes then stopped darting to and fro. She seemed to be transfixed by the information in the central part of the document. The column that named Philippa Price's mother and father. Eventually, she put the birth certificate to one side and reached for the last item in the box: the Adoption Registration Document. Within seconds of scrutinizing the final document, the penny had dropped. She looked towards me and blurted, "Jesus Christ Daphne, you were adopted. According to this, your biological parents are called Jack Jones and Pauline Price! No wonder you've been acting weird for the past few days."

Having this information confirmed by Deirdre set me off. I burst out crying. I'd kept this information all to myself for almost a week. The pent-up emotion just came out. I was like a bottle of bubbly that had just had its cork removed. Deirdre held open her arms. I didn't hesitate and hugged her tightly. I'd not been this close to anyone for a long time. The last time was probably at my parent's funeral. I received lots of sympathy hugs that particular day. The faint aroma of suntan oil from her holiday in Portugal clung to her clothing and skin. The smell wasn't unpleasant. In fact, it was quite fragrant. I sobbed uncontrollably. With my head on her shoulder, my tears disappearing into her hair. She reassured me that everything would be ok. Her soothing words worked and before long we were sat down having a cup of tea chatting things through.

"Did you have any inclination that I was adopted, Deirdre?"

"No, not really", she replied.

"It had crossed my mind once or twice over the years that you didn't seem to resemble Aunty Brenda and Uncle John very much. But I just put it down to one of those things, I suppose, especially as mum and dad had never mentioned it either. From my experience, most people who are adopted are told at a relatively young age, and generally, most of the immediate family are aware of the situation. To keep something like that under wraps from those close to you would probably be quite difficult, I imagine. Deirdre hesitated for a moment, before adding, "and have you noticed, Daphne, that your original birth name was Philippa? It's the name you have adored and always wanted. The irony is that for the first six months of your life, that's what you were called. What are the chances of that?"

I smiled and felt a warmness inside.

"Yeh, what are the chances of that. I'm still coming to terms with it all" I replied.

Deirdre disappeared into the kitchen. Probably to make another cup of tea. All of a sudden there was a shriek followed by some commotion. I rushed into the kitchen to find Deirdre with her hand under the cold-water tap.

"What's happened," I asked frantically.

"I was making a cup of tea, and I wasn't concentrating, and I poured some boiling water on my hand. I wasn't concentrating because I was thinking about you and this adoption thing. I've had a thought. I can't believe I didn't think of this sooner."

"Think of what sooner?", I asked tentatively.

"Mum and dad. They are bound to know all about this. My dad and your dad are brothers for crying out loud. They must know something. Pass me the Aloe vera gel, Daphne."

She grimaced as she rubbed some gel on the affected area. Then she turned and headed for the front door, shouting as she went,

"Hang in there Daphne. I'll be back as soon as I can and hopefully, I'll have my dad with me!"

Confession time

It wasn't until mid-afternoon that Deirdre returned. Uncle Roger was in tow. Similar to Deirdre he was sporting a lovely tan following their week in Portugal. We made a pot of tea and sat round the dining table. Uncle Roger didn't seem his normal self though. He would normally be joking around or poking fun at me. That was the way he operated. I loved him and I loved the relationship we had. I hoped this adoption thing wasn't going to affect the bond we had together.

Deirdre did the honours and filled each of our mugs with tea. Uncle Roger was looking a little bit sheepish, and this added to the somewhat awkward atmosphere in the room. As Deirdre began to slice into some shop bought carrot cake, Uncle Roger started to speak. It was unusual to listen to him talk about something other than Mystery Shopper assignments. His voice was quavering.

"Daphne, Deirdre informs me that whilst we were in Portugal, you stumbled across some important information when clearing out your mum and dad's wardrobe. I understand the information is linked to your adoption. Is this correct Daphne?"

I could feel myself welling up again, so I just nodded.

"Well, I can confirm that you were adopted as a baby. I'm really sorry that you have had to find out this information the way you did. I wish you hadn't. And now for me, this is the really awkward bit. I'm really, really sorry to tell you Daphne, that I have always known you were adopted. Aunty Anthea has known this too."

Deirdre and I glanced at each other. Despite her glowing suntan, it didn't hide the fact that Deirdre was blushing with embarrassment at what her dad was confessing to. Uncle Roger had acknowledged his daughter's embarrassment.

"There's a few more things I'd like to say that I think you should know. If it gets too much Daphne, please stop me, as I know this can't be easy for you. I can't explain why my brother and sister-in-law didn't tell you that you were adopted. We chatted about it many times over the years. I explained to them that you had a right to know. Every time I asked if they had broached the subject with you, I used to get the same response from your dad, which was, 'all in good time Roger, all in good time'.

"By the time you reached your twenties, I stopped pestering them about it because I knew I was wasting my time. It has crossed my mind once or twice whether I should tell you myself that you are adopted. But this wasn't my responsibility. The responsibility was with your parents. I have felt guilty knowing the situation for all these years and not being able to do anything about it. I have tried to deal with the guilt by supporting you in other ways such as involving you in the family business and helping with your driving lessons. I hope you understand. I've been longing this day to arrive for almost 55 years. It's a relief. I also wanted to say that Deirdre had no knowledge of the adoption until you told her earlier today. That's the truth. She is as surprised as you are."

Uncle Roger took a big gulp of tea and reached out for a piece of carrot cake. Deirdre gave him a look of disapproval. She was always encouraging him to cut out the sweet stuff and think more about his bulging waistline. With a mouthful of cake, he said,

"All this information must be very confusing and is a lot for you to absorb, so I think I'll pause for now. I feel uneasy about leaving you here on your own with all this on your mind. Do you want to come and stay with us for a few days. Aunty Anthea will make up the spare bed."

"No, I'll be alright here. I'd prefer to be on my own and think things through."

"Ok, we can continue to chat over the coming days and weeks. There's bound to be things that crop up that you want to talk about. After all, it's not every day you are told you are adopted. Have you anything you would like to ask me before I go?" he asked.

"There is one thing," I replied. "Have you any information about my biological parents?"

"I'm afraid not, Daphne," Roger replied swiftly. "As far as I'm aware, the adoption was organised through a third party so I don't think your parents would have come into contact with the biological parents. If they are still alive, they will probably be a similar age to me. Deirdre might be able to assist with any historical searches if that was of interest. She is into all that genealogy stuff. Isn't that right Deirdre?"

"It's called the Durham Family History Group, dad, and yes, I'm still a member. Daphne knows I'll support her where I can."

Deirdre and Uncle Roger stood up to leave. Deirdre gestured that she would phone me later. Then, just like Deirdre had done earlier, this time it was Uncle Roger who held out his arms. I needed a hug more than ever, so I didn't hesitate. It was like hugging a big soft teddy bear.

"No matter what happens going forward, Daphne, I'm still your Uncle Roger, and I'll always be here for you. Don't you forget that," he clarified.

"I won't, and I'll always be your crazy niece, Daphne," I said.

We hugged again.

Acceptance, the truth and a half-eaten Vanilla Slice

Accepting I was an adopted person was an ongoing process and took some time to get used to. After all, it had happened so quickly. One minute I was emptying a wardrobe as a non-adopted person. A couple of minutes later I was faced with the same task, as an adopted person. How the heck do you cope with that?

The following few weeks and months were difficult. Waking up every morning knowing I was adopted didn't exactly fill me with joy. I used to wake up every morning with this happy go lucky demeanour and untroubled. Not now. Now, my mind was on auto pilot, and I was unable to change its course of travel. Each morning, we'd go on a journey together….whether I liked it or not. The list of questions, then sub questions, was endless. Our journeys could be quite focused. The most recent one was about clarity on my 'identity'. Who was I? I began my life as a Price, albeit for a short while. Then I became a Dapper. Effectively, I'd had a foot in both camps. What would Philippa Daphne Price have turned out like, given the opportunity? How would she have been shaped? I wonder if she would have 26 pairs of red shoes and have an extensive earring collection. At the moment, I feel like a Dapper, but who knows. Maybe this 'identity' thing will change over time.

Each day, it was easy to become overwhelmed with strong emotional feelings linked to my newfound situation. Feelings ranged from anger, betrayal, abandonment, frustration and even loneliness. The first six months were the worst. On a positive note, at least I had people close to me who were there to provide support.

Tony Mathew, Uncle Roger and Aunty Anthea all did their bit to act as a sounding board and offer words of comfort. The mystery shopper assignments and driving lessons helped too. Deirdre was the star of the show though. She came round most days. We talked a lot. She was a great listener and helped me deal with my emotions. She aways had the knack of saying the right thing.

We talked about delving into my biological family history and seeing what we could discover. I even accompanied her to one of the Durham Family History Group meetings she attended. This kind of thing confused the hell out of me, but Deirdre was fascinated by research, and I gave her permission to press ahead on my behalf. If anyone could discover more about my past, she could. I had every faith in her.

Sometimes this resulted in me providing signatures or speaking to people on the phone [with Deirdre present] to confirm she was acting as my intermediary. One day she turned up at the house with a package. It contained a test tube which I had to fill with saliva. I thought it was a strange request but knew it was in my best interests, so I was happy to go along with it.

On the 9th December 2022, Deirdre turned up the house carrying a blue arch lever file and a paper bag containing an assortment of cream cakes. She'd obviously come past the bakery on route. The paper bag contained vanilla slices, iced fingers, apple turnovers and suchlike. We'd exchanged text messages earlier in the day, so I knew to expect her. The message hinted that she was hoping to update me on the research into my biological parents, Jack Jones and Pauline

Price. Together, with her friends from the Durham Family History Group, they had managed to source key information about their lives. I was extremely excited, albeit somewhat nervous. Sat around the dining table, Deirdre started to explain what had been discovered. She was ever so gentle with me.

"Daphne, when we talked about undertaking research into your family history, do you recall me mentioning that you should prepare yourself for both positive and negative outcomes?"

I nodded cautiously and soon tuned in to the tone of the conversation, and the somewhat ominous direction it was going. This didn't sound too hopeful, I thought, even to a scatty individual like me.

Deirdre continued, "I'm pleased to say that with the help of Ginette, from the Family History Group, we have managed to trace your biological parents, Jack and Pauline."

Deirdre's facial expression was slightly apprehensive, and I could sense a 'but' was just around the corner. And I was right.

"There is no easy way of telling you this Daphne, I'm afraid they have both passed away. Sadly, we have discovered that they both died in a house fire. This incident happened shortly after giving you up for adoption. They were residing at the time in the Bolton area of Lancashire. I'm really sorry, Daphne. I really am."

I sat there motionless. I felt like crying, but no tears would come. The half-eaten vanilla slice on the plate in front of me didn't seem that appetising anymore. Deep down, I had known there was a possibility they may not be alive. But to be told they had died when I was only a baby was totally unexpected. I was empty. I was helpless. I felt dead inside. I stared at my half eaten cream cake, not really knowing what to say or do next. Deirdre broke the silence.

"We have established some further information about Jack and Pauline from the records that we have been able to access. Would you like me to go through this with you now, Daphne, or do you want me to leave this until another day? You've had a lot to take in over the last few minutes."

I stopped staring at the cream cake and nodded.

"Ok Daphne, I'll continue, but just let me know if you would like me to pause or if you want me to stop."

She added, "At the time of their death, they were both 21 years old and had been in a relationship for about 18 months. The adoption file states that Pauline had a strained relationship with her family. She had left the family home at 18 after her father physically abused her. He liked his drink and was always in the pub. This often resulted in him being involved in brawls, and he was well known to the police.

"At the time of your birth, Jack and Pauline were living together in a rented room in a large townhouse. They were both working full-time, but financially, it was a real struggle for them. Pauline worked in a nearby factory that made confectionary, and Jack was an apprentice mechanic in a garage close to where they lived. Neither of them was well paid. They were loathed to give you up but didn't feel they had any other option. With no money and no family support network around them, they felt you would have a better chance with another family.

"They stayed together after you had been adopted. There is little information about how the house fire started. The newspaper clipping doesn't provide much detail. They weren't the only ones to perish, though. Other tenants in the building died, too."

Deirdre passed across the blue file she had brought with her.

"This is for you. It contains all the information Ginette and I have been able to source so far. There are copies of birth/death certificates, death registration records, an adoption file, newspaper clippings and other documents you may be interested in. The one thing we haven't been able to source are photos of Jack and Pauline, but we'll keep trying. I'm sure we'll come across some sooner or later.

"There's one more thing Daphne. As Ginette scoured the information and records available to us, she picked up on something else. She noticed in the Parish records that someone else shares the same birth date as you. 16th June 1968. They also share your original surname, Price. She is going to delve into this further when she gets the chance."

"Right, I'm going to go now. We can catch up tomorrow after I've been to hockey training."

As she stood up to leave, she said,

"I know that some of the information that has been shared with you today has been pretty grim. But hopefully, we can uncover information about your biological family that is much more positive. There are bound to be people out there who you are biologically connected to. Leave it with me."

And then she winked at me, before heading off.

Tying up loose ends

Because of the news about the adoption, and of the fate of my biological parents, Christmas was a bit of a washout. This was a shame as I normally fully enter into the spirit of the festive season. After Christmas, the weeks flew in and before I knew it, Spring had arrived.

Easter 2023 was memorable. It was memorable, as a miracle happened. I passed my driving test! Good old Patsy Dixon of Patsy's School of Motoring had managed to get me to a place that no other driving instructor had managed to do. It was unbelievable. Even Graham Chaffinch, the test examiner, whom I was on first name terms with as we crossed paths 13 times before, couldn't believe I had passed. I was suffering from 'twitching toes' leading up to the test and thought it might hinder my chances. However, Tony Mathew came to the rescue by giving me a herbal remedy which seemed to do the trick and calm my toes down.

The world record set for 'failed driving tests', which I understood to be 771 and held by a woman in South Korea was now no longer in danger. Patsy sees me as one of her greatest achievements and every time we bump into each other in the supermarket, she becomes ecstatic, dashes towards me and gives me a huge hug.

Tony Mathew now has a new female companion in his life. He met her on an online dating site. She is called Janice. Like Mrs Peterson used to, Janice can also knock out some home-produced treats. Her triple chocolate cake is to die for. Her Victoria Sponge cake isn't half bad either. As a result, Tony's cake tin is always full to brimming.

Tony is approaching his 60th birthday. He's been considering retirement for a while now and on the countdown to this, has reduced his working hours to just two shifts a week. Working reduced hours means Tony can spend more time with Janice. They are always heading off on adventures together. There is generally a tale to tell on their return. Their most recent adventure was a mini break to Barcelona and unsurprisingly, another drama ensued. They had just enjoyed a coffee following a visit to the famous Picasso Museum. They then returned to the multi-story car park where their hire car was parked. Due to the car park being busy on their arrival, they had to park on the top floor. Unfortunately, there weren't any toilets in the car park and Tony desperately needed a wee. The only place out of sight of other people was on the car park staircase, so he made his way there. He knew he shouldn't, but he was desperate. Really desperate. At the same time as relieving himself, he unwittingly created a tropical rainforest environment for those on the staircase below. After that, he and Janice left the car park pretty sharpish and in fits of laughter.

Uncle Roger is enjoying life after work. There was a concern, especially from Aunty Anthea, that he wouldn't take to retirement, but this was ill founded. He is absolutely loving it. One of the ways he is spending his leisure time is metal detecting. He was introduced to the hobby by his good friend Martin Lock, an acquaintance he'd met through work. Martin invited Uncle Roger out on one of his detecting permissions. He borrowed one of Martin's spare detectors and has been hooked with the hobby ever since. He has now bought himself his own detector along with accessories such as a pinpointer, finds pouch, spade and metal detecting trowel with holster. He certainly looks the part.

Aunty Anthea gave him an old ice cream tub to store all his finds in. It's now full of buttons, buckles, coins, bits of lead, musket balls, gunshot cartridges, ring pulls and unknown objects he dug up on nearby farmland. Deirdre helps him to research the stuff he finds. She is red-hot at that kind of thing. It takes her no time at all. His oldest find to date is a copper-alloy beehive thimble dating back to the 16th century.

Although Uncle Roger had stepped down from day-to-day operations at the Quiet Customer, he still owns the business outright, and is keen the business is managed effectively and makes a profit. The person he appointed as his replacement, was Alison Armitage. This was a decision he soon regretted. Soon after landing the role, she started to put her own stamp on things and began to implement the odd change here and there. These changes weren't welcome by other staff, particularly Judith Longstaff. Judith didn't think Alison was cut out for the position in the first place and voiced her concern in no uncertain terms to all who would listen, but out of earshot of Uncle Roger.

"You can't make a silk purse out of a sow's ear" was one of the phrases she used to express her displeasure at the new appointment.

The first change made by Alison was to axe the 'employee of the month' award. She texted all staff with her decision, explaining that the award represented 'individualism' rather than the 'encouragement of teamwork'. All the staff could see right through this decision and knew what she was really up to. Essentially, if she wasn't able to win the award anymore, nobody else was going to either. She was going to make damn sure of that.

A few months into the role and at the end of her probation period, Uncle Roger had seen enough and brought her short reign to an end, giving the following reasons for her dismissal: losing control of the finances, lack of strategy, weak leadership and poor decision making. Alison was out of her depth and went quietly. Apparently, she landed a role with one of Uncle Roger's competitors 'Close Inspection' and is back winning 'employee of the month' awards with her latest employer on a regular basis!

The blue arch lever file given to me by Deirdre, sat unopened on the dining room table for the next couple of weeks. I needed a little bit of time to get used to the idea that my biological parents had passed, before fully engrossing myself in the details of how exactly my adoption unfolded. I knew it was going to be a difficult read and I had to be right mentally. One rainy Sunday morning I felt I was in the right frame of mind to start working my way through the information in the file.

Reading this material in black and white was so emotional. The information was written in the late sixties. The style of writing was different. There were no holds barred. It told it how it was. Some of

353

the phrases used, particularly in the adoption file, were hard hitting. There was no room for sentiment. It must have been a heartbreaking experience for Jack and Pauline. Understanding the rationale for giving me up was comforting. Giving up your baby must be one of the hardest things anybody can do. There was certainly no contempt or ill feeling towards them on my part. They had a really difficult decision to make, and they made it for the right reasons. They simply gave me a better chance in life than I would have had, had I stayed with them. Essentially, from what I read, they seemed a sweet young couple who deeply cared about each other. If I'd have stayed with them, I may have perished in the house fire too.

Normally, I was pretty useless at reading lots of information and maintaining my concentration, but this stuff was riveting and held my attention. Strangely, reading about my biological parents and understanding more about them helped me better connect to them, albeit the connection was spiritual. As I trawled through the text, there was a sentence that stood out from all the rest. It was on page 5 in my adoption file from 1968. Pauline had said,

"I will always love my gorgeous Philippa and will meet her again one day in the future. I hope she forgives us."

To read this, warmed my soul. At long last, emotionally, I began to feel part of a family for the first time in my life. It was amazing.

Mystery Trip

It was the 10th July 2023 and Deirdre still hadn't explained where we were destined for on our mystery trip. We boarded a train at Newcastle train station that was bound for London Euston. The only thing I could establish from that, was that we were heading south. The only instruction I was given prior to the trip was to pack enough clothes and toiletries for a two-night stay.

Deirdre was preoccupied on the train journey. She was constantly on her phone sending messages. No sooner had one message been sent, she was on to the next. She was tapping out the messages faster than I'd ever seen before. She was in the zone, and I didn't interfere. My phone on the other hand remained silent.

London Euston station was bustling as we worked our way through the overcrowded central hall, pulling our brand new four-wheeled suitcases behind us. Deirdre had purchased the suitcases prior to the trip. Her case was black and mine was bright pink. We made our way down the escalators towards London Underground in search of the Victoria Line bound for Oxford Circus and were soon hit by that unmistakeable smell of the underground system. A warm blanket consisting of a mix of dust and grease and something vaguely metallic. A distinctive smell but not unpleasant.

Within a couple of minutes there was a rumbling sound coming from the darkness to our left. The train speedily rattled into the station, creating a vacuum of warm wind throughout the platform, accentuating that unique underground aroma. The brakes hissed and screeched as the tube train slowed down to a stop. The doors slid open revealing a carriage crammed full of passengers. We squeezed on, packed in like sardines. This annoyed Deirdre as she couldn't attend to the constant stream of messages that continued to arrive on her mobile phone. The notification messages were relentless. Where are all these messages are coming from? I thought to myself.

In the packed carriage, everyone kept themselves to themselves. Many were plugged into electrical devices and in their own little world. I took notice of other passengers; their appearance and what they were wearing. Outfits and styles I'd never come across before. It was a different scene to what I was used to. But I liked it. I didn't feel out of place. With my own unique style, I was one of them, only a northern version.

Within half an hour, we'd arrived at our accommodation. It was a plush hotel with an impressive façade. A tall woman wearing an olive-green uniform greeted us with genuine smile. Her English was fluent although she probably originated from elsewhere in the world, possibly Eastern Europe. Checking in was a smooth affair. They were expecting us, and our details soon appeared on their booking system. Deirdre asked me to go and find the hotel bar and restaurant whilst she had a quiet word with the lady on reception, so I made myself scarce. I got the feeling she wanted me out of the way for a few minutes. She was up to something and had been on edge all day. When I returned, the receptionist was giving Deirdre directions on how to get to our room.

"You are on the second floor. As you come out of the lift, turn right, through the double doors and your room is third on the right. It's number 219" she explained.

We thanked her and made our way to the room.

The hotel room was pretty standard and included a double and single bed, private bathroom, desk, armchair, cupboard, television, telephone and coffee and tea making facilities. Deirdre placed her suitcase on the single bed as if to claim that one. She looked tense. She then glanced at her watch.

"Daphne, we have just under half an hour to freshen up. I've booked us a table for dinner in the hotel restaurant. Does that sound ok?" she asked.

I considered questioning her about her rather odd behaviour over the last few hours but thought better of it.

"Yes, I'll be ready. I think I'll change out of this outfit I've been travelling in."

I rummaged in my suitcase to find my yellow dress decorated with rabbits. Before long we were stepping out of the lift and back in the hotel lobby. I was just about to head in the direction of the hotel restaurant when Deirdre gently took hold of my arm and started to steer me away from the restaurant. We were heading to some unmarked double doors.

"The hotel restaurant is over there Deirdre. We are going the wrong way."

Deirdre smiled. It was the first time she had looked at ease all day. I could see out of the corner of my eye that the woman receptionist had been joined by some other hotel staff and was looking across in my direction as if they were in anticipation of something happening. We stopped at the double doors and Deirdre turned to face me.

"Daphne, you have been probably wondering why I organised this trip to London. Well, I have a confession to make. I have a big surprise for you. A few weeks ago, do you remember when I said to you, there are bound to be people out there who you are biologically connected to?"

I nodded cautiously.

"Do you also remember when you gave me two samples of your saliva?"

I nodded again.

"Well, I sent those saliva samples off to two DNA companies for testing. Your DNA results provided a number of matches. I knew how disappointed you were to hear of Jack and Pauline's passing and that you felt so alone and didn't have anyone in the world who you were biologically related to. I wanted to do something about it. Something that would make a huge difference and put a smile on your face. I hope you don't mind, Daphne, but I've been working behind the scenes on your behalf and have made contact with lots of people who you were matched to. Do you mind?"

I started to get giddy.

"I don't mind............I don't mind!"

"Thank goodness for that because this would have been a disaster if you had minded. Welcome to your biological family," Deirdre announced, whilst slowly opening the double doors to the room.

Inside the room was a sea of smiling faces against a backdrop of colourful homemade banners. One banner read: 'Fantastic to meet you, Daphne,' whilst another simply read: 'Daphne, we love you.' Groups of people all ages, genders and backgrounds, were seated around circular tables. There must have been over 100 people in the room. Their warmth drew me in. The background music was soon eclipsed by a spontaneous round of applause. Then, a rather large gentleman with white hair got to his feet and shouted, "Three cheers for Daphne, hip hip hooray, hip hip hooray, hip hip hooray!"

Everybody went with it and joined in. The feeling was wonderful. I couldn't believe that all these people had come to this hotel to meet me. Now I understood why Deirdre was on edge and constantly on her mobile phone. She was attending to queries, providing instructions to guests, just to ensure the surprise went to plan.

Soon, my guests were leaving their seats and approaching me to say hello properly. I wasn't overwhelmed, I was embracing the attention. I was giddy and full of energy. I was hugging every person I came into contact with and listening to their stories of how they were connected to me and where they had travelled from. It was information overload, but I didn't care. Some had even brought family tree diagrams to show me exactly where I fitted in. Most guests had travelled from inside the UK, but some people had come much further, from places like Ireland, Denmark and Portugal. Two people had flown in from the USA. Some guests even played me video messages on their mobile phones from connections who would have loved to have been in attendance but weren't able to make it.

Deirdre had organised that they all wear name badges, so we all knew who was who. Everyone was chatting to each other. The buzz in the room was electric. Through the many conversations taking place, some guests found that they were meeting new relatives they never even knew existed. There were so many connections being made. There was also a free bar and a cold buffet so all guests could be suitably fed and watered. Deirdre thought it was the least she could do to thank guests for their time and for making the event so memorable.

Almost three hours into the surprise event I didn't want the euphoria to end. By this stage, I was running on adrenaline. I'd never chatted as much before in such a short space of time to so many different people. I couldn't thank Deirdre enough for what she had organised. It was like a dream come true. Similar to me, my guests didn't appear to want to leave. Selfies were relentless and contact details continued to be exchanged. The room was an explosion of non-stop chitter chatter. Suddenly, I felt a hand on my arm. It was Deirdre returning from the bar with a large glass of lemonade.

"I've brought you this, Daphne. You must be parched after all the talking you've done this afternoon. Oh, and I like to introduce you to these two lovely gentlemen."

Hovering slightly behind Deirdre's left shoulder were two middle-aged guys. I took a big gulp of lemonade. Deirdre continued,

"From your DNA results, of all the thousands of people who you were matched to, we were able to establish that these two gentlemen provided the closest matches. They can't wait to introduce themselves to you."

Deirdre stepped to one side so I could say hello properly. Both men were grinning and seemed genuinely pleased to meet me. The man to the right of Deirdre spoke first. He had a pale complexion, distinct green eyes and greying hair. He had a slim build and was wearing well fitted designer casual clothes. He was still clutching his plate from the buffet containing a half-eaten sausage roll and a chocolate covered wafer biscuit similar to a Kit Kat. His name badge wasn't pinned to his burgundy jumper properly and was at such an angle it was difficult to decipher.

"Hello Daphne, I'd have introduced myself earlier, but you've been so busy chatting to guests, I thought I'd better wait my turn" he said in a quiet, but slightly nervous voice.

I felt a strong connection to him and listened intently.

"It was such a shock when Deirdre got in touch to tell me all about you and invite me along today. It's really lovely to meet you. It really is. Meeting you, and everyone here today, is a dream come true. Just like you, I uploaded my DNA to various databases in a desperate effort to search for my biological heritage. You see, I'm adopted too!"

I reached for his hand and squeezed it tightly. He squeezed it back. I didn't quite understand who he was though and how we were connected. Although I did notice the shape of his nose was similar to mine. I could sense he was keen to continue.

"Daphne, as well as both of us being adopted, there is something else that we have in common. Something really special."

His eyes twinkled as he launched into the next few words.

"We share the same parents. I'M YOUR TWIN BROTHER!!"

I stared at him in disbelief. I was speechless.

"My biological parents are also Jack Jones and Pauline Price. I was born at 12:45 pm on the 16th June 1968. My birth name was Martin Raymond Price. I am your younger brother. Deirdre, and Ginette from Durham Family History Group have helped me unravel a few things over the last few weeks. They have been ever so good."

I couldn't believe it. Was this really happening to me, or was I about to wake up from an amazing dream? It must be happening. I could feel the warmth from his hand as he held mine.

For a moment, I felt overwhelmed and just said the first thing that came to mind.

"What's your name now?" I asked excitedly.

"Oh, sorry, I should have said."

And he tilted his badge upwards so I could read it properly.

"My adopted name is WAYNE SPINNER. I have travelled here from Cumbria. I've lived there for about 25 years now. I work for Royal Mail as a Postman," he smiled.

How many more surprises could I cope with in one day? I didn't want to let go of his hand but was conscious that the other gentleman wanted to introduce himself to me.

I turned my attention to the other gentleman, who was waiting patiently for his chance to introduce himself. I looked at him and tried to take in his appearance but my mind was reeling from this latest news. Surely, this wasn't another brother standing in front of me, and I was one of triplets?

He was wearing a dark green suit and novelty tie. His novelty tie made me smile, mainly because it was covered in tortoises and reminded me of my own tattoo. He had spiky white hair, and his nose was thin and sharp. When he smiled, his two front teeth were difficult to ignore. They were super big and long. I loved them, though. They made him unique. Just like me.

"How's it going, Daphne?" he asked.

He looked in the direction of Wayne before resuming eye contact with me.

"That must have been quite a shock to meet Wayne and find out you have a twin brother. My name is GLEN FINNAN. Thanks for inviting me along this afternoon. I'm really pleased to be here. I understand that we are first cousins."

Immediately, I noticed he seemed more relaxed than Wayne. He was a really chilled-out guy.

"I've travelled from Nottingham."

"What do you do in Nottingham?" I asked.

"I'm a manager of a large Supermarket chain. I've worked in the retail sector ever since my days at university," he said proudly.

"I'm delighted you have made it, Glen. I actually can't believe what's happened this afternoon. Meeting all these people for the first time who I'm connected to and then finding out that I have a cousin and twin brother is the icing on the cake. I can't put into words how I feel."

I had another glug of lemonade and then put the glass down on the nearby table. It was littered with leftover plates from the buffet. I gazed at my newfound cousin and twin brother lovingly. A wave of emotion was on its way, and I couldn't hold it back. Nor did I want to. My eyes starting to fill up with tears. Up until now, I'd not shown this emotion over the course of the afternoon.

My voice was quivering. "Please, can we have a group hug?" And I held out my arms.

Wayne and Glen had no hesitation in stepping forward and forming that tight huddle I so desperately needed. I closed my eyes. My head rested on Glen's shoulder. My tears rolled down the lapel on his green suit, leaving a slight stain. I had a moment or two to reflect. I wondered what kind of lives my new-found brother and cousin had led until now. A postman and a supermarket manager didn't sound that exciting on the face of it. But to take people at face value is probably not the wisest thing to do. Eventually, the group hug eased, and we formed a small circle. We held hands as if we were just about to play a game of Ring A Ring O' Roses. I looked at them both and smiled. They both smiled back.

"We have a lot of catching up to do," I said.

Wayne was the first to respond,

"Sure thing, Daphne. This is only the start of our adventure."

Deirdre

The Newcastle-bound train from London Euston was packed. Most of the passengers appeared to be work commuters, based on the number of laptops on show and the mobile phone conversations I could overhear. Daphne and I sat opposite each other on table seats next to the window. Daphne faced the direction the train was travelling. She had a thing about this and said it made her feel dizzy if she travelled backwards. It didn't bother me, though. We shared the table with two middle-aged gentlemen. They were dressed smartly, both wearing identical royal blue blazers. They were very similar in appearance, somewhat striking. They didn't say much, but the bits and pieces I did catch, I think they were Dutch. I'd attended an online Dutch Course for Beginners a few years ago and recognised a few of the phrases.

The train quietly eased out of the station, leaving the platform and main concourse behind. Alongside the railroad tracks, large blank canvases of industrial areas and concrete walls were etched in graffiti. One graffiti artist even had the gall to leave their mark on the side of a freight train car. In huge orange and blue fancy lettering, it was decorated with the word 'Cigar.' It was impressive. I'd never seen graffiti as an act of vandalism but rather as a form of creative expression. I marvelled at the artistic talent on display.

I glanced across at Daphne as she stared out the window. She looked exhausted, but at the same time, she also looked content. I hoped she was happy. She deserved to be happy. It had been a

366

difficult time for her since finding out she was adopted. I'd noticed it had changed her as a person. The happy-go-lucky Daphne I had always known had disappeared overnight. She had been replaced by someone else. Someone who always looked deep in thought and not knowing who she was anymore. She was confused rather than angry. Her head had been full of too many questions. Questions she didn't have answers to. I wanted to help her so much. To play my part. Hopefully, the event at the hotel confirmed how much she is loved and gave her a sense of identity. I longed for the old Daphne to be back.

The hard work over the last few months in trying to understand Daphne's biological heritage and organise the event at the hotel hadn't been an easy task. It seriously tested my project management abilities, especially my time management skills. Away from work [as a Project Manager at a charity that supports environmental sustainability], this had been my sole focus for months. I relished the challenge, though. Soon after Daphne had given me permission to act as her intermediary with her ancestry search, I started to receive progress updates via email from the ancestry DNA company. It soon became apparent that analysing DNA was a complex process. It was going to involve a series of chemical reactions, multiple cycles of heating and cooling and a lot of complicated equipment. It was fascinating and was my kind of thing. I would need to be patient and allow the whole process to unfold. However, this period enabled Ginette, from the Family History Group, to focus on other research, such as examining birth and death registration records and parish records and applying for the adoption file or other documents to help us discover more about Daphne's past.

Daphne's DNA results were uploaded onto her account on the 10th January 2023. Her results were intriguing. She shared DNA with approximately 900 other people. The majority of the hits were distant relatives such as fourth to sixth cousins. After looking more closely at the information on the screen, I noticed something amazing. That Daphne had two really close connections. One was a first cousin, and the other was a full sibling. I sat there in disbelief whilst at the same time, trying to work out what the hell was going on. How was it possible that Daphne could have a full sibling? I wanted to phone her immediately and tell her. Tell her that she wasn't alone in the world and that she had a biological family whom she could connect with. I couldn't, though. That wasn't the plan just yet. We had a big event to organise. Daphne would just have to wait.

Over the next few weeks, using the communication service on the website, hundreds of messages were sent out to people with whom Daphne shared her DNA. In my message, I explained that she was a late discovery adoptee and that I was acting as her intermediary in organising an event with people to whom she was biologically linked to. On the whole, the response to the invite was really positive, with approximately 75% of messages being acknowledged, of which, most were supportive and sympathetic to Daphne's situation. Some confirmed straight away they would attend the event. Others needed a little bit more time before making a commitment. For some, it was necessary to call them directly, as they needed to be reassured that this was all genuine and that it wasn't some sort of scam. As more and more people confirmed their attendance, it made sense to set up a WhatsApp group to speed up the exchange of information. One of the main challenges was assisting people who wanted to attend the event with travel expenses. With the cost-of-living prices rising, some people had limited disposable income and were finding it difficult to attend. Fortunately, dad stepped in and covered the travel expenses for those who required it. Overall, this helped to boost attendance on the day.

Even I couldn't contain my delight when Wayne replied to my invitation. Yes, for a split second, 'ice cool Deirdre' got flustered and went into meltdown. I couldn't believe I was communicating with Daphne's biological brother! We chatted a couple of times on the phone and then agreed to meet up in person. We met at a quaint café just off the A66. Wayne was nervous at first, even though I'd spoken with him a couple of times previously. He soon relaxed after I bought him a cup of coffee and a homemade scone with jam and cream. It was a chance for him to explain about his own adoptive upbringing. It had been challenging, to say the least. His parents weren't the easiest to deal with, especially his adoptive mother, who displayed dominant traits. She was assertive, controlling and selfish, and generally got what she wanted in life. She used emotional blackmail to pressure others to comply with her demands. She wasn't very affectionate, nor was she supportive of Wayne. His adoptive father was domineered by his adoptive mother. Therefore, it wasn't easy for Wayne to spend any quality time with him and build up a father-and-son relationship.

Unlike Daphne, Wayne's parents had at least told him he was adopted. They broke this news when he was about eight years of age. Like other adoptees he had spoken to, he felt his own adoption had resulted in him having a number of issues. He had experienced feelings of being "abandoned" and "not being good enough." It wasn't until his adoptive parents had passed a couple of years earlier that he had started to take steps to trace his biological heritage. With the help of intermediary support from the local authority and a very helpful Search Angel he met on Facebook, he accessed his original birth certificate and adoption file. He quickly uncovered that his original birthname was Philip Andrew Price and that his biological parents were called Jack Jones and Pauline Price. The sad news that they both died in a house fire had obviously been devastating for him.

Those who were assisting him with his ancestral search hadn't identified that he had a full sibling. Therefore, for a number of months, Wayne explained his closest DNA match was a first cousin. This was Glen Finnan. He and Glen had exchanged messages with each other but had yet to meet in person. Just as Wayne was getting used to his new biological connections, he was completely stunned one day when he logged onto his ancestry personal account to find a significant change. His closest match was now no longer a first cousin; he now shared his DNA with a full sibling by the name of

Daphne Dapper!! He now couldn't wait to meet his sister and give her a massive hug.

The train tannoy system burst into life and confirmed that Newcastle would be the next stop. Daphne didn't stir. She'd been asleep most of the journey. Her head was resting on the shoulder of the smartly dressed gentleman who was still sitting next to her. He didn't seem to mind, though. He was deep in conversation with the other smartly dressed man opposite, who I had now assumed to be related, and possibly his twin brother. They were busy amusing themselves. Of the bits I could interpret, the gist of their anecdote was about their days at college as teenagers. They were reminiscing about when they cheated in a Maths exam and got away with it. We approached Newcastle station. The train wheels clunked and screeched as the train came to a standstill. It was the end of our three-day journey to London. But for Daphne, Wayne and Glen, it was the start of a whole new journey. One in which Daphne could get to know her biological family.

An early image of Terry the Orangutan, as created by my youngest daughter, Nina.

Milton Keynes UK
Ingram Content Group UK Ltd.
UKHW021041130924
448294UK00007B/355